THE ROMANIAN ORTHODOX
CHURCH AND THE HOLOCAUST

STUDIES IN ANTISEMITISM
Alvin H. Rosenfeld, *editor*

THE ROMANIAN ORTHODOX CHURCH AND THE HOLOCAUST

ION POPA

Indiana University Press

This book is a publication of

Indiana University Press
Office of Scholarly Publishing
Herman B Wells Library 350
1320 East 10th Street
Bloomington, Indiana 47405 USA

iupress.indiana.edu

Manufactured in the United States of America

Cataloging information is available from the Library of Congress.

ISBN 978-0-253-02956-0 (cloth)
ISBN 978-0-253-02989-8 (ebook)

1 2 3 4 5 22 21 20 19 18 17

CONTENTS

ABBREVIATIONS

ADSS— Actes et Documents du Saint Siège relatifs à la Seconde Guerre Mondiale

ANR—Arhivele Naţionale ale României [The Romanian National Archives]

ASCOR—Asociaţia Studenţilor Creştin Ortodocşi din România [The Association of Christian Orthodox Students in Romania]

ASUR—Asociaţia Secular-Umanistă din România [The Secular-Humanist Association of Romania]

BOR—Biserica Ortodoxă Română [The Romanian Orthodox Church—the journal of the Holy Synod]

CDE—Comitetul Democratic Evreiesc [The Jewish Democratic Committee]

CME—Congresul Mondial Evreiesc [The Jewish World Congress]

CNSAS—Consiliul Naţional pentru Studierea Arhivelor Securităţii [The Council for the Study of the Securitate Archives]

CSIER— Centrul pentru Studiul Istoriei Evreilor din România [The Center for the Study of the History of Romanian Jews]

DIE—Direcţia de Informaţii Externe, Romanian Foreign Secret Service during the Communist period

FCER—Federația Comunităților Evreiești din România [The Federation of Jewish Communities of Romania]

INSHREW—Institutul Național pentru Studierea Holocaustului din România, Elie Wiesel [The Elie Wiesel National Institute for the Study of the Holocaust in Romania]

IOM—International Organisation for Migration

ITS—International Tracing Service

PNG—Partidul Noua Generație [The New Generation Party]

PRM—Partidul România Mare [The Greater Romania Party]

ROCOR—The Russian Orthodox Church outside Russia

USHMM—United States Holocaust Memorial Museum

WCC—The World Council of Churches

ACKNOWLEDGMENTS

THIS BOOK IS LARGELY BASED on my PhD, which I completed at the University of Manchester, United Kingdom. I would like to express my gratitude for the wise supervision of Dr. Jean-Marc Dreyfus and of Professor Daniel Langton. Their careful and gentle advice guided me always in the right direction. I am indebted to Professor Dan Stone, and Dr. Ewa Ochman for their encouragement and feedback. I am also grateful for the comments and guidance of Dr. Cathy Gelbin, Dr. Ana Carden-Coyne, and Professor Maiken Umbach who were in various moments involved as advisors on my PhD panels.

From 2010 to 2012, I was the recipient of the Saul Kagan Claims Conference Advance Shoah Studies Doctoral Fellowship, New York, which was tremendously important for the advance of this project. I am grateful not only for the financial support, but also for the advice I received from the committee members and from fellow grant recipients during our annual meetings. I should mention the names of late Professor David Cesarani and of Professors Alvin Rosenfeld, Steven Katz, Dalia Ofer, and David Silberklang, as well as the support of Saul Kagan Claims Conference Fellowship administrators Chavie Brumer and Lori Schuldiner Schor.

The University of Manchester, School of Arts, Languages and Cultures, granted me the School Award (2012–2013), and I am really thankful for this. During the last stages of the editorial preparation of the manuscript I was a postdoctoral fellow at the Yad Vashem International Institute for Holocaust Research (October 2014–January 2015) and a DRS postdoctoral fellow at the Freie Universität Berlin (2015–2016). Discussions with staff and colleagues at Yad Vashem and Freie Universität helped me often to clarify ideas and to have a broader picture on Churches' attitudes toward the Jewish community. I am especially indebted to Professors David Silberklang, Dina Porat, Dan Michman, Dr. Iael Nidam-Orvieto, and Dr. Eliot Nidam-Orvieto from Yad Vashem International Institute for Holocaust Research and to Professor Gertrud Pickhan and Dr. Gregor Walter-Drop from Freie Universität.

In Romania, I have always received valuable counsel from Dr. Alexandru Florian, Director of the Elie Wiesel Institute for the Study of the Holocaust in Romania and from Dr. Adrian Cioflâncă, the Director of the Center for the Study of the History of Romanian Jews. The same can be said about Dr. Radu Ioanid, Director of the International Archival Program, United States Holocaust Memorial Museum, who helped me with his comments, advice, and access to documentation. I am also indebted to the History Department at Ovidius University, Constanța, and especially to Professor Florin Anghel for their assistance.

A project like this would have not been possible without the help of the many librarians and archivists from Romania, Israel, and the United States who supported me with their guidance and benevolence. I am equally grateful to the Indiana University Press's reviewers and editors for their suggestions, corrections, and support.

In 2013, I benefited from a Tziporah Wiesel Fellowship at the Center for Advanced Holocaust Studies, United States Holocaust Memorial Museum. Discussions with other fellows, the feedback I received on my project, and the wealth of documentation available at the center were all very important. This book was also made possible (in part) by funds granted to the author through an Ausnit Fellowship at the Jack, Joseph and Morton Mandel Center for Advanced Holocaust Studies of the United States Holocaust Memorial Museum. The statements made and views expressed, however, are solely the responsibility of the author. I am also grateful to the Emerging Scholars Program at the Mandel Center for Advanced Holocaust Studies for its support in the preparation of the manuscript and of the book proposal.

Last but not least, I would like to express my gratitude to Ella, my wife, for her permanent support and encouragement, and to my parents who, although not academically educated, were the first to instill in me a passion for history.

Permission

Several paragraphs from chapter 1, subchapter "Patriarch Miron Cristea's political and religious influence in deciding the fate of the Romanian Jews (February 1938–March 1939)," and the first paragraph of the introduction of this book, were published previously in Ion Popa "Miron Cristea, the Romanian Orthodox Patriarch: His Political and Religious Influence in Deciding the Fate of the Romanian Jews (February 1938–March 1939)," *Yad Vashem Studies*, vol. 40, no. 2 (2012), pp. 11–34. I am grateful to *Yad Vashem Studies* for its permission to re-use that material here.

I thank the Romanian National Archives for the permission to use photographs from its collection. I especially express my gratitude to Ms. Alina Horvath, the superior advisor of the Image and Communication Department of the Romanian National Archives for her support.

THE ROMANIAN ORTHODOX
CHURCH AND THE HOLOCAUST

INTRODUCTION

IN THE SUMMER OF 2010, a scandal arose when the Romanian Central Bank decided to issue five special coins celebrating the five patriarchs[1] of the Romanian Orthodox Church. The United States Holocaust Memorial Museum (USHMM), in Washington, DC, and the Elie Wiesel National Institute for the Study of the Holocaust in Romania (Institutul Național pentru Studierea Holocaustului din România, Elie Wiesel—INSHREW), in Bucharest, protested the decision because it meant commemorating Patriarch Miron Cristea, whose term as prime minister of Romania (1938–1939) "marked the opening of a systematic campaign of anti-Semitic persecution by successive Romanian governments that resulted in the devastation of the Romanian Jewish community during the Holocaust."[2] Despite this criticism, the National Bank of Romania (NBR) went ahead and issued the coins.[3] This scandal came six years after the Romanian government publicly acknowledged the Romanian involvement in the Holocaust,[4] and it was one of the very few instances in which the Romanian Orthodox Church was publicly condemned for its anti-Semitism and, indirectly, for its role in the final destruction of Romanian Jewry.[5]

In order to avoid a serious analysis of its actions during the Holocaust, starting in 1990 the Church adapted its public language to suit various audiences. In its relations with the Jewish community, Holocaust-related organizations, and the state of Israel, it promoted a narrative that denied it ever behaved negatively toward Jews. At the same time it endorsed right-wing anti-Semites and encouraged Orthodox nationalism, reminiscent of the interwar period. The dissonance of these mixed messages is obvious, but only with a proper analysis of the Church's involvement in the Holocaust can the creation of a responsible narrative be possible. This book follows the trend of new research investigating the Romanian Orthodox Church's twentieth-century past. It breaks new ground not only in questioning the myths developed after the war but also in reanalyzing the very basis of the Romanian Orthodox Church's relationship with the Jewish community and Judaism. After the fall of Communism, some scholars looked at the Church during the interwar period, while others have examined the Communist era. This research attempts to fill an important historiographical gap by analyzing the way in which the Orthodox Church responded to its own involvement in the Holocaust and its role in shaping Holocaust memory in Romania.

This book may be especially helpful to departments studying the attitudes of Christian denominations toward Jews during the Holocaust, the church-state relationship in Eastern Europe, the building of Holocaust memory, and the revival of anti-Semitism after the collapse of Communism. Many of the documents sourced here have not been seen before and are important tools for scrutinizing the position of the Romanian Orthodox Church (and, in some situations, of other Orthodox churches in the region) toward the Jewish community and Judaism. An emphasis on the way in which Holocaust memory developed in Eastern Europe in a Communist, Cold War context may also attract interest from departments studying the history of Eastern Europe, Communism, and memory. The explosion in Central and Eastern Europe after 1990 of anti-Semitism and rightwing extremist rhetoric similar to interwar Orthodox nationalism caused historians such as Katherine Verdery to suggest that the nationalism promoted in these regions after the First World War did not die out with the emergence of Communism but remodeled and reinvented itself, retaining most of its original elements.[6] In such a context, proper research into the attitude of the Orthodox Church toward Jews during and after the Holocaust is not just about the past; it is necessary for understanding the present.

Considering the increasing socio-political influence of the Orthodox Church in postcommunist Romania and its paradoxical approach toward Holocaust memory and Judaism, the scanty research on its attitude toward the Jewish community during the Second World War is surprising. Research on the interwar anti-Semitism of the Romanian Orthodox Church and its links with the Iron Guard has been done by scholars such as Lucian Leuştean, Mirel Bănică, Roland Clark, Rebecca Haynes, and Ionuţ Biliuţă. These topics appear also, although sometimes tangentially, in works by Jean Ancel, Paul Shapiro, Leon Volovici, Radu Ioanid, Bela Vago, and Zigu Ornea. But while we know much about the anti-Semitism of the Church prior to the war, there has been no scholarly investigation on how that anti-Semitism evolved between 1939 and 1945. We know almost nothing about the attitude of the Church toward the Jewish community during the war and about its remembrance of the Holocaust.

The lack of research on the Romanian Orthodox Church's involvement in the Holocaust (and to some extent this is true for other Orthodox churches in Eastern Europe as well) could have at least two explanations. First, the Church presented itself, after the fall of Communism, as victim of various political regimes, and whitewashed its own history by hiding compromising aspects. Second, this victimization narrative was even more effective in blocking any critical analysis of twentieth-century embarrassing episodes as the Church enjoyed prestige and political influence. After the fall of Communism, the Orthodox Church became very powerful and influential in Romanian society and politics. It regularly placed first in polls researching which institution Romanians trusted the most. The numbers were outstanding, with figures between 80 percent and 90 percent of the population.[7] The Church was outperformed (by the Fire Service and the Army), with polls showing a major decline in public preference since 2012. In 2013 a poll conducted by Compania de Cecetare Sociologică şi Branding (CCSB) showed that the approval rating had dropped to 66 percent of the population, the first time since 1989 that the figure dropped below 70 percent.[8]

Many external observers were surprised by the prestige the Orthodox Church enjoyed in post-1989 Romania, but this stature was built long before the fall of Communism. In Romania, in comparison to Poland for example, the Church has been a national church, not dependent on any other external authority. The efforts of the Russian Orthodox Church at the end of the 1940s to extend its influence over the Romanian Orthodox Church were reversed at the beginning of the 1950s with a program of canonization of several Romanian saints (see chapter 7). This lack of dependence on an external authority made the Romanian Orthodox Church an essential part of state plans. The Church became an emblem of national Communism, which borrowed and reinstated many elements of the interwar Orthodox nationalism.

After 1989 the power and influence of the Romanian Orthodox Church was acknowledged by politicians, who often used it for their own political gain. Involvement in politics, although the Church never made a formal alliance with any particular party, was discussed by the Holy Synod at every major election cycle, in 1996, 2004, 2008, and 2014.[9] In 2014, for example, the Church was accused by some members of the media and many political commentators of open involvement in the presidential campaign. In the months leading to the elections, the Church accepted large financial donations from the Romanian government led by Prime Minister Victor Ponta, who was the presidential candidate of the Social Democratic Party (Partidul Social Democrat—PSD). According to some accounts, during this period the government donated more than 30 million RON (approximately $9 million) to the Church.[10] Although the Orthodox Church denied claims of political involvement raised by the incumbent president of Romania, Traian Băsescu, arguing that there was no official Church declaration of support for any one of the candidates,[11] leading members of the PSD used Church symbols and institutions extensively in their campaign. For example, in October 2014, three weeks before the first run of the presidential elections, in a special ceremony Patriarch Daniel blessed Liviu Dragnea, Ponta's lieutenant and Romania's deputy prime minister, for his and his party's financial contributions to the Church.[12]

The Orthodox Church's influence in Romanian society is significant. From key sessions of the Romanian parliament to ceremonies in small villages, such as the opening of the school academic year, Church representatives are active participants. The Church also regained the right, taken away during the Communist era, to hold religious education classes in public schools. This was balanced by the state with amendments to protect the rights of minority religions, or agnostics/atheists,[13] but many commentators deplored the fact that these classes are often used for Orthodox indoctrination.[14] In 2013, in the context of discussions on revising the Romanian constitution, the Synod of the Moldova Metropolitanate, one of the most important metropolitan seats in the Romanian Orthodox Church, decided to lobby actively so that in the new constitution religious education classes, the name of God, and the role of the Orthodox Church in the history of the Romanian people would be officially acknowledged.[15] After 1989, there were many instances when the Church tried to impose its theological views on the Romanian state. In matters such as abortion, homosexuality, sexual education, and legalization of prostitution the Romanian Orthodox Church influenced state decisions.[16] Often the Church's position on such issues expressed its conservatism.[17]

The privileged political and social position of the Romanian Orthodox Church led to a lack of serious research on the Church's recent history. Since 1990 the Church has displayed two clear tendencies, visible in the official declarations of the upper hierarchy and in the articles published in its journals. These tendencies have also shaped the position of the Church toward Judaism and the Holocaust. On the one hand, the Church presented itself as a victim of Communism, hiding the compromising collaboration of Church hierarchy with the old regime. The declaration of the Holy Synod, published just few days after Nicolae Ceaușescu's death, mentioned that, "given the regime of limited liberties imposed by the dictatorship and terror upon the entire people, our Church was subject to pressures and limitations.... We are determined to rebuild the sanctuaries of our ancestral history, churches and monasteries, victims of Ceaușescu's bulldozers."[18] The declaration did not mention that the demolition of churches was done with the accord of the Church's leadership. As in the case of the Holocaust, the Romanian Orthodox Church promoted a whitewashed narrative in relation to its Communist past, selecting only favorable historical data, hiding compromising information, and promoting a narrative of victimhood, despite much evidence to the contrary.[19]

In order to maintain this narrative, the Church opposed the pressure from civil society and state organizations, including requests for free access to the secret files of priests and members of the Church hierarchy. In 1997, for example, a Holy Synod decision opposed such an initiative of Senator Ioan Francisc Moisin. The peculiar church-state relationship in post-Communist Romania is suggested by the fact that the Romanian senate sent a letter asking the patriarchate whether or not such an initiative would be accepted by the Church. As was expected, given the circumstances of collaboration of the Church hierarchy with the Communist regime, the Holy Synod opposed the initiative.[20] The Romanian Orthodox Church also opposed attempts of the Consiliul Național pentru Studierea Arhivelor Fostei Securități (the Council for the Study of the Former Securitate Archives, or CNSAS) to access priests' files. The tensions between the two institutions grew in 2007 when the Holy Synod created a parallel commission to deliberate on the CNSAS initiative. The report of the Holy Synod's commission, which included a member of the CNSAS (and this is again telling about the peculiar institutional relations in Romania), attacked the CNSAS as "incapable, in its actual structure and state, to impartially analyze the activity of the Orthodox clerics during Communism."[21]

As other historians have highlighted, the Romanian Orthodox Church does not allow access to its archives.[22] Instead of manifesting greater openness as time goes by, in 2012 the Holy Synod enforced an even more serious ban on access. According to this decision no one could see any document of the Church without prior approval of the Holy Synod and that priority would be given to theology students.[23] It should be emphasized that, although access to the Church's archive is restricted, most of its official policies concerning the Holocaust years appear clearly in its journals. The cover-up of 1945, detailed later in this book (see chapter 4), made use of the strongest documents regarding the relations of the Church with the Jewish community during the war, and those articles constitute extremely valuable documentary evidence. Until 1947, every year-end issue of the *Biserica Ortodoxă Română (BOR)* included a summary of the decisions of the Holy Synod, this being again important documentary evidence.

Although the myth that Romania was not involved in the Holocaust was constantly challenged after 1990, with many institutions coming under serious investigation, the Romanian Orthodox Church generally avoided scrutiny concerning its attitude toward Jews during the Shoah. As in the case of its Communist past, the Church successfully managed to use its political and social influence to deflect interest and make access to documents difficult. It continued the tradition established during the Communist era of good relations with the Jewish community and the state of Israel, and avoided regular engagement in the Jewish-Christian dialogue because of fears that its dark past would come to light. However, despite these efforts to avoid any discussion about its problematic involvement in the destruction of Romanian Jewry, sometimes the skeletons in the closet disturb the general silence. In 2001 the USHMM condemned the unveiling, in a Romanian Orthodox church, of a memorial dedicated to Romania's wartime leader Ion Antonescu. The exchange of letters between the USHMM representative and Patriarch Teoctist reveal the Church's unchanged stance toward Antonescu.

In 2011 another scandal broke when *Evenimentul Zilei* (The News of the Day), one of the leading Romanian newspapers, reported that in a well-known Romanian monastery Iron Guard[24] songs were sung at the birthday celebrations of Iustin Pârvu, the dean of the Petru Vodă monastery. The Church initially tried to avoid the topic, but after several days of silence, facing the growing discontent of the newspaper and of its readers, the Orthodox patriarchate issued a press communiqué. Its last sentence stated: "The Romanian Patriarchate does not initiate and promote racist, xenophobic, and anti-Semitic movements and does not support enmity based on religious or ethnic reasons as they are contrary to the Gospel of love toward all people."[25] Despite this clear statement, the patriarchate did not directly condemn those involved in the events, or the Iron Guard, and tried to pass responsibility on to a lower authority of the Church. Moreover, in 2013, when Iustin Pârvu died, he was buried in a large ceremony, as an emblematic figure of the Orthodox Church, the burial service being officiated by the metropolitan of Moldova.

The events at the Petru Vodă monastery also show a continuous trend of supporting extremist rightwing and nationalist organizations, a trend that has been visible in Orthodox monasteries since the creation of modern Romania. This is why the space dedicated to monasteries in this book is restricted. They were not involved in rescue efforts in the way some Catholic monasteries throughout Europe were during the Holocaust. Moreover, Orthodox monasteries have been places where nationalism and sometimes anti-Semitism reminiscent of the Iron Guard period were openly promoted, both before but mostly after the fall of Communism. This is visible not only in the case of Iustin Pârvu, but also in the case of Ilie Cleopa (see chapter 9).

In the twenty-first century the subject of the Holocaust has increasingly appealed to the general public in Romania. This is due to several factors, among them the issuance of the Elie Wiesel report in 2004, the revelations about Ion Antonescu as a war criminal during the TV program "100 Greatest Romanians" in 2006, and the scandals of Holocaust denial and anti-Semitism involving Romanian officials and institutions. For years after the fall of Ceaușescu, the Romanian Orthodox Church was the most trusted institution in Romania. The decrease in polls could suggest that, as in the case of Ion Antonescu, Romanians have become more aware of the dark spots in the Church's recent past. The growing interest in the Holocaust and the willingness of young Romanian intellectuals and professionals to challenge the old/Communist narratives will make this research relevant to a larger audience outside academia.

The Romanian Orthodox Church's relationship with the Holocaust is not singular. In other Orthodox Eastern European countries the lack of academic research allowed the promotion of narratives, often untrue, that presented churches in a very positive light. Following the trend begun by Jovan Byford, who wrote about the Serbian Orthodox Church's remembrance of the controversial Bishop Nicolaj Velimirović, this book investigates claims of positive involvement in the Holocaust and hopes to open new avenues into analyzing the way in which various national Orthodox churches relate to Holocaust memory. Although still in its infancy, the research of the Eastern European Christian denominations' attitudes toward Jews and Judaism is growing. This interest comes from the realization that Christian churches played a very important role in the events of the Holocaust, but it can also be explained by the worrying return after 1990 of the rightwing Orthodox nationalism of the interwar period. In such a context an analysis of the role played in the destruction of European Jewry is crucial to avoiding a repeat of the past.

METHODOLOGY AND STATE OF RESEARCH

This book analyzes the way in which the Romanian Orthodox Church responded to its own involvement in the Holocaust and its role in shaping Holocaust memory in Romania. Knowledge about the position of the Church in key political and social moments of the last century is scanty. There is research, as pointed out before, about its interwar anti-Semitism, but almost nothing has been written about the period of the Holocaust. Recently, young historians have started to look more carefully at the Communist era, but no one has looked at the Church's remembrance of the Holocaust.

Researching the period of 1938 to the present is essential to comprehensively assess the relationship of the Church to the Holocaust. Nineteen thirty-eight was the year in which Miron Cristea, the first patriarch of the Romanian Orthodox Church, became prime minister of Romania. During his administration (February 1938–March 1939), Jews were stripped of their Romanian citizenship as he called them parasites that should be expelled from the country. He also made plans for the implementation of Romanianization policies and for the deportation of Jews. Starting from that point, this book chronologically analyzes the attitude of the Orthodox Church toward the Jewish community and the Holocaust up to 2014.

The first two chapters start with an analysis of Cristea's policies and continue with the period of the Second World War. They look at the evolution of the interwar anti-Semitism of the Romanian Orthodox Church and its position toward the Jewish community from 1938 to 1944. One of the main questions addressed in these chapters is whether the Orthodox Church was a perpetrator, a bystander, or a savior during the Holocaust. Chapters 3, 4, and 5 look at the first three years after the war and their importance in the building of the public's and the Orthodox Church's remembrance of the Holocaust. They examine the dynamic of church-state relations and how they influenced the Church's Holocaust memory from 1945 to 1948. Chapters 6 and 7 detail the period from 1948 to 1989, when Communist nationalism resurrected many elements of the Orthodox nationalist ideology of the interwar period and the Church reinforced and developed the cover-up of 1945. These chapters also analyze the way in which the Church's support of national Communism influenced its remembrance of the Holocaust. The last two chapters analyze the period from 1989 to 2014 and the way in which the Church's previous contribution to national Communism preserved its position at the heart of Romanian national identity. In this way, the Church was able to maintain its prestige after the fall of Communism. These chapters look at whether the Romanian Orthodox Church finally addressed its negative involvement in the Holocaust after 1989. The Church continued to have good relations with the Jewish community and with the state of Israel, but they were based on the false premise that the Orthodox Church had had a positive attitude toward Jews during the Holocaust. A lack of academic research has allowed the continuation of this narrative until today.

In the last fifteen years, academic interest in subjects such as the attitude of Christian institutions toward Jews during the Holocaust, or toward Holocaust memory and Judaism, has grown constantly. The turning point that signaled the beginning of this new era of research was represented by two events. In 1997, the French Catholic Church issued a public apology for its inaction during the Holocaust.[26] In 1998, the Catholic Commission for Religious Relations with the Jews, under the authority of Pope John Paul II, issued the document *We Remember: A Reflection on the Shoah*, which calls for repentance from Catholics who failed to intercede to stop the Nazi genocide. It urges Catholics to repent "of past errors and infidelities" and "renew the awareness of the Hebrew roots of their faith."[27] Although it fails to address the alleged silence of Pope Pius XII, the document was praised in major newspapers around the world as a "carefully crafted statement that goes further than the Roman Catholic Church has ever gone in reckoning honestly with its passivity during the Nazi era and its historic antipathy toward Jews."[28]

Before 1997, the attitudes of Christian denominations toward the Jewish community was touched on in general books about the Holocaust. Léon Poliakov, Raul Hilberg, Yehuda Bauer, Christopher Browning, Bela Vago, and others paid attention, sometimes tangentially, to rescue or collaboration involving churches or religious figures. Others wrote more comprehensive studies on the Catholic Church's involvement in the Holocaust. The most prominent example is John Morley's *Vatican Diplomacy and the Jews during the Holocaust, 1939–1943*, published in 1980 and based on the twelve volumes of documents made available by the Vatican after the Second Vatican Council: Actes et Documents du Saint Siège relatifs à la Seconde Guerre Mondiale (ADSS). The particular interest in the attitude of the Catholic Church in Romania was grounded in the rescue actions of Andrea Cassulo, the papal nuncio to Bucharest (1936–1947). In 1963 Theodor Lavi published in Yad Vashem Studies the article "The Vatican's Endeavors on Behalf of Rumanian Jewry during the Second World War," which was based on documents published by Msgr. A. Martini in the Jesuit periodical *La Civilta Cattolica*. In 1991 Ion Dumitriu-Snagov published *România în diplomația Vaticanului 1939–1944* (Romania in the Vatican's Diplomacy 1939–1944), based, as is John Morely's book, mostly on ADSS.

After 1998 many scholars, such as Carol Rittner, John Roth, Susan Zuccotti, Michael Phayer, Daniel Goldhagen, Frank Coppa, and Suzanne Brown-Fleming, produced work looking at the Catholic Church and the Holocaust. In 1999 Robert Ericksen and Susannah Heschel published *Betrayal: German Churches and the Holocaust*, which went further and analyzed the attitude of Protestant and Catholic institutions in Germany during the Third Reich. The book edited by Kevin Spicer, *Antisemitism, Christian Ambivalence, and the Holocaust*, also looked at the attitude of various churches across Europe during the war. Randolph Braham expanded on his earlier interest and in 2000 published *The Vatican and the Holocaust: The Catholic Church and the Jews during the Nazi Era*. Since then, scholars all over the world have written books on the attitude of Pope Pius XII during the Holocaust, defending or condemning him. In 2009, the Yad Vashem International

Institute for Holocaust Research organized a workshop where these opposing views were discussed; the proceedings have been published in *Pius XII and the Holocaust, Current State of Research.*

On Eastern Europe, the research is still in its infancy. In 2004 Jovan Byford wrote a forty-one-page article entitled "From 'Traitor' to 'Saint': Bishop Nikolaj Velimirović in Serbian Public Memory."[29] In 2008 he published *Denial and Repression of Anti-Semitism: Post-Communist Rehabilitation of the Serbian Bishop Nikolaj Velimirović.* Byford's work proved that, in the case of the Serbian Orthodox Church, the narrative of continuous positive attitudes toward Jews was problematic. In 2005 Albena Taneva produced *The Power of Civil Society in a Time of Genocide: Proceedings of the Holy Synod of the Bulgarian Orthodox Church on the Rescue of the Jews in Bulgaria, 1940–1944,* which consists mostly of published archival material. As in the case of Romania, books and articles analyzing the role of Eastern European Orthodox churches in supporting interwar anti-Semitism have been published, but they do not deal directly with the events of the war.

Holocaust memory is a very complex concept with many facets and meanings; thus, some clarification of the way in which the term is used in this book is needed. First, we must look at institutional memory and in particular at the way in which the Romanian Orthodox Church as an institution has remembered its involvement in the Holocaust. Various scholars, such as Michael Phayer, Jovan Byford, Abraham Peck, John Morley, Susannah Heschel, Susan Zuccotti, and Carol Rittner, have analyzed the Catholic, Protestant, and Orthodox attitudes toward the Holocaust. More general works looking at institutional memory by scholars such as Saul Friedländer, Randolph Braham, Jeffrey Herf, Henry Rousso, and Michael Shafir are also referenced here.

The way in which terms such as "memory," "denial," and/or "silence" are used interchangeably in this book reflects the complex ways in which the Orthodox Church relates to its past. They all offer snapshots of various positions of the Church toward the Holocaust. After the Second World War, the Romanian Orthodox Church discussed the destruction of the Jewish community, built a narrative that covered up its negative actions, and presented itself as a savior of Jews, despite much evidence suggesting the opposite. During the Communist era, although the Holocaust was not often mentioned, which suggests a preference for silence, the main ingredients of the biased Holocaust memory built in 1945, such as the narrative of permanent tolerance of the Church toward Jews, were often promoted. At the end of the 1970s and the beginning of the 1980s, in an international context in which the Holocaust gained prominence in the public discourse, the Romanian Orthodox Church returned more openly to the narrative of 1945. After the fall of Communism in 1989, the Church's institutional remembrance of the Holocaust became more complex. As discussed in chapter 9, the Orthodox Church returned to and reinforced the controversial Holocaust memory built in 1945. On the other hand, in unfavorable contexts when negative actions could have come under scrutiny, the Church preferred to remain silent, a silence which could also explain the Romanian Orthodox Church's lack of desire to be more actively involved in the Jewish-Christian dialogue.

SOURCES

Research dealing directly with the Romanian Orthodox Church during the Holocaust is almost nonexistent. Jean Ancel, in the chapter "The Cross and the Jew," from his book *Transnistria, 1941–1942: The Romanian Mass Murder Campaigns,* details the missionary activity of the Church in Transnistria.[30] In addition, in a more recent book, *The History of the Holocaust in Romania* (2012), Ancel returns to this topic but without bringing forward new material, his emphasis being on the anti-Semitism of the Church before the war, or on the missionary activity in Transnistria. The unpublished PhD thesis of Georgeta Pană looks at the Holocaust in Hungary, Romania, and Poland through comparative lenses, with a general introduction to the attitude of the Orthodox Church toward the Jewish community during the war. Apart from these three works, no other research looks comprehensively at the behavior of the Romanian Orthodox Church during the Holocaust. Books by Mirel Bănică, Lucian Leuștean, Roland Clark, Rebecca Haynes, Leon Volovici, Jean Ancel, Carol Iancu, Bela Vago, Zigu Ornea, and Boris Buzila, and articles by Paul Shapiro, Radu Ioanid, Dumitru Velenchiu, Ionuț Biliuță, and William Oldson analyze in a form or another the anti-Semitism of the Church prior to the war. Even when the war period is touched on, as in the books of Boris Buzila or Lucian Leuștean, information is scanty. As a result, research for the first section of this book, covering the period 1938–1944, was mostly based on published archival material and on primary sources. Of the published archival material there are several works that should be mentioned. Volume 2 of *Evreii din România între 1940–1944* (The Jews of Romania, 1940–1944), *Problema evreiască în stenogramele Consiliului de Miniştri* (The Jewish Problem in the Minutes of the Romanian Cabinet), edited by Lya Benjamin, although focused on political developments, contains several documents related to the problem of Jews' conversion to Christianity and the political role of the Church during the war. In 1999 Gheorghe Nicolescu, Gheorghe Dobrescu, and Andrei Nicolescu published *Preoţi în tranşee 1941–1945* (Priests in Trenches 1941–1945), which includes reports written by military chaplains and missionary priests during the war. The books by Matatias Carp and Marius Mircu, written immediately after the war, contain important documentary evidence, mostly about Romanian Orthodox chaplains. Interesting documents also appear in the twelve-volume *Documents Concerning the Fate of the Romanian Jews* published by Jean Ancel starting in 1986. Important memoirs such as that of Alexandre Safran, the chief rabbi of the Romanian Jewish community during the war, and testimonies found in archival collections in Bucharest, Jerusalem, and Washington, often refer to the attitude of the Church as an institution and the attitude of local priests during the Holocaust.

The journals of the Church are important primary sources for chapters 1 and 2 (and for the entire book). I was successful in locating and checking almost all the issues of the main central journals published by the Church from 1938 to 1945: *Biserica Ortodoxă Română* (*BOR*), *Studii Teologice* (Theological Studies), and *Apostolul* (The Apostle). Especially in the case of *BOR* the copies were scattered in several libraries in Bucharest. I also looked at regional journals such as *Luminătorul* (The Luminary), *Cuvântul Preoţesc* (The Priestly Word), and *Transnistria Creştină* (Christian Transnistria). These journals contain extraordinary documentary evidence about the attitude of the Romanian Orthodox Church toward the Jewish community during the Holocaust and the church-state relationship during the war. As in the case of the Communist period, the articles published in Church journals should be analyzed in the context of political changes and pressures.

For a comprehensive understanding of the political and social context during the war, I consulted documents in several archives in Romania, Israel, and the United States. In Romania, documents can be found in the archives of CNSAS, INSHREW, the National Archives, and Centrul pentru Studiul Istoriei Evreilor din Romania (CSIER—The Center for the Study of the History of Jews of Romania). The CNSAS archives contain material that had not yet been researched previously. In many situations I was the first person to open some files at CNSAS. Documents of the Romanian Jewish community, the Romanian Secret Services, the Department of Justice, the Romanian Gendarmerie, the Ministry of Defense, and the World Jewish Congress, among others, are in the CNSAS archive. Documents from similar institutions, but more focused on the Jewish perspective, are housed at INSHREW and USHMM. At USHMM and Yad Vashem, apart from other archival material of Romanian institutions, I looked at testimonies of Holocaust survivors. I was able in this way to assess the level of intervention of Orthodox priests in favor of or against the victims. In these two institutions, I also researched documents about postwar trials and the fate of individuals who escaped justice. Access to the documents of the International Tracing Service (ITS) and to the personal archive of Charles Kramer, who was the main person involved in the uncovering of the Valerian Trifa affair,[31] was also important. USHMM was able to provide a copy of the complete letter of Metropolitan Bălan, who protested in April 1941 against the ban on Jews' conversion to Christianity. The document was used constantly to portray the Orthodox Church as a savior of Jews, but the second part of the letter, which has never been quoted before, shows that Bălan did not try to defend the Jews.

Secondary sources relevant to the Communist period include the works of Lucian Leuștean, dealing with the Romanian Orthodox Church and the Cold War. In addition, Cristian Vasile's book *Biserica Ortodoxă Română în primul deceniu comunist* (The Romanian Orthodox Church during the First Decade of Communism) is important for assessing events at the beginning of the period. The book *Religion et nationalisme: l'idéologie de l'Église Orthodoxe roumaine sous le régime communiste* by Olivier Gillet, covering the entire Communist period, is a good starting point in understanding church-state relations from 1945 to 1989. The church-state relationship in Communist Romania is also touched on in Adrian Cioroianu's *Focul Ascuns în Piatră: Despre istorie, memorie și alte vanități contemporane* (The Fire Hidden in Stone: On History, Memory, and Other Contemporary Vanities). *Biserica Ortodoxă Română sub regimul comunist, 1945–1958* (The Romanian Orthodox Church under the Communist Regime, 1945–1958), edited by Cristina Păiușan-Nuică and Radu Ciuceanu, brings forward a selection of documents about the Orthodox Church during the Communist era. A more biased approach, sometimes defending the far-right attitudes of some in the Orthodox hierarchy, is *Partidul, Securitatea și Cultele, 1945–1989* (The Party, the Securitate and the Churches, 1945–1989) by Adrian-Nicolae Petcu. On

Israeli-Romanian relations the book by Radu Ioanid about the ransom of Jews, and the memoir of Yosef Govrin, the former Israeli ambassador to Bucharest (1985–1989), are very helpful. On the Jewish community of Romania the most balanced and comprehensive analysis is that of Liviu Rotman, in *Evreii din România în perioada comunistă* (The Jews of Romania during the Communist Era) and in the fourth volume he wrote for *The History of the Jews in Romania*. Harry Kuler, in *Evreii in Romania anilor 1944–1949* (The Jews of Romania, 1944–1949), deals with the situation of the Jewish community in the first years of the Communist period. Also useful was the memoir of Chief Rabbi Moses Rosen and several books dedicated to him written before or after 1989. Several articles analyzing the portrayal of the Holocaust in Romania during Communism helped me to gain a better understanding of this topic. Especially relevant was the article by Cosmina Guşu dealing with Holocaust memory in *Magazin Istoric* (Historical Magazine), one of the most circulated historical journals during Communism.[32] As secondary sources, reflecting the Communist narrative on Holocaust memory during this period, the book *Zile însîngerate la Iaşi: 28–30 iunie 1941* (Bloody Days in Jassy: June 28–30, 1941) by Aurel Karetski and Maria Covaci, published in 1978, is one of the clearest choices.

The majority of these works only tangentially discuss the building of Holocaust memory and the role of the Orthodox Church in this process. Research of primary sources was essential to constructing a clear view on this topic. The most important are the journals of the Church, including all the issues of *BOR* (twelve issues per year, 1948–1989), in addition to all the issues of *Ortodoxia*, the journal of the patriarchate, and those of *Studii Teologice*. The archival documents are also, of course, a valuable primary resource. CNSAS, USHMM, INSHREW, and Yad Vahsem provided dozens of files regarding the internal affairs of the Orthodox Church, church-state relations, Jewish-Christian relations, internal affairs of the Jewish community of Romania, and Israeli-Romanian relations. The judicial and secret service files of Visarion Puiu, Valerian Trifa, and Antim Nica, members of the Orthodox hierarchy, are essential to correctly assessing the building of Holocaust memory in Romania. The Israeli archives on the Israeli-Egyptian peace process of the late 1970s are also valuable for understanding Romania's minor role as a mediator in this process.

Secondary sources for the postcommunist period include Lavinia Stan and Lucian Turcescu's *Religion and Politics in Post-Communist Romania*, a careful analysis of the dynamics of church-state relations in post-1989 Romania. The book *Dangers, Tests and Miracles: The Remarkable Life Story of Chief Rabbi Rosen of Romania* helps assess Jewish-Christian Orthodox relations from the perspective of Chief Rabbi Moses Rosen, who was the leader of the Jewish community for most of the Communist period and for several years after the fall of Communism. *Autocefalie, Patriarhie, Slujire Sfântă. Momente Aniversare in Biserica Ortodoxă Romănă* (Autocephaly, Patriarchate, Sacred Service: Anniversary Moments in the Life of the Romanian Orthodox Church) is an official presentation of the Romanian Orthodox Church and is important to assessing the way in which the Church portrayed itself in postcommunist Romania. Of great importance in understanding the building of Holocaust memory in Romania is Michael Shafir's *Between Denial and "Comparative Trivialization": Holocaust Negationism in Post-Communist East Central Europe*. His article "Romania's Torturous Road to Facing Collaboration" is also essential to categorizing important concepts related to Holocaust memory such as "comparative trivialization," "state organized forgetting of the Holocaust," and "competitive martyrology." Articles published in Romanian or international journals by Paul Shapiro, Katherine Verdery, William Totok, Alexandru Florian, and Randolph Braham deal with topics such as nationalism and the revival of anti-Semitism in post-Ceauşescu Romania, the building of Holocaust memory, and the effectiveness of official acknowledgement of the Romanian involvement in the Holocaust.

Articles in the Romanian Orthodox Church's journals—*BOR, Studii Teologice, Ortodoxia*, and *Analele Bucovinei*—from 1990 to 2012 sometimes directly address the Holocaust and reinforce the 1945 myths; they are also useful for understanding the nationalism of the Church after 1989 and its hesitancy in relation to Holocaust memory. Similarly, various international documents such as US State Department and European Commission reports offer a window into the dark realities of anti-Semitism, xenophobia, racism, and persecution of minorities in post-1989 Romania. Romanian and international daily newspapers are useful for assessing the grassroots attitude toward Holocaust memory, offering important insight into the problem of Jewish-Christian relations, the influence of the Romanian Orthodox Church in postcommunist Romania, and the Israeli attitude toward Holocaust memory and its relations to the Romanian state and the Romanian Orthodox Church.

1. The title "Patriarch" corresponds to the leader of an Orthodox Church (such as the Serbian, Russian, or Romanian) who has the rank of patriarchate. In Romania, the Orthodox Church was elevated to the rank of patriarchate in 1925, and the same year Metropolitan Miron Cristea was elected as the first patriarch. In Romanian Orthodox tradition, the metropolitan of Moldova holds the "locum tenens," meaning that he is the next in line to be elected as patriarch. The title "Metropolitan" is specific to Orthodox Churches. It is a rank in-between patriarch (higher) and archbishop (lower). Metropolitans are leaders of an Orthodox metropolitanate. In Romania the metropolitanates are largely ecclesiastical administrative structures corresponding to the traditional provinces of Romania (for example, the metropolitanate of Moldova, or the metropolitanate of Bukovina).

2. "The United States Holocaust Memorial Museum Objects to Cristea Coin," press release, 20 August 2010, http://www.ushmm.org/information/press/press-releases/the-united-states-holocaust-memorial-museum-objects-to-cristea-coin.

3. Mugur Şteţ, "Press Statement of the NBR Spokesman," press release, 19 August 2010, http://www.bnr.ro/page.aspx?prid=4413.

4. See Tuvia Friling, Radu Ioanid, and Mihail Ionescu, eds., *Final Report: International Commission on the Holocaust in Romania* (Iaşi: Polirom, 2005), 7–19.

5. See Ion Popa, "Miron Cristea, the Romanian Orthodox Patriarch: His Political and Religious Influence in Deciding the Fate of the Romanian Jews (February 1938–March 1939)," *Yad Vashem Studies* 40, no. 2 (2012): 11–34. Paragraph published with the permission of *Yad Vashem Studies*.

6. Katherine Verdery, "Nationalism and National Sentiment in Post-socialist Romania," *Slavic Review* 52, no. 2 (Summer 1993): 181.

7. Gabriel Bejan, "De ce scade încrederea românilor în Biserică?" [Why Is the Romanians' Trust in the Church Going Down?], *România Liberă*, 17 April 2012, http://www.romanialibera.ro/opinii/editorial/de-ce-scade-increderea-romanilor-in-biserica-261025.html.

8. See Dan Marinescu, "De ce Biserica se duce în jos?" [Why Is the Church Going Down?], *Adevărul*, 18 February 2013, http://Adevărul.ro/news/societate/de-biserica-duce-jos-1_512271dfoof5182b8577572a/index.html. In 2015 the figure dropped even lower, to 56 percent. See "Sondaj: A crescut încrederea românilor în Preşedinţie şi a scăzut încrederea în Biserică" [Poll: Romanians' Trust in the Presidency has gone up and the Trust in the Church has gone down], *Digi24*, 22 December 2015, http://www.digi24.ro/stiri/actualitate/social/sondaj-a-crescut-increderea-romanilor-in-presedintie-si-a-scazut-increderea-in-biserica-469807.

9. See "Partea Oficială," *BOR* 114, nos. 1–6 (January–June 1996): 384–386; "Partea Oficială," *BOR* 122, nos. 1–4 (January–April 2004): 330, 339–341; "Partea Oficială," *BOR* 126, nos. 3–6 (March–June 2008): 398–400.

10. Laurentiu Mihu, "De ce se scufundă Patriarhul odată cu Ponta?" [Why Is the Patriarch Sinking alongside Ponta?], *România Liberă*, 23 October 2014, http://www.romanialibera.ro/opinii/editorial/de-ce-se-poate-scufunda-biserica-odata-cu-ponta-354543.

11. Cristina Răduţă, "BOR îi răspunde lui Băsescu: 'Implicarea politică partizană a Bisericii în campania electorală trebuie dovedită'" [BOR Answers Băsescu: 'Biased Political Involvement of the Church in the Elections' Campaign Must Be Proved], *Adevărul*, 3 November 2014, http://adevarul.ro/news/politica/bor-raspundelui-basescu-implicarea-politica-partizana-bisericii-campania-electoralatrebuie-dovedita-1_545789490d133766a87ec7b1/index.html.

12. Irina Rîpan, "Liviu Dragnea, decorat de Patriarhul Daniel. Preoţii i-au cântat vicepremierului 'Vrednic este!'" [Liviu Dragnea, Decorated by Patriarch Daniel. The Priests Sang 'He

Is Worthy' in vice-prime minister's honour], *Adevărul*, 12 October 2014, http://adevarul.ro
/locale/ramnicu-valcea/video-liviu-dragnea-decorat-patriarhul-daniel-preotii-i-au-cantat
-vicepremierului-vrednic-este-1_543a7e780d133766a8e0a1de/index.html.

13. Lavinia Stan and Lucian Turcescu, *Religion and Politics in Post-Communist Romania* (New York: Oxford University Press, 2007), 154.

14. C. Iacov, "Monica Macovei vrea sa scoata ora de religie din scoli" [Monica Macovei (Euro MP and presidential candidate) Wants to Abolish RE Classes], *Hotnews*, 12 September 2014, http://www.hotnews.ro/stiri-politic-18092064-monica-macovei-vrea-scoata-ora -religie-din-scoli.htm; see also Andreea Unturica and Cosmin Vaideanu, "Remus Cernea propune ca Religia să devină facultativă în şcoli şi să fie înlocuită cu Etica, obligatorie" [Remus Cernea (a Romanian MP) Proposes that RE Classes Become Optional and Be Replaced by Ethics Which Should Be Mandatory], *Mediafax*, 14 February 2014, http://www.mediafax.ro /social/remus-cernea-propune-ca-religia-sa-devina-facultativa-in-scoli-si-sa-fie-inlocuita-cu -etica-obligatorie-12085553.

15. Cezar Pădurariu and Andreea Saguna, "Mitropolia Moldovei şi Bucovinei cere ca predarea religiei în şcoli să fie garantată în viitoarea Constituţie a României, iar numele Dumnezeu să apară în paragrafe" [The Moldova Metropolitanate Requests RE Classes Be Secured in the Future Constitution of Romania and the Name of God Appear in Its Articles], *Adevărul*, 13 March 2013, http://adevarul.ro/locale/iasi/mitropolia-moldovei-bucovinei-cere-predarea -religiei-scoli-garantata-viitoarea-constitutie-romaniei-numele-dumnezeu-apara-paragrafe-1 _514074e300f5182b8501ce15/index.html#.

16. Stan and Turcescu, *Religion and Politics*, 171–193.

17. Sorin Cosma, "Homosexualitatea—patimă de necinste" [Homosexuality—A Shameful Vice], *BOR* 122, nos. 1–4 (January–April 2004): 171–182.

18. Sfântul Sinod [The Holy Synod], "Mesajul Bisericii Ortodoxe Române" [The Statement of the Romanian Orthodox Church], *BOR* 107, nos. 11–12 (November–December 1989): 3.

19. Vasile Miron, "Rezistenţa bisericii ortodoxe stramoşeşti în faţa presiunilor regimului ateo-comunist," [The Resistance of the Ancestral Orthodox Church against the Pressures of the Atheistic-Communist Regime], *BOR* 126, nos. 7–12 (July–December 2008): 501–518.

20. "Partea Oficiala," *BOR* 115, nos. 7–12 (July–December 1997): 392.

21. "Partea Oficiala, Viata Bisericieasca," [Official Section. Church Life], *BOR* 125, nos. 9–12 (September–December 2007): 294.

22. Vasile Cristian, *Biserica Ortodoxă Română în primul deceniu comunist* [The Romanian Orthodox Church during the First Decade of Communism] (Bucharest: Curtea Veche, 2005), 8.

23. See Sfântul Sinod, "Hotărârea nr 5944 din 5 iulie 2012 a Sfântului Sinod al Bisericii Ortodoxe Române privind modul de aprobare a accesului la documentele aflate în Arhiva Sfântului Sinod şi în arhivele centrelor eparhiale, pentru cercetarea ştiinţifică, publicistică sau de altă natură," Hotărâri ale Sfântului Sinod [Decisions of the Holy Synod], accessed 2 July 2013, http://patriarhia.ro/images/pdf/HotarariSinodale/2012/5944_Comunicare_documente _Arhiva.pdf.

24. The Iron Guard, also known as The Legion of Archangel Michael, was established in 1927 by Corneliu Zelea Codreanu (1899–1938), after separating from the National Christian Defence League of Alexandru C. Cuza (1857–1947). According to Paul Shapiro, "Faith, Murder, Resurrection: The Iron Guard, and the Romanian Orthodox Church," in Kevin P. Spicer, ed., *Antisemitism, Christian Ambivalence, and the Holocaust* (Bloomington: Indiana University Press, 2007), 142, the Iron Guard "was not unequivocally pro-monarchic and was certainly not pro-King Carol II"; it defined itself as a movement, not as a political party, was not committed to parliamentarianism, "was anti-establishment, embracing youthful 'action,' peasantist populism, and mystical religiosity as exemplified by the frequently illiterate local clergy." The

Legion had a militaristic structure, following the tradition of militaristic far-right organizations established by A. C. Cuza. They organized death squads, which committed political assassinations, including the killing of two Romanian prime-ministers (I. G. Duca in 1933, and Armand Călinescu in 1939). Most importantly, the Iron Guard was deeply religious and placed great emphasis on Orthodox Church teachings and mysticism.

25. Vlad Stoicescu, "Reacția Patriarhiei în cazul 'Refrene legionare la «Petru Vodă»': Nu e responsabilitatea noastră" [The Reaction of the Patriarchate in the Case 'Legionary Songs at Petru Vodă': It is not Our Responsibility], *Evenimentul Zilei*, 21 February 2011, http://www.evz .ro/detalii/stiri/reactia-patriarhiei-in-fata-controversei-de-la-petru-voda-nu-e -responsabilitatea-noastra-921.html.

26. See Patrick Henry, "The French Catholic Church's Apology," *French Review* 72, no. 6 (May 1999): 1099–1105.

27. Commission for Religious Relations with the Jews, *We Remember: A Reflection on the Shoah*, accessed 16 July 2013, http://www.vatican.va/roman_curia/pontifical_councils/chrstuni /documents/rc_pc_chrstuni_doc_16031998_shoah_en.html.

28. "The Vatican's Holocaust Report," *New York Times*, 18 March 1998, http://www .nytimes.com/1998/03/18/opinion/the-vatican-s-holocaust-report.html.

29. Jovan Byford, "From 'Traitor' to 'Saint': Bishop Nikolaj Velimirović in Serbian Public Memory," *Analysis of Current Trends in Antisemitism*, no. 22 (2004): 1–41.

30. Transnistria was a large territory (44,000 km2) in Southern Ukraine that was under Romanian administration from August 1941 to February–March 1944. Its size at the time was comparable to Bessarabia, delineated in the west by the Dneister River (separating it from Bessarabia), in the east and north by the Southern Bug River (separating it from the German Reichskommissariat Ukraine), and in the south by the Black Sea. The current separatist republic of Transnistria is of a much smaller size (4,163 km2) and is reminiscent of the Soviet presence in Moldova and Ukraine.

31. Valerian Trifa became in 1951 the Bishop of the Romanian Orthodox Church in America, without Communist approval. His previous Iron Guard past, which will be detailed in chapter 7, started to resurface at the beginning of the 1960s. The Romanian Communist authorities and the Jewish community collaborated in the uncovering of Trifa.

32. Cosmina Gușu, "Reflectarea Holocaustului în revista Magazin Istoric" [The Holocaust as it Appears in 'The Historical Magazine' Review], *Holocaustul. Studii și Cercetări* 1, no. 1 (2009): 151–160.

1

A DANGEROUS "SYMPHONIA"

The Church-State Relationship and Its Impact on the Jewish
Community of Romania before June 22, 1941

ALTHOUGH THE STARTING POINT OF the systematic physical destruction[1] of the Romanian Jewish community is believed to be the summer of 1941,[2] the traces of anti-Semitic policies leading to the Holocaust should be sought in the years prior to the 1941 invasion of the USSR, especially in the policies implemented after December 1937. Anti-Semitic policies were increasingly discussed in Romania in the 1920s and 1930s, but the Goga-Cuza government of December 1937–February 1938 was the first one to radically and irreversibly promulgate such laws. The most important was the Law for the Revision of Citizenship, which in the end stripped Romanian citizenship from 225,222 Jews, representing more than one-third of the entire Jewish population of Romania.[3] The Orthodox Church, the main Christian denomination in Romania, to which a majority of 72 percent of the population belonged during the interwar period, was very much involved in the anti-Semitism of the 1930s. Directly or indirectly, the Church supported far-right parties and intellectual movements in their anti-Jewish discourse. But most importantly the increasing involvement in the politics of the country, made eloquent by the nomination of Patriarch Miron Cristea as prime minster of Romania in February 1938, led to a complicity of the Church in the anti-Semitic policies of various Romanian governments from 1938 to 1944.

In order to understand the context in which the drama of the Holocaust took place in Romania and the role played by the Orthodox Church in the destruction of the Jewish community, we need some background information. The following pages present a brief history of the Romanian Jews and of the Romanian Orthodox Church's religious and political attitude toward Judaism prior to 1938. They also highlight several particularities of the Holocaust in Romania.

The Jews of Romania—a brief introduction

Although evidence about the presence of Jews on Romanian territory since the times of the Roman Empire was debated for a long time,[4] historiography based on several archaeological findings suggests that Jews settled in the Roman provinces of Dacia since the second century A.D.[5] During the early medieval period, merchant Jews, most of them of Sephardic background, started to settle in the Wallachia and Moldova principalities.[6] At the beginning of the sixteenth century, Jews from Poland and Galicia, of Ashkenazi origin, emigrated toward these territories, as demonstrated by headstones in cemeteries of major cities such as Botoşani, Iaşi, Neamţ, and Bucharest.[7]

The principalities of Wallachia and Moldova, which came under Ottoman rule by the fifteenth century, were generally favorable to Jews, some of them holding important positions in the administrative apparatus.[8] In the nineteenth century, the fate of Jews living on Romanian territory was strongly linked with political and territorial developments. In 1859, Wallachia and Moldova united, forming the first modern state of Romania. In the Constitution of 1866, article 7 stipulated that "Romanian citizenship may be acquired by Christians only."[9]

After the Russian-Ottoman war of 1877, at the Berlin Peace Conference Romania was recognized as an independent state, one of the conditions of this recognition being the award of full emancipation to the Jews.[10] In the context of increasing anti-Semitism in the Russian Empire many Jews fled to the eastern and northeastern parts of Romania. If at the beginning of the nineteenth century the Jewish population in the two provinces was estimated at around 20,000, at the end of the century it was around 300,000.[11] Until 1918, only about 2,000 Jews had received Romanian citizenship, a fact which shows the reluctance of the Romanian authorities to put into practice the conditions of the Berlin Peace Treaty. Beginning in 1876, Jews had to undertake military service, although they could not become officers. Before the First World War, Jews mostly supported leftist parties. According to Haiko Haumann, they could not assimilate in Romanian society before 1918, and this was mainly because they did not have equal rights.[12] After the First World War, Romania doubled its territory: Transylvania and Bukovina (which had been part of the Austro-Hungarian Empire), Bessarabia (which had been part of the Russian Empire), and Quadrilater (Southern Dobruja, which had been part of Bulgaria) were added to the Old Kingdom of Romania. These territories had large Jewish presence. In the 1930 census, the Jewish population was 756,930 (4.2 percent of the total population).[13]

In Wallachia the Jewish community was mainly a Sephardic one. In Moldova, Bukovina, northern Transylvania, and Bessarabia, most Jews were of Ashkenazi background. Due to their closeness to the Pale of Settlement (the region of Imperial Russia where Jews were allowed permanent residency) and to Galicia (now western Ukraine), important Hassidic centers could be found in these regions, especially Bukovina and northern Transylvania.[14] Due to their different traditions, the Jews of Greater Romania were not a homogeneous community. Reform Judaism of the German and Hungarian types that could be found in Transylvania never took root in Wallachia. On the other hand, the acculturation of the Wallachia Jews (southern Romania), accompanied by the adoption of a Romanian identity, was not entirely mirrored in other parts of the country.[15]

In the first decade of Greater Romania's existence (1918–1928), the number of Jewish students attending Romanian universities increased, especially in the two most important student centers of the interwar period: Iași (Moldova) and Bucharest (Wallachia).[16] In parallel with this process, the Jews, especially those in Bessarabia, developed a very organized system of Jewish education.[17] Although there are no statistics on the extent of linguistic acculturation among Romania's Jewish communities during the interwar period, in Ezra Mendelsohn's opinion the Jews of Bessarabia, Bukovina, northern Transylvania, and Moldova continued to speak Yiddish, while the German and Hungarian orientations remained very much alive in Bukovina and Transylvania. "The new generations learned Romanian in school; in Bukovina for example, the great majority of Jewish children attended government schools, and the same was true in Transylvania.

Acculturation did not necessarily imply the decline of orthodoxy, at least not in its Transylvanian stronghold."[18] Many Romanian Jews contributed to the cultural life of the country, in various fields their performance being outstanding.[19]

The Jewish community of Romania suffered great losses during the Holocaust. Most of the Jewish population in northern and eastern Romania was killed, while the population of the Old Kingdom was largely saved due to the failed plans to deport the Jews from these territories to Belzec. After the war, most of the approximately 400,000 Jewish survivors left Romania, the majority of them emigrating to Israel. At the end of the Communist era only 20,000 Jews were still in Romania and by 2006 the number, according to the Federation of Jewish Communities of Romania, was 9,351.[20]

The Romanian Orthodox Church and the Jews prior to 1938

In 1859 Wallachia and Moldova, two principalities which had been under Ottoman suzerainty for more than four centuries, united under the leadership of Alexandru Ioan Cuza in what is known as the Vechiul Regat (the Old Kingdom) of Romania. In 1872 the political quest for independence of the new state was mirrored by the Orthodox Church; the two metropolitanates of Wallachia and Moldova exited the jurisdiction of the Constantinople Patriarchate and the Metropolitan of Wallachia was elevated to the rank of metropolitan-primate. On April 25, 1885, seven years after the Congress of Berlin confirmed the independence of Romania from Ottoman rule, the Church became autocephalous (self-governing). On February 25, 1925, seven years after the creation of the Greater Romania, the Romanian Orthodox Church was elevated to the jurisdictional territory of a patriarchate, being in dogmatic, liturgical, and canonical communion with the other sister Orthodox Churches.[21] The metropolitan-primate, Miron Cristea, became the first patriarch of the Romanian Orthodox Church (1925–1939). During the interwar and war period the Romanian Orthodox Church was divided into five metropolitanates (this is a category specific to Eastern Orthodoxy, similar to some extent to Western archbishoprics), largely corresponding to the historic provinces of Romania. Some of the interwar metropolitans, such as Nicolae Bălan, the metropolitan of Transylvania (1920–1955), Visarion Puiu, the metropolitan of Bukovina (1935–1940) and of Transnistria (1942–1943), Tit Simedrea, the metropolitan of Bukovina (1941–1945), and Irineu Mihălcescu, the metropolitan of Moldova (1939–1947), were influential personalities and played an important role in the Holocaust. In 1939, after the death of Miron Cristea, the Romanian Orthodox Church elected Nicodim Munteanu as the second patriarch of the Church (1939–1948).

The Romanian Orthodox Church has not had a clear and distinct theology concerning Judaism and the Jews; most of the time the guidelines have been represented by Eastern Orthodox Church fathers' writings and some late medieval Church laws. The Orthodox Church manifested from an early stage a dualistic approach toward Jews, and this was mainly because of the way in which the Church and the state had worked together since medieval times. For example, in a seventeenth-century Church document called the Govora Law (1640) Jewish-Christian relations were forbidden: "Any priest who will have any relation with the Jews, will call them brothers, or will eat at the same table with them will be excluded from the Church."[22] On the other hand, Jews who converted to Christian Orthodoxy were, under Prince (Ruler) Matei Basarab's state law of 1652, able to become priests and to pursue an ecclesiastical career.[23] The Orthodox theological approach to the conversion of Jews was stipulated in a law from 1764 called "Law/Ordinary Regarding the Way in which the Yids can be accepted for baptism." According to this law, which still represents the guidelines of the Romanian Orthodox Church, Jewish converts had to complete a pre-catechization and a catechization process before being considered for baptism. The rules were strict: before the catechization began, the aspiring Jewish convert had to pass a series of tests. After the pre-catechization period, the catechumen (aspiring convert) was assigned to a "knowledgeable priest" who "would lead him to the Christian teachings, but, most importantly, would introduce him to the true faith and moral life." The catechization period varied, the most common being forty days in which the catechumen had to attend Church services and fast. During the entire period, "the priest will always have to be careful and to enquire whether the catechumen wants to be baptized truly for the sake of faith, or [is] driven by other reasons."[24] This emphasis on doubt in the case of an aspiring Jewish convert was suggestive of the distrust of the Orthodox Church. This distrust would continue and would also be felt during the 1938–1942 debates about the conversion of Jews. After the catechization period, the neophyte faced a public examination, and only then could the baptism take place. Although the 1764 law mentions the Jews in particular, the precepts of the law were largely similar to the Orthodox (and Catholic) laws regarding the conversion of heretics.

After the 1859 union of Wallachia and Moldova, the Romanian Ortho-dox Church received several blows that affected its political influence, among them the 1864 land reform of Alexandru Ioan Cuza, which expropriated large parts of its properties. Although the nineteenth-century Romanian politicians, inspired by the French model, promoted a more visible separa-tion of church and state,[25] this does not mean that the Orthodox Church's influence at the grassroots decreased. Its unchanged popular prestige be-came more visible after the First World War. In 1918, new territories of Austria-Hungary, Russia, and Bulgaria joined Romania in what is known as the Great Union (*Marea Unire*). These new additions were recognized by the Great Powers in the post–First World War peace treaties. The Great Union was the realization of a dream held for decades by many Roma-nians, but the new realities of Greater Romania were far from simple. Due to the ethnic and religious diversity of the new provinces, after 1918 roughly 30 percent of the new state's population was non-Romanian, as opposed to 8 percent before the war. Almost the majority of the 30 percent non-Romanians were non-Orthodox as well. "The Orthodox Church remained dominant, but its faithful dropped from 91.5 percent in 1899 to 72.6 in 1930."[26] A patriarchate report from 1935 reveals that 12,375,850 people, out of 18,057,028, the entire population of Romania according to the 1930 cen-sus, declared themselves to be Orthodox.

> The Orthodox clergy numbered 8542 priests, 7868 of which received salaries from the state, 380 salaries from private funding, 188 were retired while 106 priests were without any state salaries. The composition of the clergy showed that most of them had only elementary theological education. Only 76 priests had doctoral degrees in theology, 1446 had university degrees, while 3287 had completed seven or eight years in a seminary and 537 only four years. In addition, the priests were helped by 10,452 cantors; 9166 received state support and 1268 private funding.[27]

The 1930 census revealed that in Romania 6,029,136 people were illiterate and, most importantly, 14,405,898 of the population was rural. This led Lucian Leuștean to argue that "the large number of rural clergy with a relatively low level of education was directly linked with the political and economic tra-jectory of Romania, as due to the traditional character of Orthodoxy, peas-ants tended to support the political position of their local clergy."[28]

In this context, the political game of the Church became decisive in in-terwar Romania, both for the politicians who tried to gain votes and for the Church who sought a return to a strong political position. The Romanian Orthodox Church became a patriarchate in 1925, and the role of the first patriarch, Miron Cristea, in taking advantage of interwar politics was essential. He understood that the Great Union of 1918, with its destruction of ethnic and religious homogeneity, was a golden opportunity for the Church to regain the positions it had lost since the creation of modern Romania. Cristea advocated a return to the days when the church and the state supplemented each other.[29] The interdependence of church and state would be made more manifest during the dictatorships of Carol II and Ion Antonescu. When Nicodim, the second patriarch of the Church, praised Carol II in 1940 as being Constantine the Great, this was not a figure of speech. It was a vision the Church shared at the time, in which the ruler and the Church should work together, as in the old times, for the prosperity of the nation. Famous pictures showing Patriarch Nicodim standing at the right-hand side of Ion Antonescu during some of his speeches or pictures of metropolitans participating in rallies of the Romanian army suggest the strong links between the Church and these institutions.[30] The Church enjoyed being seen at the core of the state's chain of command, legitimating and encouraging it.

This political role of the Romanian Orthodox Church had a great impact on the Jewish community of Romania. Before 1938 this aspect became visible in the fact that all far-right anti-Semitic political parties and movements claimed to be inspired by and to have at their core the Church's dogma and history. Although Patriarch Cristea disliked the Iron Guard, an extreme rightwing, anti-Semitic, and antiestablishment movement, he supported other extremist figures such as A. C. Cuza and Octavian Goga. Other important members of the Church's hierarchy openly promoted the Iron Guard too, sometimes in spite of royal and Church orders. One example, among others, well-reported in the media at the time and which had a great impact on the public was the funeral of two Iron Guard volunteers killed in 1937 in the Spanish Civil War. Metropolitans Visarion Puiu of Bukovina and Nicolae Bălan of Transylvania held special services for them despite an official ban. The Orthodox Theology faculties at most universities were focal points of radical anti-Semitism, and many Orthodox priests were actively involved in far-right parties. For example in the 1937 general election, 33 out of 103 parliament candidates of the Iron Guard (renamed Totul pentru Țară—All for the Country) were Orthodox priests.[31] Iron Guard and other

THE ROMANIAN ORTHODOX CHURCH AND THE HOLOCAUST

far-right parties' strong presence in places with a significant Jewish population[32] and the role of Orthodox priests in promoting far-right policies[33] alienated the Orthodox and the Jewish communities even more. According to the *Final Report of the Elie Wiesel International Commission on the Holocaust in Romania*, "in 1938, Alexandru Răzmeriţă, a Romanian Orthodox priest, described a plan for the total elimination of the Jews in the cities and their deportation to forced labor camps in the countryside. Attempts to escape the work camps would be punished by execution."[34] To the encouragement of far-right parties and movements should be added the open and virulent anti-Semitism of Patriarch Cristea who, in 1937, in a now well-known attack, called the Jews parasites who suck the bone marrow of the Romanian people and who should leave the country.

> One has to be sorry for the poor Romanian people, whose very marrow is sucked out by the Jews. Not to react against the Jews means that we go open-eyed to our destruction. . . . To defend ourselves is a national and patriotic duty. This is not 'antisemitism' [sic]. Where is it written that only you, the Jews, have the privilege of living on some other people's back and on our back, like some parasites? You have sufficient qualities and opportunities to look for, find and acquire a country, a homeland that is not yet inhabited by others. . . . Live, help each other, defend yourselves, and exploit one another, but not us and other peoples whose entire wealth you are taking away with your ethnic and Talmudic sophistications.[35]

The way in which Cristea's declarations of 1937 influenced his policies as prime minister (February 1938–March 1939), is discussed later in this chapter.

In his analysis of the church-state relationship in Orthodox Romania, Olivier Gillet is right in pointing out that in medieval Eastern Europe there was no struggle for supremacy between the church and the state as there was in the West, and that the church-state separation increasingly advocated in Western Europe since the Enlightenment was not really applied in the East.[36] Gillet points out that the Romanian Orthodox Church adapted every time to the political contexts of the last century, following the Byzantine tradition of church-state relationship. This is how we should understand the Church's collaboration with various and significantly different regimes, from the fascist dictatorship of Ion Antonescu to the Communist dictatorship installed after 1945.[37] This culture of adaptability, or *symphonia* as it is called by Lucian Leuştean, put the Orthodox Church in a powerful position, at the center of the state's politics.[38] Both Leuştean and Gillet suggest that, despite many political changes, nothing about the Church's influence in Romanian politics and society has changed from 1938 to the present day.

The game of political power, the support of the rightwing movements, and cultivated anti-Semitism put the Church in a dangerous position. All these factors contributed to a mingling of the Church with anti-Semitic policies. At the beginning of 1937, the Holy Synod, led by Patriarch Cristea, expressed a clear desire to get rid of foreigners and its support for any policies that would revise the citizenship status of the Jews.[39] It is not surprising that when the Goga-Cuza government adopted the law for the revision of citizenship in January 1938 it was saluted in the Church's press as the spiritual rebirth of Romanianism.[40]

Particularities of the Holocaust in Romania

Romania was, at the time of the Holocaust, still a relatively young state. The 1859 union of Wallachia and Moldova under the leadership of Alexandru Ioan Cuza and the creation of the Old Kingdom of Romania were clearly steps toward self-determination. The new state unilaterally declared its independence from the Ottoman rule in May 1877, during the Russian-Turkish War, and was officially recognized by the Great Powers at the Berlin Peace Conference of 1878. In 1866, in order to preserve the new state, Romanian politicians invited Karl of Hohenzollern-Sigmaringen to become the new king of Romania. Given his German heritage, the newly renamed Carol I refused pressure to declare war against Austria-Hungary and Germany in 1914. Romania entered the First World War only in 1916, after Carol I's death. After 1918, Romania's territory almost doubled, adding the new provinces of Transylvania, Bukovina, and Bessarabia, which had substantial Jewish communities. In 1923, the new constitution granted civil rights to the Jewish population, Romania being the last country in Europe to do so. However, the attitude of various interwar Romanian governments toward Jews ranged from grudging acceptance of their equality before the law, under pressure from foreign powers, to overt anti-Semitism.[41] The anti-Semitic policies were more openly promoted after King Carol II called the National Christian Party (Partidul Național Creștin, or PNC) of A. C. Cuza and Octavian Goga to form a government in December 1937. Although this government was removed from power two months later under pressure from France and the United Kingdom, its policies continued to be put in practice during 1938 and the first part of 1939 by the governments led by Miron Cristea, the patriarch of the Romanian Orthodox Church. In the summer of 1940, in the context of German advances in Western Europe and the loss of territories gained by Romania after the First World War, more anti-Semitic policies were passed. King Carol II's dictatorship (February 1938 through September 1940) ceased when the king was forced to abdicate by a coalition, which was openly pro-German, formed by General Ion Antonescu and the Iron Guard, also known as the Legion of Archangel Michael (hence the name of its members, Legionnaires). The Legionary State (September 1940 to January 1941) ended with an open conflict, known as the Legionary Rebellion, between Antonescu and the Iron Guard. During the clashes of January 21–23, 1941, 120 Jews were killed in the Bucharest pogrom. After the elimination of the Iron Guard, Ion Antonescu remained the sole leader of Romania. He maintained the previous relation with the Reich and on June 22, 1941, Romania joined Germany as an ally in the war against the USSR. This moment also signifies the beginning of the physical destruction of the Romanian Jewish community.

The Holocaust in Romania was, from many points of view, unique in European Jewry's destruction. In the opinion of Raul Hilberg, considered to be one of the world's foremost scholars of the Holocaust, "Besides Germany itself, Romania was thus the only country that implemented all the steps of the destruction process, from definition to killings."[42] The Romanians had their own plan for a final solution, inspired by the German model but with significant particularities. Some of the most important were the religious dimensions of Romanian anti-Semitism and the discrepancy in the destruction process.

The first dimension is suggested by the fact that the Church supported and encouraged extreme rightwing, anti-Semitic parties and movements in a quest to regain its former role in Romanian politics. At the same time the idea that Orthodoxy was the core of Romanian national identity ensured that anti-Semitism and the Holocaust in Romania were more grounded in religious ideology. Even racial elements such as blood, or people (*neam* in Romanian), were interpreted in a religious register. This mixture of religion and politics, and the vanishing line between church and state, detailed later, led to a great involvement of the Romanian Orthodox Church in the Holocaust.

The second important difference between the Romanian and German final solution is suggested by the chronological development of the Holocaust in Romania. Soon after the start of the war against the USSR it became obvious that the Romanians were implementing a program of annihilation of Jewish communities. In the summer of 1941 a series of pogroms took place in Moldova, Bukovina, and Bessarabia. The Romanian army and gendarmerie,[43] the German army, and units of the Einsatzgruppen D (SS death squads), perpetrated them,[44] sometimes with the participation of Romanian civilians.[45] Concomitantly, the Romanian authorities began to deport Jews from these territories to the Dniester River in what is known in the historiography of the Holocaust as the "hasty deportations."[46] Although stopped for several weeks due to discontent from the German army, which complained that the movement of troops eastward was being hindered, these deportations restarted in the autumn of 1941. Many Romanian Jews, mostly from Bessarabia, Bukovina, and Moldova, were deported to Transnistria, a territory in southern Ukraine that came under Romanian control in August 1941. From 1941 to 1944, thousands of Romanian and Ukrainian Jews died in Transnistria in direct shootings or due to starvation, sickness, and cold.[47] According to the *Final Report*, between 280,000 and 380,000 Jews died in territories under Romanian control.[48] In addition, more than 25,000 Roma (that is, 12 percent of the Roma population living in Romania in 1942) were deported to Transnistria during the war. Although some were killed by gendarmes on arrival, they were not targeted for organized executions, as was the case with the Jews. Most of the deported Roma died from hunger and illness. Although the exact number of those killed is not known; the highest estimate is 19,000, Dennis Deletant suggesting that "it is almost certain that more than half [of the 25,000 Roma deported] died."[49]

Despite a continuous crescendo in the implementation of anti-Semitic policies from 1937 to 1942, in October 1942 the Romanian authorities suddenly and unexpectedly changed their attitude toward Jews. While initially agreeing with German plans for the deportation of all remaining Romanian Jews to Belzec, Ion Antonescu changed his mind due to discontent with German demands that Romania increase its war efforts and lack of assurances from Hitler regarding Romanian territorial claims. The decision of October 1942 to halt the deportations was reinforced at the beginning of 1943 when it became clear after the Battle of Stalingrad that Germany could lose the war. Antonescu spared the remaining Jews in order to use them as bargaining chips with the Allies should the Axis powers lose. As a result, about half of the Romanian Jews, mostly from the Old Kingdom of Romania, survived the war.

PATRIARCH MIRON CRISTEA'S POLITICAL AND RELIGIOUS INFLUENCE IN DECIDING THE FATE OF THE ROMANIAN JEWS (FEBRUARY 1938 THROUGH MARCH 1939)

Patriarch Miron Cristea (1868–1939) was an influential and powerful personality both inside and outside the Romanian Orthodox Church.[50] He was very much involved in Transylvania's decision to join Romania after the First World War and was the leader of the Transylvanian delegation (the second on that delegation was the Greek-Catholic Archbishop Iuliu Hossu) that handed in the official proclamation of unification to King Ferdinand on 5 December 1918.[51] He became the first patriarch of the Romanian Orthodox Church (1925–1939), and was one of the three members of the Regency from 1927 (the death of King Ferdinand) to 1930 (the return of King Carol II).[52]

At the beginning of February 1938 King Carol II abolished the government of Octavian Goga and A. C. Cuza, one important factor in this decision being the strong negative reaction from France and the United Kingdom against its anti-Semitic measures. Amid the increasing power of the Iron Guard (whom the king considered his worst enemy) and a very turbulent political climate, Carol II dissolved the parliament, the constitution, and all political parties on 11 February 1938, and instituted his own dictatorship with Patriarch Cristea as prime minister. Anti-Semitic measures were the most important part of Patriarch/Prime Minister Miron Cristea's political program, which he presented to the king soon after nomination. The first five paragraphs were about such policies; only from the sixth paragraph onward did the program address other economic, financial, and social problems. First the program was meant to "promote the national idea" by the "reparation of historical injustice toward the Romanian dominant element." When practical policies were concerned, the third paragraph called for a "reexamination of the acquisition of citizenship after the war and annulment of all naturalizations made fraudulently and contrary to the vital interests of the Romanians. This reexamination will also promote broader economic participation by the Romanian element." The next paragraph went beyond the Goga-Cuza policies, announcing "the organization of the departure from the country of foreign elements that, recently established in the country, damage and weaken our Romanian ethnic national character. Romania will cooperate with other states that have an excess of Jewish population, helping [the Jews] to find their own country."[53] Prime Minister Miron Cristea continued the policies of the Goga-Cuza government, such as the stripping of Jews of their Romanian citizenship.[54] But he also advocated new and more extreme measures. Deportation and Romanianization, the other two main aspects of his anti-Semitic program, visible in the paragraph quoted above, would be key features of the Holocaust in Romania later on, and the patriarch of the Church was one of the main promoters of them starting in 1938. Regarding Romanianization, in one of his speeches quoted in *Apostolul*, the journal of the Romanian Orthodox Patriarchate, in May 1938, Cristea said:

> But we cannot go further with our tolerance and indolence without putting under threat the very future and Romanian character of our country. After the war many infidels,[55] many foreigners, [and] Jews invaded us, so many that we cannot endure on our bodies that many parasites sucking away our vitality. . . . There are institutions, factories, [and] professions where 50, 60, 70, 90, and even 95 percent of the beneficiaries are foreigners, and we, Romanians, are their slaves in our own country.[56]

In his 1939 New Year speech, given at the Royal Palace, Cristea outlined the government's accomplishments in 1938 and his plans for 1939. A special section of the speech was dedicated to "The Primacy of the Romanians":

> Foreigners that are no longer needed as specialists will be stripped of their right to live in Romania. Especially concerning the Jews, the government has taken measures to stop any mass invasion of the Jews from Central Europe. The review of citizenship status started and continued and for those that could not prove their citizenship, or acquired it through unauthorized means, we created a special status, considering them what they always were—foreigners, under control. To them we have applied the laws for the protection of national work.[57]

In an article published in *Apostolul* as a follow-up to the New Year speech, entitled "The Restoration of the Autochthonous in Their Historic Rights," Cristea's plans for the Romanianization process were unveiled: "His Holiness the Patriarch considers state action necessary for the reinforcement of the autochthonous element, in the quest for regaining the lost positions, lost because of the historic vicissitudes."[58] The plan was meant primarily to enforce the employment of Romanians to the detriment of "foreigners." It was to be applied over a period of ten years, with a progressive increase of the Romanian element in every profession and harsh penalties for those "who would try to sabotage the nationalization of the work force."[59] At that time, Romanianization meant, it seems, mostly the reinforcement of the autochthonous element in different professions and not, as subsequent measures would stipulate, the spoliation of Jewish businesses and properties. The patriarch died a few weeks later, and Romanianization was dropped from the public debate for more than a year after his death.

Miron Cristea saw the Jews as a threat to the very existence of Romanian people, as parasites, as promoters of decadence, as invaders.[60] In 1938 the Church press became flooded with anti-Semitic materials,[61] especially the official journal of the patriarchate, which acted both as a religious and political review. But most importantly, in March 1938, one month and a half after the issuance of the Law for the Revision of Citizenship, the Holy Synod adopted a decision to ban the conversion to Orthodoxy of any Jew who could not prove his/her Romanian citizenship.[62] This decision, which was a clear politicization of a religious act, was not surprising because a year before the same Holy Synod had expressed open support for such an initiative.[63]

Patriarch Cristea's "mania" against the Jews, as it was called by the British ambassador to Bucharest,[64] was important in shaping both state and Church policies against the Jewish community of Romania. However, it would be a mistake to believe that Miron Cristea was the only person to blame for the Orthodox Church's anti-Semitism before the war. Visarion Puiu, the metropolitan of Bukovina, fought a veritable war against Jewish banks and enterprises.[65] Metropolitan Bălan of Transylvania offered his public support for the Iron Guard when he held funerals for the two Iron Guard victims of the Spanish Civil War. His links with far-right personalities, including A. C. Cuza or Octavian Goga, were notorious. Professors at the Faculties of Orthodox Theology like Nichifor Crainic (1889–1972) and Teodor Popescu (1893–1973) openly promoted extreme anti-Semitism. But the strongest argument that the Church was not just a victim of Cristea's mania against the Jews is the Holy Synod decision in June 1939, four months after Miron Cristea's death, to stick with the previous regulation and to ban any baptism of Jews who could not prove their Romanian citizenship. The 1939 decision went a step further in making acceptance of Jews with Romanian citizenship into the Church harder.[66]

The death of Miron Cristea (March 6, 1939) brought a more relaxed attitude toward the Jewish community both politically and religiously. The process of stripping Jews of their Romanian citizenship eased and the plans for Romanianization were put aside. In July 1939 the law that required the predominance of ethnic Romanians in factories was annulled.[67] After March 1939 the official journals of the Church did not contain as many anti-Jewish articles as before and the Church's public outbursts of anti-Semitism were rarer. This should be seen in the context of Carol II's dictatorship and his censorship policy; it may be yet another argument that Cristea, not Carol II, was the main promoter of anti-Semitic policies from February 1938 to March 1939.

After Cristea's death, in June 1939 the Romanian Orthodox Church held elections for a new patriarch. In an address to the Electoral College, Metropolitan Bălan of Transylvania, one of the most important and influential personalities of the Church, made clear his refusal to accept the patriarchal seat, his only reason being that he wanted to continue his service in Transylvania.[68] At the same time, another candidate, Metropolitan Visarion Puiu of Bukovina, expressed the same refusal.[69] Visarion Puiu was disliked by King Carol II who, starting in 1937, supported Puiu's replacement as Metropolitan of Bukovina.[70] The reasons for this dislike were linked to Puiu's anti-Semitic, pro-Iron Guard, and pro-German policies.[71] Bălan was also an anti-Semite and his pro-German and pro-Iron Guard attitudes were well-known,[72] so it would be safe to assume that the two public "refusals" were influenced by the king. It should be emphasized here that the elections were held when King Carol II's power was at its peak. Later developments could also shed light on these two refusals. In 1942 great tensions arose inside the Church: Patriarch Nicodim's authority was contested by Metropolitan Bălan, who acted for a period as the true leader of the Church. Moreover, the tensions of 1942 had regional connotations (see chapter 2). It is likely that King Carol II, who probably was aware of the situation inside the Church, forced the two "refusals" as a way of preventing an internal ecclesiastical war.

Both Visarion Puiu and Nicolae Bălan would play important roles later during the Holocaust. Although an anti-Semite, Metropolitan Bălan would be influential in halting the deportation of Jews from the Old Kingdom to

Belzec in 1942. Visarion Puiu, on the other hand, became the head of the Orthodox Mission in Transnistria from November 1942 to December 1943. He would be condemned to death in absentia by the Communists after the war for his support of state policies in Transnistria, among other reasons.[73]

In June 1939 The Romanian Orthodox Church elected Nicodim Munteanu as the new patriarch. In Romanian Orthodox tradition, the metropolitan of Moldova holds the "locum tenens," meaning that he is the next in line to be elected as patriarch. However, the circumstances of Nicodim's election as metropolitan of Moldova in 1936 are unclear.[74] He accepted the patriarchal seat only because every other contender refused the role. He was old[75] and, as events would show, lacking backbone. He was not in the same league as Patriarch Cristea or Metropolitan Bălan. While those two influenced decisions, created opportunities, and led the Church, Nicodim seemed to be more a victim of circumstances than a creator of policies. From the articles he wrote before and during the war, it seems that he had two major convictions (or obsessions) and both of them would bring him a lot of trouble after the war: he hated the Bolsheviks and he considered the Jews as the main creators and promoters of Bolshevism.

The Church returned to promoting strong anti-Semitism in its official press after the loss of Bessarabia and Bukovina in June 1940. At the same time, Carol II's dictatorship started to crumble. The Jews were blamed in both lay and religious press for the loss of these two historical provinces of Romania and for their alleged mocking and attacking of the retreating Romanian army.[76] As many documents suggest, people of various ethnic backgrounds perpetrated the few incidents against Romanian troops.[77] Nevertheless, the anti-Semitic propaganda emphasized and exaggerated the alleged Jewish guilt. In the summer of 1940, with Carol's dictatorship losing power and legitimacy, a set of anti-Semitic laws similar to the Nuremberg Laws were passed in Romania.[78] In the long run, they and others issued at the beginning of 1941 were meant to expel the Romanian Jews from the economic, financial, and social life of the country. As a result, the Holy Synod of the Romanian Orthodox Church faced requests for help from Jews converted to Orthodoxy (see chapter 2).

From 6 September 1940, when King Carol II abdicated, to January 22, 1941, when the Iron Guard tried to seize control of the state, Romania was ruled by a coalition of General Ion Antonescu and the Iron Guard in what is known as the Legionary State. In his special message after the Iron Guard came to power in September 1940, Patriarch Nicodim took a moderate tone, or, as Mirel Bănică says, he was "lacking enthusiasm."[79] It is apparent that in his approach to the Iron Guard Nicodim followed the same line as his predecessor, fearing the antiestablishment and violent policies of the Legion and its power to undermine the Church. Despite Cristea's and Nicodim's hesitancies toward the Iron Guard, its large influence on the Church's grassroots continued to grow. For example, in January 1941, after the unsuccessful putsch of the Legion, 422 out of 9,000 people arrested were Orthodox priests.[80] During the Legionary State the Iron Guard tried to force a reorganization of the Church. They asked, among other things, for the priests to become more involved in politics and thus to play the Iron Guard's political game.[81] This is apparent in an exchange of letters between Patriarch Nicodim and General Antonescu published in a well-known Romanian newspaper. The patriarch opposed the proposed reorganization, and it is not surprising that he welcomed the ejection of the Iron Guard from government in January 1941.[82] Nevertheless, the friction between the patriarchs of the Church and the Iron Guard were not based on different policies toward the Jews. Moreover, the Church, released from the danger of an inopportune Iron Guard, adopted their extreme anti-Semitism, so after January 1941 in the Church's press the racial and religious aspects of anti-Semitism were more openly promoted.

NOTES

1. This term appears in Tuvia Friling, Radu Ioanid, and Mihai Ionescu, eds., *The Final Report of the Elie Wiesel Commission for the Study of the Holocaust in Romania* (Bucharest: Polirom, 2005), 120–126. It is used in the title of the sub-chapter describing the first pogroms in the summer of 1941 ("The Iași Pogrom: The First Stage of the Physical Destruction of Romanian Jewry") as a way of highlighting the distinction between previous anti-Semitic measures designed to destroy the community and the campaign of physical violence and murder.

2. See George Voicu, ed., *Pogromul de la Iași (28–30 Iunie 1941): prologul Holocaustului din România* [The Jassy Pogrom (29–30 June 1941): The Prelude of the Holocaust in Romania] (Iași, Romania: Polirom, 2006), 11.

3. Carol Iancu, *Les juifs en Roumanie (1919–1938): de l'emancipation a la marginalisation* (Paris, Leuven: Peeters, 1996), 312.

4. Nicolae Gudea, "Were There Jews in the Provinces of Dacia (Ancient Romania) during the Roman Era?," in *The History of the Jews in Romania*, vol. 1, *From the Beginnings to the Nineteenth Century*, ed. Paul Cernavodeanu (Tel Aviv: Goldstein-Goren Diaspora Research Center, 2005), 16.

5. Silviu Costache, *Evreii din România: Studiu de Geografie Umană* [The Jews of Romania: Study on Human Geography] (Bucharest: Editura Universității București, 2004), 32–33.

6. Constantin Rezachevici, "The Jews in the Romanian Principalities, Fifteenth to Eighteenth Centuries," in Cernavodeanu, ed., *The History of the Jews in Romania*, 1:37.

7. Costache, *Evreii din Romania*, 44.

8. Ibid., 64.

9. Carol Iancu, "The Struggle for the Emancipation of Romanian Jewry and Its International Ramifications," in *The History of the Jews in Romania*, vol. 2, *The Nineteenth Century*, ed. Liviu Rotman and Carol Iancu, 121.

10. Haiko Haumann, *A History of East European Jews* (New York: Central European University Press, 2002), 195.

11. Ibid., 194–195.

12. Ibid., 196.

13. Sabin Manuilă, ed., *Recensământul general al populației României din 29 decemvrie 1930* [The Census of Romania's Population, 29 December 1930] (Bucharest: Institutul Național de Statistică, 1938), 2, xxiv.

14. Ezra Mendelsohn, *Jews of East Central Europe between the World Wars* (Bloomington: Indiana University Press, 1983), 98.

15. Ibid., 174.

16. See Irina Livezeanu, *Cultural Politics in Greater Romania: Regionalism, Nation Building, and Ethnic Struggle, 1918–1930* (Ithaca, NY: Cornell University Press, 1995), 235–240.

17. Mendelsohn, *Jews of East Central Europe*, 199.

18. Ibid.

19. See Nicolae Cajal and Hary Kuller, eds., *Contribuția evreilor din România la cultură si civilizatie* [The Contribution of Romanian Jews to the Culture and Civilization] (Bucharest: Hasefer, 2004), 180–700.

20. Federația Comunităților Evreiești din România, Membrii FCER [The Federation of Jewish Communities of Romania, FCER Members], accessed July 2, 2013, http://www.jewishfed.ro/index.php/despre-noi-mainmenu-127/14-prezentarea-fcer/24-5-numar-de-membri-obiective-generale-de-activitate.

21. For a short presentation of the history of the Romanian Orthodox Church, see http://patriarhia.ro/history-of-the-romanian-orthodox-church-355-en/.

22. Gheorghe I. Petre-Govora, ed., *Pravila bisericească de la Govora* [The Church Law from Govora] (Bucharest: Academia Română, 2004), 71.

23. Episcop [Bishop] Dr. Antim Nica, "Pe urmele apostolatului românesc" [Retracing the Romanian Apostolate], *Biserica Ortodoxă Română (BOR)* 63, nos. 11–12 (November–December, 1945): 572.

24. Ibid., 573–575.

25. Lucian N. Leuștean, *Orthodoxy and the Cold War: Religion and Political Power in Romania, 1947–65* (London: Palgrave Macmillan, 2009), 25–38.

26. Ibid., 48.

27. Ibid., 47.

28. Ibid.

29. See Ion Popa, "Miron Cristea, the Romanian Orthodox Patriarch: His Political and Religious Influence in Deciding the Fate of the Romanian Jews (February 1983–March 1939)," *Yad Vashem Studies* 40, no. 2 (2012): 15.

30. See "Biserica în misiune" and "Evenimente și solemnități din trecutul bisericesc," especially "Miron Cristea Prim Ministru," "In timpul guvernării legionare," "In timpul guvernării antonesciene," and "Alte procesiuni și sărbători religioase," Fototeca Ortodoxiei Românești, http://fototecaortodoxiei.ro/.

31. Paul Shapiro, "Faith, Murder, Resurrection: The Iron Guard and the Romanian Orthodox Church," in *Antisemtisim, Christian Ambivalence, and the Holocaust,* ed. Kevin P. Spicer (Bloomington: Indiana University Press, 2007), 151.

32. Paul Daniel Quinlan, *Regele Playboy: Carol al II-lea de România* [The Playboy King, Carol II of Romania] (Bucharest: Humanitas, 2001), 205.

33. Leuştean, *Orthodoxy and the Cold War,* 51. Leuştean says that almost two thousand priests were directly involved in the Iron Guard.

34. Friling, Ioanid, and Ionescu, eds., *Final Report,* 50.

35. Leon Volovici, *Ideologia naţionalistă şi „problema evreiască": eseu despre formele antisemitismului intellectual in Romania anilor '30* [Nationalist Ideology and "The Jewish Question": Essay on the Forms of Intellectual Anti-Semitism in 1930s Romania] (Bucharest: Humanitas, 1995), 75.

36. Olivier Gillet, *Religie şi naţionalism. Ideologia Bisericii Ortodoxe Române sub regimul comunist* [Religion and Nationalism. The Ideology of the Romanian Orthodox Church under the Communist Regime] (Bucharest: Compania, 2001), 18–19.

37. Ibid., 107.

38. Leuştean, *Orthodoxy and the Cold War,* 189.

39. Shapiro, *Faith, Murder, Resurrection,* 149.

40. Patriarhul României Miron Cristea, "Renaşterea spirituală a Românismului prin tainele şi luminile Bisericii Creştine" [The Spiritual Rebirth of Românianism (i.e., Romanian nationalism) through the Sacraments and the Lights of the Christian Church], *Apostolul* 14, nos. 1–2 (1–31 January 1938): 2.

41. Yehuda Bauer, *American Jewry and the Holocaust: The American Jewish Joint Distribution Committee, 1939–1945* (Detroit: Wayne State University Press, 1982), 335.

42. Raul Hilberg, *The Destruction of the European Jews* (Chicago: Quadrangle Books, 1961), 485.

43. The term "gendarmerie" is derived from the medieval French expression "gens d'armes," which translates to "armed men." During the interwar period, the Romanian gendarmerie was mostly tasked with policing the countryside. As the Second World War began, the gendarmerie returned under the authority of the Ministry of War. It took over its military police duties and became involved in the deportation of Jews and Roma to Transnistria in 1941 and 1942.

44. See Dennis Deletant, *Hitler's Forgotten Ally: Ion Antonescu and His Regime, Romania 1940–1944* (London: Palgrave Macmillan, 2006), 143–149.

45. Radu Ioanid, *The Holocaust in Romania: The Destruction of Jews and Gypsies under the Antonescu Regime: 1940–1944* (Chicago: Ivan R. Dee, 2000), 98–99.

46. Friling, Ioanid, and Ionescu, eds., *Final Report,* 134–136.

47. Avigdor Shachan, *Burning Ice: The Ghettos of Transnistria* (New York: Columbia University Press, 1996), 195.

48. Friling, Ioanid, and Ionescu, eds., *Final Report,* 179.

49. Deletant, *Hitler's Forgotten Ally,* 187, 195.

50. Some of the information in this section appeared previously in Popa, "Miron Cristea." Published here with the permission of *Yad Vashem Studies.*

51. Leuştean, *Orthodoxy and the Cold War,* 39.

52. Keith Hitchins, *Rumania 1866–1947* (Oxford: Clarendon, 1994), 413.

53. Patriarhul României Miron Cristea, "Apelul guvernului către ţară" [The Appeal of the Government to the Country], *Apostolul* 14, no. 4 (15 February 1938): 44–45.

54. CNSAS, D11433, "Instrucţiuni şi ordine referitoare la reglementarea cetăţeniei evreieşti 1930–1939" [Instructions and Orders Related to the Regulation of Jewish Citizenship

1930–1939], 67(?). According to this account, published in the Monitorul Oficial on 26 November 1939, 617,396 persons had their citizenship revised; this is 84 percent of the entire Jewish population. Of those, 225,222 persons lost their Romanian citizenship.

55. "Liftă" in Romanian, which is an insulting word used by the Orthodox to designate people of other religions. See http://dexonline.ro/definitie/lifta.

56. Patriarhul Miron Cristea, "Patriarhul Miron Cristea binecuvântează și îndrumă tinerimea Română" [Patriarch Miron Cristea Blesses and Guides the Romanian Youth], *Apostolul* nos. 8–10 (15–30 May 1938): 136.

57. Patriarhul Miron Cristea, "Primatul etnicului românesc" [The Primacy of the Romanian Ethnicity], *Apostolul* nos. 1–2 (1–31 January 1939): 7–8.

58. "Repunerea băștinașilor în drepturile lor istorice" [The Restoration of the Autochthonous in Their Historic Rights], *Apostolul* nos. 1–2 (1–31 January 1939): 29.

59. Ibid., 30.

60. See Popa, *Miron Cristea*, 23, 29.

61. All the anti-Semitic aspects of Cristea's political program were widely publicized and Jews were presented as Communists or promoters of decadence. Some of these articles spoke about a "Jewish invasion." See Ioan Al. Brătescu-Voinești, "Comunismul," *Apostolul* 21 (1–15 December 1938): 303–306, and "Statistica evreilor în lume" [Statistic on the Number of Jews in the World], *Apostolul* no. 16 (1–30 September 1938): 239.

62. "Supliment" [Supplement], *BOR* 56, nos. 5–6 (May–June 1938): 5, 16.

63. Shapiro, *Faith, Murder, Resurrection*, 149.

64. William Oldson, "Alibi for Prejudice: Eastern Orthodoxy, the Holocaust, and Romanian Nationalism," *East European Quarterly* 36, no. 3 (Fall 2002): 303–304.

65. See Ion Popa, "Visarion Puiu, the Former Romanian Orthodox Metropolitan (Archbishop) of Transnistria—A Historical Study on His Life and Activity," *Holocaustul. Studii si Cercetări* 6, no. 1 (2013): 182–203.

66. "Supliment" [Supplement], *BOR* 57, nos. 9–10 (September–October 1939): 21–22.

67. Vladimir Solonari, *Purifying the Nation, Population Exchange and Ethnic Cleansing in Nazi-Allied Romania* (Washington, DC: Woodrow Wilson Center, 2010), 51.

68. "Declaratia IPS Sale Mitropolitul Nicolae Bălan" [Declaration of His Holiness Metropolitan Nicolae Bălan], *Apostolul* 15, no. 12 (1–30 July 1939): 141–142.

69. Ibid., 142.

70. Dumitru Velechiu, "Mitropolitul Visarion Puiu, un martir al demnitatii ortodoxe" [Metropolitan Visarion Puiu a Martyr of Orthodox Worthiness], *Analele Bucovinei* 11, no. 1 (2004): 67, 72–73.

71. CNSAS, D8927, "Chestiunea Preoțească în Vechiul Regat, 1940–1943" [The Priesthood Issue In the Old Kingdom, 1940–1943], "Nota Privind Inlocuirea Mitropolitului Visarion Puiu, signed by C.D., 15 May 1940," 7.

72. Ibid. The same note includes Metropolitan Bălan: "It is presumed that a group of high priests, headed by Metropolitan Bălan, are involved in pro-German politics."

73. Dumitru Stavrache, *Mitopolitul Visarion Puiu: documente din pribegie (1944–1963)* [Metropolitan Visarion Puiu: Documents from Wandering] (Pascani, Romania: Moldopress, 2002), 7.

74. Leuștean, *Orthodoxy and the Cold War*, 53.

75. He was 75 when elected and he lamented over this aspect. See "Cuvântarea IPSS Nicodim Munteanu, Noul Patriarh al României" [The Speech of His Holiness Nicodim Munteanu, the New Patriarch of Romania], *Apostolul* 15, no. 12 (1–30 July 1939): 146.

76. Pr. Dimitrie Balaur, "Atrocitațile evreilor in Basarabia" [The Atrocities Committed by Jews in Bessarabia], *Apostolul* 16, no. 10 (October 1940): 324.

77. See the 4 July 1940 report of Alfred Lorner, German Consul in Galați, in Ottmar Trasca, Dennis Deletant, *Al Treilea Reich si Holocaustul din România: 1940–1944. Documente din Arhivele Germane* [The Third Reich and the Holocaust in Romania: 1940–1944. Documents from German Archives] (Bucharest: Editura INSHREW, 2007), 132 (German) and 138 (Romanian translation).

78. Lya Benjamin, Sergiu Stanciu, Nicolae Cajal, and Ion Șerbănescu, *Evreii din România între anii 1940–1944* [The Jews of Romania from 1940 to 1944] (Bucharest: Hasefer, 1993), xxvii.

79. Mirel Bănică, *Biserica Ortodoxă Română: stat și societate în anii '30* [The Romanian Orthodox Church—State and Society in the 1930s] (Iași, Romania: Polirom, 2007), 242.

80. Leuștean, *Orthodoxy and the Cold War*, 54.

81. Bănică, *Biserica Ortodoxă Română*, 235–239.

82. Nicodim, Patriarhul României, "Ispita. 21–23 Ianuarie 1941" [Temptation. 21–23 January 1941], *BOR* 59, nos. 3–4 (March–April 1941): 129–131.

2

PERPETRATOR, BYSTANDER, OR SAVIOR?

The Romanian Orthodox Church and the Holocaust (1941–1944)

THE ROMANIAN ORTHODOX CHURCH DEFINED its attitude toward Jews prior to June 1941, the start of the war against the USSR. In 1937, almost one year before the law for the revision of citizenship was passed, the Church openly expressed its support for such measures. Patriarch Cristea, as prime minister of the country, implemented a strong anti-Semitic program as a result of which many Romanian Jews were stripped of their Romanian citizenship and marginalized. He openly spoke about "the First Solution," a term generally used in Holocaust historiography to describe the German plans for the deportation of Jews in 1938–1941. Cristea advocated deportation of all Jews from Romania, and made plans for Romanianization. Romanianization, an adaptation of the term "Aryanization," describes the process of spoliation of Jewish or Roma property and its passing into the hands of the state.[1] In the Romanian case, it also meant the replacement of Jewish workers, in various sectors of economy, with ethnic Romanians. In the Church's publications, starting in 1938, the Jews were portrayed as the main supporters and promoters of Communism, and old stereotypes and myths were revived—such as the idea that the Jews were promoters of decadence and enemies of "Românianism," the term used to describe Romanian national and ethnic identity. The number of Jews in the country was exaggerated, giving vent to claims of a "Jewish invasion."

But most importantly, during the dictatorships of Carol II and Ion Antonescu, an interconnection between the church and the state was increasingly visible. In June 1940 Patriarch Nicodim praised Carol II by comparing him to Constantine the Great, a direct allusion to the Byzantine model in which the distinction between religious and political spheres was not very clear.[2] At public appearances, state and church officials were often seen together, and a close relationship between the church and military officials was made evident in public appearances. The Church, through its patriarch or other high-ranking officials, was always present at important public ceremonies. This suggests its strong influence and role in Romanian society and how it worked to support and encourage state policies. This had tremendous effects on the Romanians' attitude toward Jews during the Holocaust. Eighty percent of the population lived in the countryside where the Church was the most trusted institution and where the sermons and advice of village priests were followed without hesitation. In this context, images of Church clergy standing alongside political or military officials published in lay and religious press, gave credence and legitimacy to state policies against Jews. In the long run this led to Orthodox Romanians' hatred for, or at the very least apathy about the fate of the Jews.

THE CHURCH'S PRESS AND THE HOLOCAUST

On June 22, 1941, Romania joined Germany in its war against the USSR. Initially the war was seen as a way of recuperating Bessarabia and Bukovina, taken by the Soviets one year before, but in the summer of 1941 Romanian troops crossed the Dniester River into Ukraine. On August 19, 1941, the Romanian government decreed that Transnistria, the area between the Bug and Dniester rivers occupied by Romanian and German armies was to be under Romanian control. The Tighina Treaty (August 30, 1941) enforced the decision.[3] The area included the Black Sea port of Odessa, which became the administrative capital of Transnistria during the Second World War.

Aspects related to the Holocaust as reflected in the Church's central journals

The war against the USSR was presented as a holy war in *Biserica Ortodoxă Română*, the official and the most representative journal of the Romanian Orthodox Church. In the May–June 1941 issue there was only one note published (due to the fact that probably the issue was almost completed when the war broke out) in the Internal Review section, entitled "The Holy War of Restoration." The war started on June 22, 1941, was described as "the holy war for the liberation of our brethren, who have the same blood and the same law, from the bondage of Bolshevik tyranny." The note emphasized that the ongoing fight was for the "restoration of faith and the elevation of the Cross."[4]

This Christian dimension of the war against the USSR was even clearer in the encyclical of the war published by Patriarch Nicodim in the next issue of *Biserica Ortodoxă Română (BOR)*. The first paragraph expressed joy at the possibility of recovering Bessarabia and Bukovina. Then, Nicodim addressed his readers directly:

My dear Romanians, men and women,
Our country is at war with the Godless people. Our leader was right when he called this war a holy one, because it seeks not only the realization of the national cause—restoration of our borders—but also the destruction of the apocalyptic dragon of bolshevism, which transformed the godly Russia into a nest full of all kind of crimes. A nest of all who declared war against God Himself, who sought to spread in the whole world their terrible poison.[5]

Although at the time of publication the Judeo-Bolshevik propaganda and the messianic ideology of the war had strong German influences,[6] Nicodim's message was not new to the Church. A red thread runs from Nicolae Păulescu and through Nichifor Crainic to Patriarch Nicodim's declaration, what might be called a Romanian Orthodox channel. One of the first to lay the foundation for political anti-Semitism in Romania, Dr. Nicolae Păulescu (1869–1931) "had seen the conflict against Jews in religious terms, as a great battle between 'divine Christianity' and 'demonic Judaism,' and called for the mobilization of the entire Christianity."[7] This message was carried forward by Orthodox theologians such as Nichifor Crainic, or later, by Teodor Popescu.[8] Some imagery used by Nicodim in his encyclical, like "nest of all who declared war against God" or "apocalyptic dragon," were linked to the Judeo-Bolshevik propaganda of the Church before the war. In the *Apostle*, the official journal of the patriarchate, a 1938 article, "Communism," blamed the Jews for all the atrocities committed by the Bolsheviks in Russia during Stalin's reign of terror. The Jews were portrayed as the main actors in the atheist destruction of Russia.[9]

In the January–April 1942 issue of *BOR*, in the context of massive Jewish deportations to and deaths in Transnistria, the article "[The] Communist Anti-Christianity" was published. Written by Teodor Popescu, professor at the Faculty of Orthodox Theology at the University of Bucharest, the article expressed the Church's longstanding opinion in this matter. The article, which ran to thirty-seven pages, depicts the Bolsheviks in very harsh words: "The Bolshevik atheist is not human, but beast. For him there are no sacred relations, nor human feelings; he lost the sensibility and sentiments of a normal human being. Family, parents, children, friends, love, charity, meekness, compassion, goodness, justice, are nothing in the register of Communist values."[10]

The author pretended that Bolshevism was proved to be full of Satanism and demonism. Speaking about the Bolshevik persecutions in Russia, he calls the Communists "atheist beasts" with a "demonic face." Most importantly, he offers vivid details of the atrocities the Bolsheviks had reportedly unleashed upon Orthodox Christians in the USSR.[11] Toward the end of the article, the author clearly identifies the Jews as the main creators and supporters of Bolshevism:

> Communism has, at its basis . . . the Jews, permanent adversaries of Christianity, ideologists and promoters of all main anti-Christian doctrines. . . . Nietzsche, especially, awoke the beast in nineteenth-century man. Karl Marx armed him with socialist-philosophical theories and set on against God and the Church, and Russian Communism, instigated by Judaism, organised it in the atheist state. Its goal: to finish once and for all with religion and the Church.[12]

The timing of this article was crucial. Published in the first months of 1942, after the pogroms of the summer of 1941 and the direct or indirect killings in Transnistria in the winter of 1941–1942, the article, especially the ample space dedicated to atrocities, could be seen as an excuse for inaction. Anyone who read in parallel this article and the books of Marius Mircu or Matatias Carp about the killing of Jews would be surprised to find the same vivid images of atrocities. The article supported the passivity of the Orthodox clergy and regular members toward the sufferings of the Jews in this period; that is, if you help them you help the demons, the persecutors of our brothers. This article, and others, worked as a consciousness polluter; it was used to sanitize prejudice and justify inaction in behalf of the victims. This could explain what Jean Ancel defines as the schizophrenic attitude of the Romanian Orthodox Church in Transnistria, its ability "to separate Christian acts—the founding and renovation of churches, the self-sacrifice of evangelical [missionary] priests, the mass baptism and marriage ceremonies, etc.—from the atrocities committed against the Jewish people virtually simultaneously, sometimes only meters away."[13]

The attack against the Jews in this time of tragic destruction was made directly by Patriarch Nicodim himself. In the encyclical for fasting, the army, and the land, published in the same January–April 1942 issue of *BOR*, Nicodim says:

> But, while sitting near us, the Bolshevik dragon spread poison upon us from outside the country. And inside he found wretched souls who became his mercenaries. Let us praise God that these Satan's soldiers were found mostly among the sons of the foreigners, the ones that called upon themselves and upon their children the curse, since they hanged on the Cross the Son of God, the Redeemer of our souls.[14]

It should be noted that beyond the Judeo-Bolshevik ideology, this quote promotes religious anti-Semitism. In the Church's official publications Jews were now depicted as murderers of God, Satan's soldiers, and cursed, wretched souls. Through the voice of its most important personality, the Church legitimized hatred of the Jews during a time when hundreds of thousands of them were being killed in Transnistria. As for the patriarch himself, this was his position, published in the official journal of the Church. Later on, during Communist efforts to rewrite the past, Nicodim would be characterized as a person concerned with the fate of Jews, sometimes even as their savior.

The patriarch's unsympathetic attitude could also be seen in his other actions during the war. For example, in October 1941 Nicodim congratulated Ion Antonescu for the conquest of Odessa.[15] He said nothing about the hundreds of Jews hanged on the streets of the city, or about the thousands killed in retaliation for the alleged bombing of the Romanian army headquarters. The beginning of 1943 found Nicodim offering King Michael I and Marshal Antonescu "the Victorious Cross" a medal specifically created by the Romanian Orthodox Church to celebrate "the advance of the Cross in Bolshevik Russia." In his speech, the patriarch emphasized again the sacred connotations of the war and the indestructible links between the Church and the Romanian state, but said nothing about the killing of hundreds of thousands of Jews.[16]

While the state dramatically changed its attitude toward Jews in the autumn of 1942, concerned with the possibility that Germany might not win the war, the Church continued its anti-Jewish discourse. In the summer of 1943, the Church's journals adopted Nazi propaganda about the massacre of Vinnytsia (a town in Ukraine). Visarion Puiu, the head of the Orthodox mission in Transnistria, was one of the Eastern European Churches' representatives to witness the unveiling of the mass graves in the town. The Germans pointed to them as proof of Bolshevik cruelty, but later research showed that some of the victims were Jews killed by Einsatzgruppe C after the invasion of the USSR. It is likely that in the mass graves of Vinnytsia there were over-burials—that the same mass graves used by Soviets during the reign of terror (1936–1938) were used by the Germans later.[17]

The way in which *BOR* portrayed the Bolshevik massacre was profoundly anti-Semitic. Like the article "Communism," published before the war, these reports almost entirely overlooked Stalin's guilt for the reign of terror, instead laying the entire blame for the atrocities on the Jews. After describing in the first report the mass graves and the way in which the NKVD carried out the atrocities,[18] the second report attacked the Jews. According to this report, "in many cases the reason for arrest was a denunciation made by a Jew." The author offers some stories in which the Jews, because of their alleged superior position in the Bolshevik state, took advantage and denounced anyone who did not show proper reverence toward them. The report concludes, "According to the witnesses' accounts given to authorities, it is estimated that 20 percent of the arrests were made because of a Jewish denouncer." The Ukrainian police who made the arrests were presented as "Judaized police." The fact that the article showed no doubt about the mass graves of Vinnytsia was strange, coming from a Church that had witnessed German and Romanian massacres on the Eastern Front. The conclusion of the report had a propagandistic tone: "Only after the victory in the war against Bolshevism will the population be completely aware about the wrath that has passed over her and awake to a new life."[19]

In 1943 the year-end issue of the Church's official journal dedicated thirteen pages to a laudatory article about the book *Transfigurarea Românismului* (The Transfiguration of Românianism) by Nichifor Crainic.[20] The book was a continuation of the prewar nationalist message of the strongly anti-Semite Crainic. Crainic criticized the poet, philosopher, and theologian Lucian Blaga, who espoused a more moderate kind of nationalism and who refuted the idea that the Church should be considered the core of Românianism. This attack was reminiscent of the interwar disputes about Romanian nationalism, and the fact that the Church published a laudatory review of the book at the end of 1943 is suggestive of its attitude at the time: that nationalism and Orthodoxy were the core of Românianism.

Aspects related to the Holocaust as reflected in the
Church's regional journals

The Church's regional publications were sometimes even harsher in their anti-Semitic attacks. This is more disturbing when one realizes some of these publications came from places that had large Jewish populations, or places to which Jews had been deported. In *Luminătorul* (The Luminary), the official review of the Bessarabia metropolitanate, the May–June 1941 issue included an article defending the use of violence—when it was for a just cause.[21] One of the strangest examples of the way in which the Romanian Orthodox Church distorted the Christian message in order to suit the nationalist agenda is an article in the same issue entitled "We Shall Love One Another," with the subtitle "Only Christians among Themselves."

These articles published at the beginning of the war implicitly suggested that Christian compassion and love was not and should not be available to Jews. An article entitled "The Samaritan Medical Work in Our Holy War," published in January–February 1942, when the death toll of Jews in Transnistria was greatest, did not mention the suffering of Jews at all, and the Samaritan work of the title was reserved only for ethnic Romanian soldiers. During the war the review promoted religious anti-Semitism: the Jews were seen as "cursed by Jesus,"[22] "the sons of the Devil,"[23] as the ones that "in the plan of a divine justice execute the curse of wandering,"[24] the ones who "violated their alliance with Jehovah."[25] Economic and racial anti-Semitism were also promoted: the Jews were portrayed as Mammon's slaves, idolaters, and liars.[26] Even more disturbing was the publication at the beginning of 1944 of a "good" article about the Jews. It was entitled "Saved by the Cross"[27] and consisted of stories about Jews who allegedly were not deported because they painted crosses on their houses. The article did not show any kind of remorse or compassion for the fate of the hundreds of thousands of people killed.

The level of hatred espoused in this Orthodox journal of the Bessarabia metropolitanate is sometimes extraordinary. An article published in March–April 1942 and entitled "What Do the Canons Say about the Conversion of Jews to Christianity?" starts with a full page of anti-Semitic and conspiracy theories and prejudices. In the author's view Jews were a chosen people tasked with the mission to receive the Messiah. Instead of fulfilling their mission, they "answered with malice and murder, with betrayal and hatred." Jews are presented as "sons of God at the beginning; at the end sons of the devil; [they] made a covenant with Yahve, now a coalition with Satan." These common themes of religious anti-Semitism are accompanied by conspiracy theories. "These crucifiers of Christ, these persecutors of Christians, in their obsessive thirst for world domination, are promoters of subversive currents and the main cause of world crisis, social disturbances, political strife, and modern immorality." In the author's view, "The soul of the contemporary man will not find peace until every Jewish trace is eliminated from the world's spirituality."[28]

Cuvântul Preoțesc (The Priestly Word), published by the metropolitanate of Bukovina, had in its year-end 1941 issue one of the harshest anti-Semitic attacks ever published in a Romanian Orthodox Church journal. The article, entitled "Against Simony," had as its central theme outrage against priests who had accepted money in exchange for baptizing Jews. The outrage was not primarily at the priests' behavior as at the fact that through this method the Jews escaped death. The author said from the beginning that "there are not enough words to express the satisfaction brought by this law (i.e., Decree Law 711 of March 18, 1941, which forbade the conversion of Jews) to the cause of Românianism which is Christian from its birth." The converted Jews were portrayed as wolves entering a stable. The author quoted Jesus's words: "Do not give dogs what is sacred; do not throw your pearls to pigs. If you do so, they may trample them under their feet, and turn and tear you to pieces" (Matthew 7:6). In this metaphor, the Jews are the dogs and the pigs, and the pearls represent Christian baptism. The attack against converted Jews used vitriolic language: Jews were "a bunch of Kikes" (*o liota de jidovi*) and "The Yid wanders howling like a lion in wilderness. . . . The wriggles of the Jew are ineffective." The ineffectiveness of their struggles is explained proudly by the author: "Today, in the most glorious time for Romania, near the Cross the sword is watching. We are certain that all Romanians, bearers of the Cross and of the sword, will fulfil their duties, like the soldiers on the front line, without bargaining."[29] As in other articles published in Transnistria, this one not only condemned the Jews but also defended and even encouraged the use of violence against them, and even their killing.

The articles from *Luminătorul* and *Cuvântul Preoțesc* appeared at the end of 1941 and beginning of 1942, a period when tens of thousands of Jews from Bessarabia and Bukovina were deported to and killed in Transnistria.

The timing, the way in which Jews were portrayed, and the language of hatred used against them show how far the Orthodox Church, in these regions, inspired by the discourse in the capital, went down the road of promoting and legitimizing anti-Semitism.

The Romanian Orthodox Church created, after the beginning of the missionary campaign in Transnistria, a journal entitled *Transnistria Creştină* [Christian Transnistria]. In its first issue, published at the beginning of 1942, the joy that the Jews had been destroyed was unequivocally expressed: "... proclaiming the resurrection of Christ out of the tomb which was sealed a second time by *the sons of perdition* [emphasis in original]. The darkness collapsed and Satan's sons disappeared from the face of God, hiding *in the deepest parts of the Earth*."[30]

The "sons of perdition" and "Satan's sons" were two phrases used frequently in Church journals to refer to Jews. Later in the same article, another indirect reference to Jews was made: "As Jesus in the old times drove out of the Temple with the whip and with lightening and thunders, so we have driven out the money changers from the beautiful Moldavian realm."[31]

Jews were portrayed as Bolsheviks, so the hatred toward Communists was directed toward them as well. Expressions like "Communist Yids," or "the Communist Yid state" were frequently used in the pages of the journal.[32] At the beginning of 1943 an article about the missionary activity of Niceta turned into an attack on Jews: "Hence the Satan and the Yids invaded ... [and] the sacred places were destroyed, or desecrated by the Yids." The article proposes deportation and possibly annihilation very clearly: "Let us drive out Satan from the Romanian realm. ... [We have] to do the work of Our Redeemer, where the Satan and the Yids have destroyed."[33]

These articles were published mostly after Visarion Puiu took over from Iuliu Scriban as head of the missionary campaign in Transnistria. It is clear that the articles published in regional newspapers, in places with a substantial Jewish population, were sometimes more aggressive than those published in the capital, but that should be seen in context. As pointed out earlier, these publications worked as consciousness polluters; their articles were meant to sanitize anti-Jewish prejudice and hatred. Through them, the Church acted as a moral perpetrator, legitimizing and sometimes directly encouraging violent policies against the Jews.

The involvement of the Romanian Orthodox Church in Transnistria and the trial of priests for their violence against Jews

At the end of the Second World War a series of trials were carried out by the Communists in Romania. These started as early as March 1945 and involved different figures that had taken part in the events of the war. The most notorious case of a Church representative tried for events of the war was that of Visarion Puiu, former metropolitan of Bukovina (1936–1940) and former metropolitan and head of the mission in Transnistria (1942–1943). Puiu, who had fled to the West in August 1944, was condemned to death in absentia in 1946.[34] His prosecution did not directly mention his attitude toward Jews, although his support of state policies in Transnistria was stated. (See chapter 5.)

Out of hundreds of documents related to the postwar trials, many mention priests;[35] most of them were condemned for their involvement in the Iron Guard, but although their actions might have involved violence against Jews, this aspect was rarely touched on. For example, a document from the gendarmerie headquarters in Târgu-Mureş makes reference to a priest who, during the Legionary Rebellion of January 1941, after seizing the village hall "took over through the use of terror the business of a Jew, forcing him to cede the property and to sign a contract certifying that."[36] But such cases where Jews are mentioned in Communist trials as direct victims of Legionnaire priests' abuses are rare. The Communist prosecutors were more concerned to prove affiliation of these priests to the Iron Guard than their violence against Jews. However, in a large file found at the CNSAS with war criminals who were directly involved in the destruction of the Jewish community, a number of priests are mentioned. In the file, among other lists of persons who were tried or were selected to face trial, is one entitled "A Table with War Criminals Reported to the People's Tribunal through the Juridical Bureau." This list, compiled by the Romanian office of the World Jewish Congress in 1946, contains 684 names of people involved directly in the killing of Jews. Twelve of those named were Orthodox priests.

Priests' involvement in the destruction of Jews, according to this file, varied. Four of them were involved in the looting of Jewish property. Five were involved in anti-Semitic propaganda and instigation of deportation of Jews to Transnistria. One took an active part in the killing of Jews during the Bucharest pogrom. One "instigated the assassination of Jewish soldiers," but the document does not specify whether those Jewish soldiers were Romanian soldiers killed before the war, or Soviet soldiers. One of the priests was involved in "blackmail and physical abuse against Jews." All twelve were from places that witnessed the physical destruction of Jews during the Holocaust—Bukovina (six, all of them from Dorohoi County), Bessarabia (one), Moldova (two), Bucharest (one), and Transnistria (two, both from Obodvca).[37] The involvement of these priests in the Holocaust went beyond anti-Jewish propaganda promoted in the Church's journals. They did not just write against Jews but actively participated in their physical annihilation. The reluctance of the Communist prosecutors to mention the Jewish suffering, at least in the first phase of the trials when many Legionary priests were prosecuted, suggests that many other priests participated actively in the killing of Jews.

The involvement of some priests in the Holocaust, as portrayed in this file, is not the only instance in which Church clergy and institutions went beyond propaganda, supporting more directly the murder of Jews. Marius Mircu, who wrote his account about the Holocaust in Romania immediately after the end of the war, relates a story about the chaplain of the Roman (a town in Moldova) garrison who, on one occasion when he heard people shouting "the Russians are coming," ran scared. In fact, the shouting was a joke. The laughing soldiers asked, "What happened to you, father?" "The Communist Yids [*Jidanii comuniști*] followed me. Only my courage saved me."[38]

The Orthodox chaplains in the Romanian army largely encouraged the Judeo-Bolshevik myth. The book *Preoți în tranșee* (Priests in Trenches), which consists mainly of reports of Orthodox chaplains from the front line, relates many cases of chaplains boasting of preaching anti-Judeo-Bolshevik sermons. For example, in his report of August 18, 1941, captain-priest Nicolae Petrache writes, "Walking to the holy place, we found only ruins and rubble, in a place that was a very beautiful church. This is the work of Communism and Judaism [*Jidovism*]." Later in the report, he mentions that "I am preaching to the crowd about the indebtedness Ukrainians owe to the brave crusaders who fight under the protection and shadow of the cross for the destruction of Communism and Judaism [*Jidovism*]."[39] In his report, the military dean, Major Gheorghe Ureche, writes that "in this parish there was a second priest, Mizumschi Mihei, who three days before our arrival was shot by the Judeo-Bolshevik barbarians."[40] It was significant that, in the Romanian language, in his order of barbarianism, the Jews are mentioned first.

The Orthodox involvement in Bessarabia, Bukovina, and Transnistria was not limited to promoting anti-Judeo-Bolshevik propaganda. The mixture of politics, military strategy, medieval superstitions, and religion is demonstrated by the fact that a cross was carried in front of Romanian troops when they crossed the Dniester River.[41] The priests were seen as one of the main tools in promoting state policies in these territories. In an address to the active chaplains of the Romanian Army Headquarters/Inspectorate for Military Chaplaincy, on July 20, 1941, the speaker clearly states, "I want to remind you [of] the important duties you have as chaplains. . . . Encourage and stimulate the soldiers. Show them that the war today is a crusade of Christianity against godlessness. Brilliant results up to now prove that we are fighting for a just and holy cause."[42]

The priests in the army acted like governmental appointees. For example, captain-priest Floroiu Nicolae mentions in his report that "on December 8th I preached to the Fourth Company about: 'Why are we in Ukraine' and on December 9th at the Head Company: 'Moral and national reasons that brought us here'." This was when tens of thousands of Jews were dying in the same territory.

Another problematic aspect related to the attitude of the Romanian Orthodox Church during the Holocaust is represented by the religious missionary campaign in Transnistria. Its main scope was the re-Christianization of a territory seen in Orthodox imaginary as cursed and tainted by atheistic Communism. This was done via public gatherings where priests "re-educated" the population about Christian values, and through baptism, including re-baptism of adults. According to Boris Buzilă, who wrote a history of the Bessarabian Orthodox Church, "in the first weeks after Liberation [July 1941], the Church in Bessarabia developed an intense missionary activity both in Bessarabia and in Transnistria, with the help of the Patriarchate, the state, and other sister Churches from beyond the Prut River [the Old Kingdom of Romania]."[43] This campaign was backed by some of the most representative figures of the Church, such as Metropolitan Bălan of Transylvania and several bishops. In the summer of 1941 a missionary administration was created and Iulius Scriban, a well-known professor at the Faculty of Theology in Bucharest, was named the head of the missionary campaign.

Jean Ancel, writing about the Romanian Orthodox missionary campaign in Transnistria, details the political reasons for this religious offensive and the stages in the chronology of the mission. He also references some interesting documents, other than the ones mentioned previously in this chapter, about anti-Semitic attacks by members of Church hierarchy involved in the campaign.[44] In priests' reports from Bessarabia and Transnistria, baptisms are most frequently mentioned, but baptisms of atheists, not of Jews. It appears to have been a kind of competition—who could bring back to faith more atheists.[45] Ancel puts this campaign of baptism face to face with the physical destruction of Jews. He concludes by speaking about the schizophrenic attitude of the Church, mentioned previously,[46] and about the grassroots impact of the campaign: "This outlook—and the willing participation of the Romanian Orthodox Church in achieving the administration's goals—freed Romanian citizens from weighing their actions against universal humanistic values."[47] According to Ancel, "the Jews never caused disagreement between the administration and the Romanian Orthodox Church."[48] The missionary campaign in Transnistra, the attitude of the Romanian Orthodox chaplains, and the action of priests who actively participated in the physical violence against Jews took the Church toward a more active involvement in the destruction of the Jewish community during the Holocaust.

JEWISH REQUESTS FOR HELP AND THE PROBLEM OF CONVERSION

The problem of conversion of Jews was discussed several times by the Romanian Orthodox Church prior to and during the Second World War. In March 1938, a few days after Patriarch Miron Cristea became prime minister, the Holy Synod banned the baptism of Jews who could not prove Romanian citizenship. This could be an expression of Patriarch Cristea's politico-religious role. When, as prime minister, he openly promoted anti-Semitic policies, there was a desire shared by both the patriarch and the Church to replicate those policies in the life of the Church too. Although controversial, the Holy Synod's decision of March 1938 was not surprising. In June 1939, after Cristea's death, without state pressure, the Holy Synod decided to maintain the ruling of March 15, 1938. Moreover, the new decision hardened the conditions of baptism even for Jews who were Romanian citizens.[49]

In August 1940, the anti-Jewish legislation hit the Jewish community of Romania hard and requests for help addressed to the Holy Synod did not take long to appear. In its December 1940 meeting, the synod discussed a request for help from N. Solomonescu, a Jew converted to Orthodox Christianity. Mr. Solomonescu asked the Orthodox Church to intervene with the state authorities so that Jews baptized more than thirty years earlier could be exempt from the August 8, 1940 law's provisions. The Holy Synod's decision in his case was that "as the baptism of the Jews cannot invalidate the running provisions and laws concerning the defense of race, the requester will be advised to reclaim his civil and political rights on juridical channels."[50]

If previous decisions of the Holy Synod were directed against Jews who could not prove their Romanian citizenship, now all Jews were affected. It should be emphasized that Mr. Solomonescu was a baptized Jew who was now a faithful Orthodox Christian. The request concerned Jews baptized more than thirty years ago, whose belonging to the Orthodox faith and Romanian nation could not be doubted. Even given these circumstances, the synod refused to consider any requests for help. In this way, not only did the Church turn its back on its own faithful but, more importantly, it became a promoter of racial policies by making distinctions between its members based solely on ethnic grounds.

The Romanian state officially forbade the conversion of Jews on March 18, 1941. *BOR* published Decree No. 711 in its March–April 1941 issue:

> The ethnic being of our People must be preserved from interference with Jewish blood. The Jews have nowadays the possibility of hiding their ethnic origin by converting to our national religions. In order to avoid such a crime in our national community, it is necessary to modify article 44 from the law of religions, in the sense that the Jews could not convert to any other religion.[51]

Initially the Church just published this announcement in its official journal, without any other comment. The first reaction came from Metropolitan Nicolae Bălan of Transylvania who spoke openly against it. In an address to Radu Rossetti, the minister of education and religions, dated April 2, 1941, he protested on the ground that the state "cannot be a master over something that does not belong to it; that is the grace and the will of redemption that belongs to God."[52] Hence, Bălan says, Decree Law 711 should be abolished. Later citations of this letter always quote the first part, entirely overlooking the second part, in which Bălan clearly mentions that his protest is not in favor of Jews. The narrative about his intervention in favor of Jews is so strong that the reading of the complete letter (available at the USHMM) comes as something of a shock. Not only that Bălan is not concerned with Jews' fate, but he even suggests a better solution for the "avoidance of the amalgamation of Romanian and Jewish blood," namely forbidding mixed marriages. He also stresses that for the Transylvania metropolitanate "the problem of Jews' baptism was not an issue," because this Church body was at the forefront of promoting Românianism.[53]

In its June 1941 meeting, the Holy Synod mirrored Bălan's reaction: it expressed its distaste for state interference in the Church's business, but made clear that as far as the protection of race was concerned, it was obeying state regulations:

> As a result of discussions in which H. H. Metropolitans Irineu of Moldova and Tit of Bukovina took part, the Holy Synod, after receiving the commission's proposal, decides:
> The State has all the right to enforce any necessary laws that would help the protection of the Country and the People's very existence. The Church however cannot abdicate from its mission given by the Holy Creator: "Therefore go and make disciples of all nations, baptizing them in the name of the Father and of the Son and of the Holy Spirit." Hence the Church cannot stop the baptism of those who ask for it for their own redemption, but baptism does not invalidate in any way the present laws and provisions for the defense of race.[54]

It seems that Metropolitan Bălan was not part of the commission that discussed the issue, but he made a speech at the beginning of the day. Although opposing the idea of a conversions' ban, the Church made clear that it supported the state in its racial policies. The first and the last sentences of the Holy Synod's decision made this aspect evident.

After the outbreak of war on June 22, 1941, the massive pogroms in Moldova, Bessarabia, and Bukovina, and the start of deportations to Transnistria in the autumn of 1941, the Holy Synod faced new requests for help. In its October 23–24 meeting a request from the Bishopric of Hotin for permission to baptize a Jewish teenager named Ruhlea Peiril was discussed. She was sixteen and her parents had died in the war, most likely killed by Romanian or German troops in the massacres of 1941. Although it acknowledged these tragic circumstances, the synod's decision showed once more the Church's lack of sympathy: "The issue is passed to the local priest who will solve it according to the canonical laws and the laws of the Country."[55] The laws of the country forbade the conversion of Jews, so indirectly the Holy Synod forbade the priest and the Bishopric of Hotin to baptize Ruhlea

Peiril. The Bishopric of Hotin's confusion about whether such baptisms were allowed was not unique. According to Jean Ancel, at the beginning of the missionary campaign in Transnistria, Iulius Scriban, the head of the mission, likewise did not know whether or not to baptize Jews. After an exchange of letters between the patriarch and Scriban, which show again the patriarch's submissiveness to the state,[56] the mission's conclusion was that "in order to preserve the race . . . the Patriarchate has forbidden priests to baptize Jews into the faith, [imposing] disciplinary and criminal penalties [for doing so]. These norms apply to the priests in Transnistria as well, since they are subject to the Romanian Orthodox Mission."[57]

The confusion could come from the fact that, in the summer and autumn of 1941 before the settlement of the Romanian mission, many Ukrainian local priests continued to baptize children and to encourage intermarriage in order to help Jews avoid deportation.[58] In most cases these efforts were in vain, because the Romanians did not want to accept the validity of these conversions. Another explanation for Scriban's position could have to do with his mild anti-Semitism. The anti-Semitic articles he wrote for Church journals before the war were some distance from the rhetoric of Nichifor Crainic and Teodor Popescu, his colleagues at the Faculty of Theology. This was the main reason for an ample campaign of denigration against him, which started by the middle of 1942. He was accused of being too closely linked to the Jews. Although there was no evidence that he tried in any way to save or to minimize the suffering of Jews in Transnistria, he was judged for "his close relationships with some Jews from the capital city" and "for being an intermediary between the Jews in the capital and those in Transnistria."[59] In the end Scriban was replaced by the more pro-German Visarion Puiu, the former metropolitan of Bukovina.

Ruhlea Peiril's case was probably the last occasion on which the Holy Synod discussed the conversion of Jews or requests for help from Jewish victims. This could mean that the Church had made its position clear. From 1938 to 1941, on several occasions the Holy Synod publicly declined to offer any help. Moreover, these decisions were part of the Church's campaign to rid Romania of Jews. Only this can explain the refusal to help even Jews who were committed Orthodox faithful.

The lack of other synod discussions on the Jewish problem is significant in another way. The Jewish community of Romania, through different channels (either directly through Chief Rabbi Alexandre Safran and president

Dr. Wilhelm Filderman, or indirectly through the queen mother or various other personalities) asked the Church for help in stopping the deportations, first to Transnistria, then, in 1942, the foreseen deportations to Belzec.[60] The fact that there were no debates on these desperate requests shows the Orthodox Church's lack of interest in the fate of the Jewish community.

According to Lya Benjamin, "the Orthodox Patriarchate, in a report from March 2, 1942, informed the Prime Minister that although the new legal instructions acted as an impediment to the Church's redemptive mission, it respected entirely the law and did not baptize any Jews."[61] However, there were priests at the local level who baptized Jews during this period. The Romanian Police issued several lists of Jews converted after March 1941. The overall impression one gets is that, although they were in the religious minority, the Roman Catholic, Greek Catholic, Calvinist, and Evangelical churches baptized more Jews than the Romanian Orthodox Church. For example, an October 1942 document of the Ministry of the Interior monitoring the conversion of Jews after March 1941 suggests that out of 256 persons, 44 were converted to Orthodoxy and 157 to Roman Catholicism.[62] Another document about Jewish converts in Kishinev suggests that thirty-two persons were converted to Roman Catholicism and only four to Orthodoxy.[63] Out of those four persons only two were converted by Romanian priests. According to a census carried out in May 1942 on persons with "Jewish blood," "from 292,149 Jews [Jews still in Romania after killings, deportations and border changes], 4,631 were converted Jews; from this number, in spite of interdictions, 1,311 Jews converted from August 9, 1940 to May 20, 1942."[64]

As far as conversion is concerned, the Orthodox Church was more of a bystander compared with the efforts made by other denominations in Romania, and especially by the Roman Catholic Church. The Catholic Church sustained a strong campaign of conversion during the Holocaust in Romania, including in the capital city of Bucharest and, in most cases, Jews converted to Catholicism were saved because the Romanian authorities feared the international influence of the Vatican. Jews converted to other faiths were most often deported. Sometimes the conversion, because it was a violation of the law, was in itself a reason to be deported.[65]

THE ROMANIAN ORTHODOX CHURCH AND THE RESCUE EFFORTS

Although the large majority of available documents incriminate the Romanian Orthodox Church for its attitude during the Holocaust, both as a moral and active perpetrator and as a bystander, there are some important exceptions. Two Orthodox metropolitans allegedly played an important role in stopping the deportations of Jews, and one Romanian Orthodox priest has been awarded Righteous Among the Nations status.

In the summer of 1941, in an attempt to stop Jewish deportations to Transnistria, the chief rabbi of Romania, Alexandre Safran, and Dr. Wilhelm Filderman, head of the Federation of Jewish Communities, approached, among others, the metropolitan of Bukovina, Tit Simedrea. Although an anti-Semite who had attacked Safran in the Romanian senate the year before, Simedrea showed compassion toward the chief rabbi, promising to speak with Ion Antonescu on his behalf. He also "met with the military governor of Bukovina, General Calotescu, and was able to persuade him to intervene personally to halt the deportation from Czernowitz [Cernăuți]."[66] The deportations were later renewed, but the alleged intervention of Metropolitan Simedrea could have been significant, not necessarily in the number of persons saved, but in the manifestation of benevolence, rarely coming from a member of the Orthodox hierarchy. The halting of deportations from Czernowitz and the protection of around 20,000 Jews during the war had multiple reasons, mostly related to the economic interests in the region. Whether Simedrea was influential in this process is a matter for further research. Supporting the alleged intervention in favor of Jews are reports that during the Holocaust Simedrea hid a Jewish family in the metropolitanate compound. This was offered as evidence in the quest to obtain Righteous Among the Nations status for the former metropolitan. In the end, Simedrea was refused status, and this could shed light on the veracity of this story.

Jean Ancel, in one of his books about the Holocaust in Romania, suggests that the 1943 New Year's Day sermons in the Bukovina Metropolitanante included a request to help Jews, but the document Ancel cites is actually a Romanian Secret Service note, simply acknowledging rumors that such an event may have happened;—even the agent was not sure whether such sermons had been preached.[67]

Not all the evidence supports the likelihood of Metropolitan Simedrea's rescue efforts. The article "Against Simony," which contains one of the most virulent attacks against Jews, was published in *Cuvântul Preoțesc*, a journal of the Bukovina Metropolitanate, and it is debatable whether metropolitan Tit Simedrea was aware of its publication. In 1941, in a speech to the Bukovinian Church Assembly, Simedrea described the war against the USSR as a

holy war, a theme very much emphasized in the pages of *Cuvântul Preoțesc*.[68]
He said: "Therefore, the legitimate gladness brought by the glory of our
armies, and the steadfast belief of the nation that it wages a holy war, justifies
the trust in the righteousness of this war. . . . This is the Bolshevik man, with
whom the most diligent people in the study of the Bible allied to wage war
against Christian Europe."[69] Tit Simedrea's attack on Jews here is explicit.
Although he expresses a clear sympathy for the Jews, whom he sees as "the
most diligent people in the study of the Bible," he condemns them for sup-
posedly allying with the atheist Soviets against Christian Europe.

The campaign asking for Simedrea to be awarded Righteous Among the
Nations status was unsuccessful.[70] Although Yad Vashem has not made public the reason behind the decision, it is very likely that despite some positive
actions by the former metropolitan of Bukovina, there were also dark spots,
such as the ones highlighted above, that contributed to the final negative
outcome.

The other Romanian Orthodox metropolitan who allegedly intervened
in favor of Jews was Metropolitan Nicolae Bălan of Transylvania. Nicolae
Bălan had expressed strong anti-Semitism and his links with the Iron Guard
were well-known. He encouraged by personal action the Orthodox mission
in Bessarabia and Transnistria (with poisonous effects on the Jews of these
territories) and was seen by the Germans as a more desirable person to lead
the Romanian Orthodox Church because of his pro-German attitude.

In August 1942, plans had been made by the Germans to deport all Jews
from southern Transylvania to Poland. Facing this situation, the Jewish
community decided to approach Metropolitan Bălan. Why Bălan and not
the patriarch? Some documents suggest that Bălan acted in the summer of
1942 as the real leader of the Church and a veritable war between the patriarch and metropolitans representing different provinces of Romania had
broken out. According to Chief Rabbi Alexandre Safran, Bălan, surpris-
ingly, offered to intervene with Marshal Ion Antonescu on behalf of the
Jews.[71] Safran describes in a dramatic tone the way in which he approached
Bălan and their meeting:

> I followed him out into the rambling courtyard and saw him to his car. I felt
> that I was seeing him off on a mission that would decide the fate of tens of
> thousands of Jews, and, in trembling voice, I told the metropolitan that his
> enterprise was of a major significance for the Jews of Romania. Once he was
> in his car, he took my hand, looked straight at me and told me to remember

that day . . . . At 3 o'clock in the afternoon, the telephone rang. A powerful voice spoke to me in a grave timbre. It was Metropolitan Bălan. He informed me that he had obtained from Marshal Antonescu the cancellation of the deportation order for the Jews of southern Transylvania. The miracle—yes, the miracle—had happened. The Jews of southern Transylvania had been saved from deportation to Poland; in fact, their very lives had been saved.[72]

Although Alexandre Safran's account cannot be supported by other evidence, apart from some unsubstantiated similar claims used in the later Communist narrative, there may be some truth to this story. Bălan's action, although paradoxical, could be understood in the context of the tensions within the Church and of his quest to exercise leadership.

The rescue actions of the Orthodox Church's upper hierarchy were not consistent. Even if we are to believe these accounts, excepting the summer of 1941, when Metropolitan Simedrea of Bukovina spoke out against the deportations to Transnistria, and the summer of 1942 when Metropolitan Bălan allegedly intervened to halt the deportation of southern Transylvanian Jews to Poland, there is no evidence that either man continued to be concerned with the fate of Jews. Both Metropolitan Bălan and Tit Simedrea helped for a very short period of time. For them the rescue efforts were not a priority.

In 1942, Patriarch Nicodim forwarded several letters to various Romanian authorities on behalf of converted Jews who had asked for his help. Documents found at the USHMM show that he did so on at least three occasions, in April, May, and October 1942.[73] These interventions were preceded by a letter Nicodim sent to Ion Antonescu on March 26, 1942 in which he asked what he should do about the baptized Jews.[74] The state reply to Nicodim's letters was unfavorable[75] and the patriarch did not push any further with his interventions. A few more letters, which have surfaced at CSIER in Bucharest, were forwarded by the Romanian patriarchate to various Romanian institutions in 1942. Most were signed by other administrators of the patriarchate. These, like the letters forwarded and signed by Nicodim himself, did not plead for the converted Jews who were asking for help but rather used minimal, official language, which only acknowledged the receipt of those letters and asked the forwarding institution to solve the cases as it considered lawful.

Nicodim's action was not consistent. His efforts were sporadic and only on behalf of a very few converted Jews. He did not have the passion to help the victims like the queen mother, or Andrea Cassulo, the papal nuncio to Romania. Moreover, on February 23, 1942, Nicodim sent a letter to Ion Antonescu in which he complained that while the Romanian Orthodox Church had complied with the state regulations and did not baptize Jews, the Catholic Church was permitted to continue the process of conversions. He asked for stricter measures against those who continued to baptize Jews.[76]

In an explanatory report written to the Communist Secret Police in 1963 when he became their agent, Antim Nica, former vice head of the Romanian Orthodox mission in Transnistria, boasted of helping Jews in Transnistria. He brought as evidence a letter from the Norwegian Lutheran mission in Transnistria that certified his active involvement in facilitating the Norwegian Lutherans' help to the converted Jews.[77] He also implied in the report that his action in favor of Jews was the reason for the tensions between him and Visarion Puiu, the head of the Romanian Orthodox mission, but the document he attached did not support this claim.[78] Reading the articles written by Nica during the war it is obvious that he was not an avid anti-Semite, but his efforts to present himself as a savior of Jews lack proper arguments. He asked for the letter from the Norwegian mission immediately after the war, and tried to use his alleged help of Jews politically. Nica would become influential in the cover-up of 1945.

On the Yad Vashem list of Righteous Among the Nations, forty-three Romanian (and eleven Bessarabian) men and women who had saved Jews during the Holocaust are mentioned. One of them is the Orthodox priest Gheorghe Petre. He received the recognition in 2004 for "saving many Jews in Crivoi-Ozero ghetto in Transnistria."[79] Gheorghe Petre was sent to Transnistria as a missionary priest in 1942. He facilitated the distribution of supplies from the Old Kingdom to the Jews in Crivoi-Ozero and Trei Dube ghettos.[80] According to Georgeta Pană, he was arrested and in 1943 he appeared before the martial court. In 1944, he was released for lack of evidence.[81]

Although not on the list of Righteous Among the Nations, other Orthodox priests helped Jews during the Holocaust. According to some accounts, Father Lozonschi from the Sf. Gheorghe Church in Iași sheltered Jews in his church during the pogrom of June 27–29, 1941. Another priest, Father Răzmeriță from Iași, died during the pogrom, but the circumstances of his death are not entirely clear. Most sources indicate that he left his home, which was located near a synagogue, to defend Jews who were being beaten by bands of vandals. He was killed either intentionally or by accident, being mistaken for a Jew. The eulogy published in the journal *Mitropolia Moldovei* in September 1941 was silent about the circumstances of his death, avoiding any mention of the pogrom against the Jews.[82] Toma Chircuță, a priest of the Zlătari Orthodox Church in Bucharest, defended the Jews who tried to shelter during a bombardment in 1944. Father Paul Teodorescu, from Războieni saved one Jew who was buried alive alongside corpses removed from a death train in Târgu Frumos.[83]

Priest, novelist, and public personality Gala Galaction defended the Jews in writing and in action. In the winter of 1941, he asked priest Gheorghe Cunescu to donate money to a sick Jewish woman whose husband had been deported to Transnistria. According to another report, when he saw Jews clearing snow on Bucharest streets Galaction took the shovel from a Jew and worked for a time in his place—as a sign of solidarity.[84] He, alongside philosopher Constantin Rădulescu-Motru, spoke often against anti-Semitism. These examples, although scanty, prove that in the Orthodox Church there were a few priests who understood that the first mission of any church is to manifest charity; a lesson forgotten by the highest authorities both before and during the Holocaust.

One of the major problems related to these positive examples is the fact that they are mostly unknown. Although the Romanian Orthodox Church used several positive examples in the cover-up of 1945, some of those were controversial and even untrue. The rescue efforts of the priests mentioned in the paragraph above were, and to a large extent still are, not known. In some cases, such as that of Father Răzmeriță, no one brought the priest's actions to the attention of Yad Vashem, a sign of the Church's disinterest in researching these priests' efforts, possibly because that would involve the Church properly analyzing its own actions during the Holocaust.

INTERNAL AND EXTERNAL RELATIONS OF THE ROMANIAN ORTHODOX CHURCH DURING THE HOLOCAUST YEARS

The legitimization of state policies against Jews and the support of violence against them followed a long tradition of Church anti-Semitism. Given the church-state relationship in the interwar period and its encouragement of anti-Semitism in the 1930s, the Church's active involvement in the destruction of the Romanian Jewry is not a great surprise. Still, in some instances the Church seemed to be paralyzed, unable to respond to the cries of innocent victims. Documents discovered in Romanian archives have now put the entire activity of the Romanian Orthodox Church during the Holocaust years in a new perspective.

After the death of Patriarch Miron Cristea, tensions within the Romanian Orthodox Church surfaced. For a time they were kept under control by King Carol II, who forced Metropolitan Nicolae Bălan and Metropolitan Visarion Puiu, both of them known to be pro-German, to publicly withdraw from the patriarchal race of June 1939.[85] But the tensions resurfaced when Carol II was forced to abdicate on September 6, 1940. In April 1941, it was Metropolitan Bălan of Transylvania, and not the patriarch, who addressed the Ministry of Religions regarding the law banning the conversion of Jews. It was one of the first instances when Bălan acted like the real leader of the Church.

A veritable internal war broke out inside the Church by the middle of 1942. According to a Romanian Secret Service document dated August 4, 1942, "the news about the retirement of Patriarch Nicodim is of great topicality, being imminent."[86] The same source said that the patriarch retired, away from the public sphere, at the Neamț Monastery, refusing to deal with any patriarchal duties. The reason given in the document was that "the Patriarch says . . . his name was discredited among priests." A Romanian Secret Service note dated September 4, 1942 mentions that Bishop Ghenadie of Buzău had a heart attack after Metropolitan Bălan threatened him with deposition. The note ends with a comment that sheds an entirely new light on internal Church relationships in Greater Romania: "These circles [priests' circles] are indignant at Metropolitan Bălan of Transylvania's interference in the business of the Orthodox Church from the other side of the Carpathians [the Old Kingdom]. They are of the opinion that these conflicts could bring great troubles within the Church."[87]

It is ironic that while being the core of Romanian nationalism, the Church itself was divided. While it played the role of uniter of all Romanians, the Church's provinces were at war with each other, with Old Kingdom provinces openly expressing worries about the stronger influence of the Transylvanian side. These tensions were the focus of the Priests' National Congress in Czernowitz in the second part of September 1942. Again a Romanian Secret Service note helps us to see inside the fighting: "In the introduction, it must be mentioned that between Patriarch Nicodim and Metropolitan Tit Simedrea on one hand, and Metropolitans Bălan and

Popovici on the other hand, there is a conflict having the following reason: the Patriarch supports Metropolitan Tit Simedrea for the future candidacy as Metropolitan Primate [offering him *locum tenens* as future patriarch] to the detriment of Metropolitan Bălan."[88] The province-driven aspect of this conflict is again outlined by the combatants: Nicodim and Simedrea represented the Moldovan side, while Bălan and Popovici represented the Transylvanian side.

Patriarch Nicodim's preference for Simedrea may have had other explanations too, and they should be sought in developments at the Metropolitanate of Bukovina. From 1936 to 1940 the metropolitan of Bukovina was Visarion Puiu. King Carol II increasingly lobbied for his removal after 1937, due in part to Puiu's openly anti-Semitic and pro-German policies. For about a year (1939–May 1940) Puiu's situation was unclear, and then in May 1940 he was removed from his post and replaced by Tit Simedrea.[89] During the Legionary State (September 1940–January 1941) Puiu was reinstated with the help of the Iron Guard.[90] He was again removed and replaced in March 1941 with Tit Simedrea, who remained metropolitan of Bukovina for the duration of the war.[91]

Germany's interest in the internal tensions of the Romanian Orthodox Church is made evident by a Romanian Secret Service report from November 1942: "The tensions within the Orthodox Church have been discussed with great concern by the German legation in Bucharest."[92] The Germans considered Metropolitan Bălan as being pro-German and Patriarch Nicodim, although not seen as an anti-German, was believed to have a pan-Slavic orientation. The real question, according to this document, was whether the tensions were "just internal quarrels, or this fight [had] a political connotation too, in the sense that the Orthodox Church would be more pro-German under Metropolitan Bălan than under Patriarch Nicodim."[93] The political interference in the Church's business is also suggested by the fact that at the end of September 1942 Ion Antonescu, the leader of the country, summoned Patriarch Nicodim for a meeting in Predeal. The patriarch refused to go "because he feared some troubles as a result of his audience with the Marshal."[94] It is likely that Antonescu, aware of the tensions inside the Church, tried to solve them by intervening personally. We do not know whether Antonescu had in the end any role in easing the conflict, but it is worth mentioning that the relationship between Antonescu and Bălan was not harmonious. In February 1941, Bălan openly expressed his disapproval of the instauration of the Antonescu regime and the elimination of the Iron Guard.[95] Antonescu himself was aware of Bălan's strong personality and although he maintained an amiable relationship with him, feared his influence and leadership. For Antonescu, Nicodim's submissiveness was much more preferable.

All these tensions inside the Church shed an important light on the events of the Holocaust. First, it must be said that the tensions did not have at their basis any concern or sympathy toward the Jews. This was an internal battle for power between different personalities representing different provinces of Romania. The Romanian state and the German legation were interested in this internal war, but the choice was between a pro-German (Nicodim), and a stronger pro-German position (Bălan). Regarding the fate of Jews, it is worth mentioning that while thousands of them were dying in Transnistria, the Church was paralyzed by this internal battle for supremacy. Even if the Church had been concerned with their fate, which did not seem to be the case, its attention was elsewhere. The battle for power was more important for the Romanian Orthodox Church during the Holocaust years than the fate of hundreds of thousands of innocent people.

The attitude of the Romanian Orthodox Church during the Holocaust: some definitions and comparisons

The involvement of the Romanian Orthodox Church in the Holocaust is complex and often hard to categorize. This complexity comes from at least two sources: one is the difficulty of defining who or what the Church is, and the second is the non-uniform attitudes of the clergy. This book sees and analyses the Church as an institution: a part of civil society, a political player, and a moral authority. This is why it pays attention first and foremost to representative institutions such as the Holy Synod, the Patriarchate, and the central and regional journals, as they have been the voice of the Church. The examination of clergy's actions, on the other hand, offers a better understanding of how the Church's institutional policies were implemented on the ground. Through their actions and attitudes, priests shaped the attitude of the population and defined or explained the larger trends of the Church toward the Jews.

In the interwar period, and especially after February 1938 when Patriarch Miron Cristea became prime minister, the Romanian Orthodox Church rediscovered the magic of being at the center of political power. During the dictatorships of Carol II and Ion Antonescu, the line between religion and politics in Romania almost entirely vanished. The Church worked for the state and the state worked for the Church, as in medieval times. The Church legitimized the military campaign against the USSR and the state's policies toward the Jews and the state, in return, banned emerging evangelical denominations and enforced participation in Church services. During the Holocaust, in its central and regional press, the Church supported the state's anti-Judeo-Bolshevik propaganda. Sometimes its anti-Semitic discourse went further and portrayed the Jews as Satan's soldiers, depraved profiteers, "cursed by Jesus," "sons of the Devil," those who "in the plan of a divine justice execute the curse of wandering," and the people who "violated their alliance with Jehovah." The Church also promoted economic and racial anti-Semitism: the Jews were portrayed as Mammon's slaves, idolaters, liars, and depraved. These articles worked as conscience polluters, destroying the people's sense of moral duty to save the victim, encouraging their inaction, and on a few occasions even expressing joy at seeing the Jews destroyed. The language used in Church publications was sometimes extremely virulent; metaphors in which Jews were presented as dogs or pigs, and expressions such as "a bunch of Yids" (*o liota de jidovi*) were used. Given this violent language, it is not surprising that in some cases regular priests went further and committed physical violence against Jews.

The Church's silence during the Holocaust can be seen in its missionary activity in Transnistria. Not only did it not raise any concern about the many victims killed in this territory, but through the missionary priests and the military chaplains it encouraged anti-Judeo-Bolshevik propaganda that presented Jews as enemies of the state. Its silence can also be seen in its official reaction to pleas for help and in the Church's attitude toward the conversion of Jews. The Holy Synod of the Church refused to help any converted Jew, although in some cases the converts had been Orthodox faithful for more than thirty years. Some documents show that Patriarch Nicodim forwarded in 1942 several letters to the Romanian authorities on Jews' behalf. However, in this Nicodim was not consistent. His efforts were sporadic and only for very few converted Jews. Moreover, in one of his famous encyclicals, published in April 1942, he presented Jews as Communists, "Satan's soldiers . . . the foreigners, the ones that called upon themselves and upon their children the curse, since they hanged on the Cross the Son of God, the Redeemer of our souls."[96] Other stories of rescue presented after the war as part of the whitewashing process also have major problems. In April 1941, Metropolitan Nicolae Bălan protested against the state's ban on Jewish conversion, but Bălan made clear that his intervention was not in defense of Jews. According to Chief Rabbi Alexandre Safran's memoir, it seems that Bălan did indeed intervene in 1942 and his call to Ion Antonescu might have played a role in the postponement of deportations to Belzec. However, the postponement should be seen in the larger context of German-Romanian relations at the end of 1942 and of Romania's foreign policy during the war years. There are other stories of rescue, which unfortunately are not widely known, in which a few Romanian Orthodox priests risked their lives for the sake of Jews. Gheorghe Petre was the only Romanian Orthodox priest awarded Righteous Among the Nations status by the Yad Vashem.

The involvement of the Romanian Orthodox Church in the Holocaust was different from that of most denominations in Europe. Not only did the Church not raise its voice against the persecution of Jews like the Bulgarian Orthodox,[97] Danish Lutherans, and some Protestant groups in the Netherlands did, but because of the church-state relationship, the Romanian Orthodox Church legitimized the politics of hatred. The number of clergy intervening in favor of victims, publicly or privately, was far less in Romania than in Catholic France and Poland, or in the Protestant Netherlands and Denmark.[98] In Romania, the minority denominations (Roman Catholics especially, but also the Greek Catholics, the Lutherans, and the Calvinists) were far more involved in rescue efforts than the Romanian Orthodox Church, although even in these cases it is hard to separate the saving role from the desire to proselytize, and further research will have to analyze this aspect.

NOTES

1. See Ștefan Cristian Ionescu, *Jewish Resistance to "Romanianization," 1940–1944* (London: Palgrave Macmillan, 2015), 34–66.

2. Patriarch Nicodim Munteanu, "Laudation," *BOR* 58, nos.7–8 (July–August 1940): 515–517.

3. Tuvia Friling, Radu Ioanid, and Mihai Ionescu, eds., *The Final Report of the Elie Wiesel Commission for the Study of the Holocaust in Romania* (Bucharest: Polirom, 2005), 138.

4. Comitetul de Redacție [Editorial Board], "Războiul Sfânt de Dezrobire" [The Holy War of Restoration], *BOR* 59, nos. 5–6 (May–June 1941): 337.

5. Nicodim, Patriarhul României, "Cuvântul Bisericii pentru Războiul Sfânt" [The Church's Message on the Holy War], *BOR* 59, nos. 7–8 (July–August 1941): 377–381.

6. Friling, Ioanid, and Ionescu, eds., *Final Report*, 94.

7. Georgeta Pană, *Antisemitismul religios din perspectivea Holocaustului* [Religious Anti-Semitism from a Holocaust Perspective] (Bucharest: University of Bucharest Press, 2008), 127.

8. Nichifor Crainic, *Ortodoxie și etnocrație* [Orthodoxy and Ethnocracy] (Bucharest: Cugetarea, 1938), 163–164. "Europe is not agitated today by a simple social war or by an ideological one; today Europe is agitated by war of the Talmud against Christ's Gospel. The democratic regime of the last century with its liberties after the world peace gave to the Jewish people a crazy courage and a sacred drunkenness of the White Horse Messianism."

9. Ioan Al. Brătescu-Voinești, "Comunismul," *Apostolul* 14, no. 21 (1–15 December 1938): 303–306.

10. Teodor Popescu, "Anticreștinismul comunist" [The Communist Anti-Christianity], *BOR* 60, nos. 1–4 (January–April 1942): 19.

11. Ibid., 21–22.

12. Ibid., 48–49.

13. Jean Ancel, *Transnistria, 1941–1942: The Romanian Mass Murder Campaigns* (Tel Aviv: Tel Aviv University, 2003), 1:483.

14. Nicodim, Patriarhul României, "Cuvânt pentru post, pentru oștire si pentru ogor" [Message for the Fast, Army and Land], *BOR* 60, nos. 1–4 (January–April 1942): 7.

15. "Cronica interna, telegrama trimeasă Domnului Mareșal Ion Antonescu" [Internal Chronicle, the Telegram Sent to Marshal Ion Antonescu], *BOR* 59, nos. 9–10 (September–October 1941): 600–601.

16. "Crucea Biruitoare" [The Victorious Cross], *BOR* 61, nos. 1–3 (January–March 1943): 5–9.

17. See Irina Paperno, "Exhuming the Bodies of Soviet Terror," *Representations* 75, no. 1 (Summer 2001): 89–118. See also David Watts, "Erwin Bingel: Eyewitness to Mass Murder at Uman and Vinnitsa in the Ukraine," Holocaust Research Project, 2009, accessed 10 January 2012, http://www.holocaustresearchproject.org/einsatz/bingel.html.

18. "Masacrul bolșevic de la Winnitza văzut de delegațiile bisericești străine" [The Winnitza Bolshevik Massacre as Seen by the Foreign Churches' Delegates], *BOR* 61, nos. 7–9 (July–September 1943): 437–440. The spelling of the Ukrainian town in this Romanian language article is rather similar to German (Winniza), than Romanian (Vinița), this being another indication of the article's German inspiration.

19. "Cum aresta NKVD?" [How Did the NKVD Arrest People?], *BOR* 61, nos. 7–9 (July–September 1943): 446.

20. Nichifor Crainic, "Transfigurarea Românismului," *BOR* 61, nos. 10–12 (October–December 1943): 517–529.

21. IC. C. Grumăzescu, "Iisus și războiul" [Jesus and the War], *Luminătorul* 74, nos. 5–6 (May–June 1941): 296–300.

22. Titus Bogdănescu, "Viața lui Iisus, Judeii" [The Life of Jesus, the Jews], *Luminătorul* 75, nos. 3–4 (1942): 174.

23. Nic. Ch. Cănănău, "Ce spun canoanele despre primirea în Creștinism a Iudeilor?" [What Do the Canons Say about the Conversion of Jews to Christianity?], *Luminătorul* 75, nos. 3–4 (1942): 196.

24. Ibid., 205.

25. Bogdănescu, *Viața lui Iisus, Iudeii*, 174.

26. Ibid.

27. Pr Al. Enache Dubasari, "Salvați prin cruce" [Saved by the Cross], *Luminătorul* 77, nos. 2–3 (1944): 31–33.

28. Nic. Ch. Cănănău, "Ce spun canoanele," 196-205.

29. Pr. George Antonescu, "Impotriva Simoniei" [Against Simony], *Cuvântul Preoțesc* 8, nos. 8–10 (1941): 4.

30. David Portase-Prut, "Bat clopotele până la Bug, Gânduri pascale" [The Bells Toll Up to the Bug, Easter Thoughts], *Transnistria Creştină* 1, no. 1 (January–March 1942): 15.

31. Ibid., 16.

32. See, for example, Andrei Baleasnai, "Ororile Bolşevismului" [Bolshevik Hideousness], *Transnistria Creştină* 2, nos. 1–2 (January–February 1943): 79–82.

33. Constantin Tomescu, "Trans Nistrum," *Transnistria Creştină* 2, nos. 1–2 (January–February 1943): 2–5.

34. CNSAS, DIE 142, Privitor la Visarion Puiu [File no. 142 Regarding Visarion Puiu], Serviciul de Informaţii Externe [Foreign Office Secret Service—DIE], "Referat despre Visarion Puiu, Conspirativ "OLIVIU", din 31 August 1955 al Ministerului Afacerilor Interne, Direcţia I," 66.

35. CNSAS D8175, Referitor la foştii guvernanţi şi funcţionarii din Transnistria învinuiţi pentru crime de război, cf. art. 14 din Convenţia de Armistiţiu—documente din perioada 1944–1945 [Regarding the Former Government Officials and Functionaries of Transnistria Prosecuted for War Crimes According to Article 14 of the Armistice Convention—Documents from 1944–1945], "Ministerul Afacerilor Interne, Cabinetul Ministrului, Nota No 27.617 din 5 Ianuarie 1945," 173.

36. CNSAS D13273, Preoţi Operaţi 1945 [Priests Filed in 1945], "Nota a Inspectoratului de Jandarmi Mureş," 47.

37. CNSAS D8177, Identificarea, Arestarea şi Judecarea Criminalilor de Război. Masacrul Impotriva Evreilor, 1944–1950 [Identification, Arrest, and Trial of War Criminals. The Massacre against Jews, 1944–1950], "C.M.E, Secţiunea din Romania, Serviciul Statistic şi de Documentare, Biroul Juridic," 200–232.

38. Marius Mircu, *Pogromurile din Bucovina si Dorohoi* [The Pogroms in Bukovina and Dorohoi] (Bucharest: Glob, 1945), 13.

39. Gheorghe Nicolescu, Gheorghe Dobrescu, and Andrei Nicolescu, *Preoţi în tranşee 1941–1945* [Priests in Trenches, 1941–1945] (Bucharest: Fed. Print, 1999), 10–11.

40. Ibid., 24.

41. Ibid., 46.

42. Ibid., 18.

43. Boris Buzilă, *Din istoria vieţii bisericeşti din Basarabia 1812–1944* [A History of the Bessarabian Church 1812–1944] (Bucharest: Fundaţiile Culturale Române, 1996), 362.

44. Ancel, *Transnistria*, 1:474, 476.

45. Niculescu, Dobrescu, and Nicolescu, *Preoţi în tranşee*, 14. "After a quarter of a century of Bolshevik atheism, the families from the territory invaded by the Red Army were alienated from the Orthodox faith. The military chaplains had the task of reinstalling normality. 'In Transnistria I baptized 636 children, 40 of them from Catholic families' said chaplain Fărtăiş Zaharia. . . . The captain chaplain Gheorghe Alexandru . . . baptized 1,904 children aged from one week to 22 years old (885 boys and 1,019 girls), this number is added to the ones baptized in Odessa, 487 (that makes a total of 2,391 Christenings)."

46. Ancel, *Transnistria*, 1:483.

47. Ibid.

48. Ibid., 1:481.

49. "Supliment," *BOR* 57, nos. 9–10 (September–October 1939): 21–22.

50. "Supliment," *BOR* 59, nos. 1–2 (January–February 1941): 39–40.

51. "Cronica internă" [Internal Chronicle], *BOR* 59, nos. 3–4 (March–April 1941): 253.

52. USHMM, RG 25.021 M, reel 100, 35–36.

53. Ibid.

54. "Supliment," *BOR* 59, nos. 11–12 (November–December 1941): 16.

55. Ibid., 33.

56. Ancel, *Transnistria*, 1:481.

57. Ibid., 1:478.

58. Ibid., 1:439.

59. CNSAS D8927, Chestiunea Preoțească în Vechiul Regat [The Priesthood Issue in the Old Kingdom], "Nota no. 9 din 3 iulie 1942," 255.

60. Alexandre Safran, *Resisting the Storm, Romania 1940–1947: Memoirs* (Jerusalem: Yad Vashem, 1987), 53–54.

61. Lya Benjamin, "Dreptul la convertire și statutul evreilor convertiți în perioada regimului antonescian" [The Right to Conversion and the Situation of Converted Jews during the Antonescu Regime], *Studia et Acta Historiae Iudaeorum Romaniae*, ed. Silviu Sanie and Dumitru Vitcu (Bucharest: Hasefer, 1998), 3:248.

62. CNSAS D11374, Comunitatea Evreilor din Romania, 1942–1943 [The Jewish Community of Romania, 1942–1943], "Ministerul Afacerilor Interne, Cabinetul Secretarului de Stat, no. 2474 din 29 Octombrie 1942," 166.

63. Ibid., "Inspectoratul Regional de Poliție Chișinau, Serviciul Siguranței, no. 40157 din 13 Martie 1943," 245–247.

64. Benjamin, *Dreptul La convertire*, 246.

65. CNSAS D11381, Comunitatea Evreilor din Romania, 1943–1949 [The Jewish Community of Romania, 1943–1949], "Tabel nominal cu evreii care au fost trimisi in Transnistria pentru ca au trecut la religia Creștină dupa 21 Martie 1941" [Table with Jews Who Were Deported to Transnistria because Converted to Christianity after 21 March 1941], 57.

66. Avigdor Shachan, *Burning Ice: The Ghettos of Transnistria* (New York: Columbia University Press, 1996), 128.

67. Ancel, *Transnistria*, 2:408.

68. See Traian Saghin, "Ave crux, spes unica!" [Hail Cross, Our Only Hope!], *Cuvântul Preoțesc* 8, nos. 8–10 (1941): 1.

69. Tit Simedrea, "Cuvântarea IPSS Tit Simedrea Mitropolitul Bucovinei cu prilejul deschiderii adunării eparhiale" [The Speech of His Holiness Tit Simedrea, the Metropolitan of Bukovina at the Opening of the Church Assembly], *Cuvântul Preoțesc* 9, no. 5 (May 1942): 1–3.

70. Mirela Corlățan, "Un mitropolit român a adus Yad Vashem în fața instanței" [A Romanian Metropolitan Has Taken Yad Vashem to the Court], *Evenimentul Zilei*, 1 February 2011, http://www.evz.ro/detalii/stiri/un-mitropolit-roman-a-adus-yad-vashem-in-fata-instantei-919902.html.

71. Safran, *Resisting the Storm*, 100.

72. Ibid., 100–101.

73. USHMM, RG 25.021, reel 100, 90, 100–101, 129–131.

74. Ibid., 83.

75. Ibid., 87, 100.

76. Ibid., 79.

77. CNSAS R 319280, Dosar Personal al Agentului, Numele Conspirativ "VALER" [Personal File of the Agent, Code Name "VALER"], "Memoriu" [Explanatory Report], 17–37.

78. Ibid., "Anexa 3," 52.

79. The Righteous Among the Nations, INSHREW, accessed 25 January 2012, http://www.inshr-ew.ro/ro/holocaustul-din-romania/drepti-intre-popoare.html.

80. "Petre Family," The Righteous Among the Nations, Yad Vashem, accessed 19 June 2013, http://db.yadvashem.org/righteous/family.html?language=en&itemId=4420764.

81. Pană, *Antisemitismul religios*, 223.

82. Gheorghe Samoilă, "Grigore Resmeriță (1896–1941)—preot martir," accessed 25 June 2013, http://frgheorghe.wordpress.com/grigore-razmerita-1896-1941-preot-martir/.

83. See Ionuț Fantaziu, "Arhive: 'Sub o conductă de apă au fost îngropați 2.500 de evrei" [Archives: Under a Water Pipe Were Buried 2,500 Jews (An Interview with Radu Ioanid)], *Evenimentul Zilei*, 1 July 2011, http://www.evz.ro/detalii/stiri/radu-ioanid-steaua-romaniei -ramane-la-vadim-sau-la-wiesel-936170.html.

84. Pană, *Antisemitismul religios*, 223, 224.

85. CNSAS D8927, "Nota privind înlocuirea Mitropolitului Visarion Puiu, C.D, 15 May 1940," 7.

86. Ibid., "Nota 8, 4.08.1942, Corpul Detectivilor, grupa a II-a," 273.

87. Ibid., "Notă din 4.09.1942, a Corpului Detectivilor," 280.

88. Ibid., "Nota informativă No 33445 S din 26.09.1942," 311–312.

89. "IPS Mitropolit Tit Simedrea, Conducatorul Eparhiei Bucovinei" [HH Metropolitan Tit Simedrea, the Head of the Bukovinean Seat], *Luminătorul* 7, no. 7 (July 1940): 8.

90. CNSAS D8927, "Corpul Detectivilor, Secția I-a, No 11, 3.10.1940," 58.

91. I.B., "Învestirea și Instalarea IPS Mitropolit Tit Simedrea" [The Investiture and the Installation of HH Metropolitan Tit Simedrea], *Luminătorul* 8, no. 4 (April 1941): 2–3; see also CNSAS D8927, "Radiotelegrama no. 23975 din 25 Martie 1941, Direcția Generală a Poliției, Serviciul Radio," 101.

92. Ibid., "Notă a Corpului Detectivilor, Grupa a III-a, din 1 Noiembrie 1942," 330.

93. Ibid.

94. CNSAS D8927, "Nota 5791 din 30 Septembrie 1942 a Corpului Detectivilor, Grupa a II-a," 301.

95. Ibid., "Nota 544, sursa SSI, din 6 Februarie 1941, Confidențial, Personal," 82.

96. Nicodim, "Cuvânt pentru post," 7.

97. See Albena Taneva, *The Power of Civil Society in a Time of Genocide: Proceedings of the Holy Synod of the Bulgarian Orthodox Church on the Rescue of the Jews in Bulgaria 1940–1944* (Sofia: Sofia University Press, 2005), 55–56.

98. See Carol Rittner, Stephen D. Smith, and Irena Steinfeldt, eds., *The Holocaust and the Christian World: Reflections on the Past, Challenges for the Future* (London: Kuperard, 2000), 74–103.

3

THE JEWISH COMMUNITY OF ROMANIA AND THE ROMANIAN ORTHODOX CHURCH IN THE AFTERMATH OF THE HOLOCAUST (1945–1948)

THE WAY IN WHICH THE Romanian Orthodox Church related to the Holocaust at the end of the Second World War has shaped its attitude toward Holocaust memory up to today. After August 23, 1944, when Romania switched sides and joined the Allies, the Church had to tread a tightrope between hiding its past involvement in the Shoah and forging good relations with the Jewish community, as required by the Communist regime. The involvement of the Orthodox Church in supporting and encouraging anti-Communist actions before and during the war made it extremely vulnerable to the new power.

Supported by the Soviet Union, which maintained a significant military presence in Romanian territory from August 1944 into the second half of the 1950s, the Communists became increasingly influential in Romania in the aftermath of the Second World War. A government led by Petru Groza was imposed in March 1945. In the elections of November 1946, although the democratic forces won a majority, the Communists falsified the results and claimed victory.[1] Despite protests from Western powers, the 1946 elections and the subsequent steps of 1947 led to the new regime taking full control of the country. On December 30, 1947 King Michael I was forced to abdicate and Romania became a People's Republic.[2] Traditional political parties were abolished and their leaders imprisoned.

From a religious perspective, 1945–1948 was a time of transition and submission. In February 1948 Patriarch Nicodim died in suspect circumstances[3] and was replaced with Justinian, known in historiography as "the red Patriarch"[4] due to his close links with the leadership of the regime.[5] In the same year, the Greek-Catholic Church was abolished, and the Romanian Orthodox Church took full advantage of this; Greek Catholic churches were transferred to the Orthodox Church and Greek Catholic priests forced to become Orthodox priests. Those who refused were imprisoned.[6] 1948 was also the year in which the Jewish community elected a new chief rabbi, preferred and, according to some accounts, imposed by the new regime.[7]

THE JEWISH COMMUNITY OF ROMANIA AT THE END OF THE WAR

At the end of the Second World War, the Jewish community of Romania and the Romanian Orthodox Church found themselves in situations that contrasted significantly with their status before the war. The Romanian Jewish community, persecuted and threatened with total annihilation after June 1941, lost approximately half of its people in the Holocaust. The survivors, physically and mentally affected by the event, still faced prejudice and injustice in a Romanian society in which anti-Semitism did not die overnight. Large parts of eastern and northeastern Romanian Jewry were killed by the Antonescu regime in pogroms (in the first months of the war against the USSR) and, after deportation to Transnistria, in mass shootings and from hunger, sickness, and cold.

The Romanian state, soon after the end of the war, minimized the number of victims. According to Radu Ioanid, the Romanian delegation at the Paris Peace Conference claimed that 1,528 Jews had died in Transnistria and 3,759 Jews had died on Romanian territory. Ioanid calls this a gross falsification.[8] We know today that in just one pogrom, in Iaşi (June 27–29, 1941), up to 13,000 Jews were killed.[9] Liviu Rotman states that about 200,000 Romanian Jews were deported to Transnistria and 150,000 of them died. To this number he adds 60,000 Romanian Jews who perished in the pogroms during the summer of 1941.[10] The Elie Wiesel Commission for the Study of Holocaust in Romania, in its *Final Report* issued in 2004, states that between 280,000 and 380,000 Jews were killed in territories under Romanian control, around 200,000 of them being Romanian Jews.[11] Places that before the war were Jewish strongholds were left empty, with no Jews at all.[12] Roughly 110,000 Jews from northern Transylvania (which came under Hungarian control in August 1940) died in Auschwitz, sharing the horrific fate of the Hungarian Jews.[13]

In 1947, the Romanian section of the World Jewish Council took a census of the Jewish population of Romania. The result showed 428,312 Jews (out of about 750,000 before the war), including the survivors from northern Transylvania and, according to Hary Kuller, more than 20,000 Jewish refugees from the neighboring countries that were still in Romanian territory in 1947 awaiting emigration.[14] That so many survived can be explained by the vacillating attitude of the Antonescu regime toward the Jewish population. As pointed out earlier, most of the Jews of the Old Kingdom escaped the Holocaust; although they initially agreed to German requests for the deportation of all remaining Romanian Jews to Belzec, in October 1942 the Romanian authorities changed their mind.

The survivors of the Holocaust in Romania faced difficult social, medical, legal, and political problems.[15] A large number of orphaned Jewish children were cared for by organizations from inside and outside Romania.[16] During the war, thousands of Jews had been displaced.[17] Many of these people could not return home because their property had either been destroyed or given to non-Jewish Romanians. The problem of restitution and of the elimination of all anti-Semitic legislation was raised by the Jewish community immediately after Romania joined the Allies in August 1944. While the Romanian governments of late 1944 and early 1945 eliminated the anti-Semitic legislation and proclaimed a return to the democratic constitution of 1923, in practice, due to bureaucratic barriers and strong anti-Semitic prejudices, the Jews faced discrimination long after August 1944. As far as the problem of restitution was concerned, the situation was even more complicated. Different governments that came to power during this period, representing different political organizations, opposed the restitution of property, claiming it would create social unrest.[18]

In the first months after the end of the Antonescu regime the Romanian Jewish community was still in collective shock, "dominated by the fear of a possible return to the subhuman state to which it was condemned."[19] In spite of this constant fear of the past, there is evidence that Jews commemorated and remembered the victims. Besides services commemorating the dead,[20] special services of burying soap that was believed to be made from humans killed in concentration camps are mentioned in several archival documents.[21]

From a political point of view, the Jewish community faced increasing pressure from the Communist regime. The small number of Jews in leadership positions within the Communist Party was rather a liability.[22] Their interference in the life of the community became increasingly visible. The Communists, often with the help of Communist Jews, went as far as to push aside, without any remorse, the Jewish leaders who, during the war, had fought for the very survival of the Jewish community, such as Wilhelm Filderman, the president of the Federation of Jewish Communities, and Alexandre Safran, the chief rabbi.[23] If initially the Communists tried to control and to influence the existing Jewish organizations, they soon dropped that approach and created new organizations, such as the Jewish Democratic Committee, which was supposed to act as liaison with the new regime.[24] Alexandre Safran says in his memoir that what Antonescu did not achieve—namely the destruction of Jewish institutions—the Communist regime did in the first phase of its power.[25]

In December 1947, Alexandre Safran chose to remain in exile because of the major political and religious changes taking place in Romania, and in June 1948 Moses Rosen was elected as the new chief rabbi. Rosen was born in Moinesti, in Moldova, the eastern part of Romania, in 1912. He was the son of the local rabbi.[26] In 1931, he studied law at the University of Bucharest, where he encountered virulent anti-Semitism. The same year he started his rabbinical studies in Vienna and Romania, but he was unable to complete them until 1938, after he had finished his military service in the Romanian army.[27] In May 1940, he was offered the post of rabbi in Suceava, but in July 1940, after the withdrawal of Romanian troops from Bessarabia and Bukovina, he was arrested, "being considered a Bolshevik."[28] He was released in September 1940 on the eve of the Iron Guard's ascension to power.[29] In the next few years he was briefly rearrested several times and, in the Târgu Jiu camp, he became acquainted with Romania's future Communist leaders.[30] During the war he settled in Bucharest, where he was initially the rabbi of a small synagogue. Later he became the rabbi of one of the main synagogues in the capital. After the war he held several positions of responsibility in the Bucharest Jewish community before being elected chief rabbi in 1948.[31]

In his memoir Rosen acknowledges that he was approached before the elections by Israel Bacal, a Communist and a prominent Jewish Democratic Committee (CDE) member, about becoming a candidate for the post.[32] According to Liviu Rotman, the fact that Rosen was a political prisoner during the war and had leftist sympathies, as shown in his relations with the

Social Democratic Party, "were warranties for the regime that Rosen would become the ideal collaborator."[33] Documents of the Romanian Secret Service describe the joy of the Communist secret agents when he was elected,[34] suggesting that he was preferred and supported by the regime.

To all the problems highlighted above should be added the persistence of anti-Semitism. Sometimes the Communist authorities revived anti-Semitism in order to distract attention from grave social or economic problems. For example, in 1946, during a period of social unrest as a result of hunger caused by that summer's severe drought, rumors of blood libel and allegations about the kidnapping of Christian children were spread, apparently by top government officials.[35] Old prejudices, developed since the creation of modern Romania, were still common after the war. Jews were widely seen as anti-Romanian, lazy, financially rapacious, and morally decadent.[36] A June 1945 police document in Suceava (northeast part of Romania, with a substantial Jewish population), describes measures against profiteering: "Orders will be given for the destruction of profiteering, the profiteers will be arrested, and the chauvinistic and reactionary Jews should be sent for internment in camps."[37] The tone is vehement and the idea of camps for Jews clearly persisted in some minds. In May 1945 serious tensions arose in the Botoșani district (also in northeast Romania) between the Jews and a subordinate officer.[38] Although it was almost nine months since the official anti-Semitic policies of the Romanian state ceased, the subordinate officer continued to mock and verbally and physically abuse Jews. At the beginning of 1946 a series of anti-Semitic attacks (mostly desecration of synagogues and cemeteries) took place in Transylvania. An attack in Hațeg (a town in southern Transylvania) persuaded the Federation of Jewish Communities in Romania to make an appeal to the prime minister of the country.[39]

These examples of grassroots anti-Semitism were increasingly accompanied by the political anti-Semitism/anti-Zionism that exploded after 1948. The period from 1945 to 1948 saw an increase in anti-Semitism among politicians, rather than a more general, structured political anti-Semitism,[40] which came later. Interestingly—and this shows the schizophrenic attitude of the Romanian politicians—anti-Semitism went hand in hand with public outbursts of (hypocritical) gestures of benevolence toward Jewish leadership. Alexandre Safran, in his memoir, vehemently condemns the hypocrisy shown by some Communist politicians.[41]

Immediately after Romania switched sides and joined the Allies on August 23, 1944, the Romanian Orthodox Church began covering up and rewriting its recent past. In the first three years after the end of the Second World War the Church was under siege. Beginning in 1945 the Communist regime made increasingly clear its intention to use the Church. Articles published in Church journals were used to enforce this new reality. For example, an article written by Lazăr Iacob and published in *BOR* in July 1945 was a veritable tract on the church-state relationship, which he claimed had to be reassessed according to the new regime's interest. In the opening sentences the author emphasizes the primacy of the state: "By birth a man becomes lawfully subject to the State. By spiritual rebirth, by baptism, he receives juridical capacity, legal status in the Church too." The words are very cleverly chosen. By birth a man "becomes"; by spiritual rebirth he just "receives" a legal status in the Church "too." The spiritual dimension is adjunct to submission to the state. Making his argument about the primacy of the state, Iacob brings into the discussion the possible tension that could appear between the two citizenships: "From the double citizenship of a man springs rights and duties both in the spiritual and secular domains. But a lawful subject cannot be divided. This is the reason why the cooperation of the two institutions, their harmony, is an absolute imperative for the good of man and society." After this, it is only one step to the most important question: When tensions appear between the two institutions, the church and the state, which one has priority?

> The favorable settings in which the State exists and functions create favorable conditions for the activity of the Church too. Tensions and agitations within the Church have unpleasant consequences for the State, a State that wants to secure quietness and peace for its citizens. . . . If it would step out of the spiritual domain, the Church could produce serious damage to the State. The many conflicts between the State and the Church in the West plainly prove this truth. As a measure of avoiding such situations, the State has secured its control and the supervision of all religions' activities, exercising this right as an emanation of State suzerainty.[42]

This is a bold declaration that the state would henceforth exercise its power in its relationship with all religions in Romania. Iacob makes clear that the

Church is facing a siege and not demolition: "For the State the activity of the Church is of a great importance, because the religious notion is one of the most important factors for social solidarity. Through the Church the State has in front of it an organized collectivity."[43] In postwar rural Romania, the Church was a means for reaching the masses, and the regime would use it both to promote its policy and to legitimate its authority.[44] The Church was very much trusted by the majority of Romanians and the Communist regime could not ignore that reality.[45] On the contrary, to gain the trust of the masses, representatives of the state often participated in religious services, a custom that continued throughout the Communist era.[46]

Lazăr Iacob (1884–1951), the author of the article, was born in Bihor, the province of Transylvania, and made a career as a professor of canonical law. As dean of the Faculty of Law in Oradea he was involved in clashes with Jewish students who contested the historiography about Romanian settlement in Transylvania during and after the Roman conquest of Dacia.[47] At the time of the article's publication, Iacob was a professor of church law at the Faculty of Theology, University of Bucharest.[48] Even before the war he defended the preponderance of the state in relation to the Church and his theological approach seemed to follow the Byzantine tradition that the king (emperor) was chosen by God and thus the Church should be an extension of the state.[49]

In August 1944, the new regime created an institution called the "Union of Patriots' from which later on appeared the "Union of Priests."[50] According to the secret service, the way in which Communist messages were to be transmitted through the Church was decided at a priests' meeting in September 1945, and Petru Groza, the new prime minister of the country, called the Orthodox Church "the church of the state."[51] Priests were lured into betraying their traditional political parties in exchange for ecclesiastical or political positions.[52] In 1946 Petru Groza asked for the creation of a "diplomatic structure" of priests to carry out the state's external political agenda and, according to some secret cables, he asked for a new patriarch.[53] Members of the Church hierarchy who were known for their far-right stand before and during the war were under surveillance[54] and Patriarch Nicodim was increasingly seen as undesirable. Often, clergy with a troubled past were promoted precisely because they could be easily blackmailed and controlled by the regime.[55] A summary of the Holy Synod's meetings of 1947, published in the year-end issue of *BOR*, mentions the rise of Teoctist Arăpaşu (future patriarch, 1986–2007), to the rank of archimandrite.[56] Such mention, at that point in time, had political significance, expressing the support of the regime for that person.

In August 1947 Irineu Mihălcescu, the metropolitan of Moldova, who held the *locum tenens* (being the first in line to succeed the patriarch), was forced to retire to the Agapia Monastery, where he died soon after in suspicious circumstances.[57] He was replaced by state decree with Ioan Marina, who less than three years before was just a priest in Vâlcea county.[58] On February 27, 1948, half a year after the removal of Irineu Mihălcescu, Patriarch Nicodim died, again in suspicious circumstances, and Ioan Marina became the new patriarch of the Romanian Orthodox Church under the name Justinian.[59] The fate of Patriarch Nicodim during this period (1945–1948) is very interesting. Although officially he got along with Communist policies, such as consolidating relations with the Russian Orthodox Church or whitewashing the recent past, secret archives show that he had a tense relationship with the new regime. By the end of 1945 Nicodim's dislike of the Soviets was made obvious in several instances.[60] In May–June 1947, during the visit of Alexei, the Patriarch of the Russian Orthodox Church, Nicodim entered into a direct confrontation with his guest, emphasizing the independence of the Romanian Orthodox Church. The dialogue was so embarrassing for the Romanian Communist officials that they started to make plans for Nicodim's departure.[61] After the episode with the Russian patriarch, Nicodim was forced to retire to the Neamț monastery.[62] Rumors about his dismissal circulated during 1947. Metropolitan Bălan hoped that, finally, he could become patriarch and made preparations for a putsch in the summer of 1947.[63] The last days of the second patriarch of the Romanian Orthodox Church are veiled in a strange atmosphere. According to secret reports, he was seriously ill, but he moved suddenly to Bucharest at the end of February 1948, where he died unexpectedly. A document found in the CNSAS archives that was supposed to have been burned (but was still in the file) mentions the return of the patriarch to Bucharest, which was not seen favorably by the regime. It is likely that Nicodim's sudden return from his imposed exile was the last straw that determined his elimination.[64]

The process of replacing the old echelons of the Church continued in the following years, one of the major episodes in this process being the reorganization of the Orthodox monasteries at the beginning of the 1950s. Still, 1948 was the decisive year for the Church because it signified the end of one era and the beginning of another: the end of Nicodim's reign (which itself is split in two major periods: before and after August 23, 1944) and the beginning of Justinian's and Communist rule. The election of Justinian was the defining moment in the process of replacing the old elite with a new one, obedient to the Communist regime. Indeed, 1948 was the climax of a process of radical changes that began as early as August 1944. However, we should be careful not to think of this as "the Communist takeover of the Church," lest responsibility for compromising decisions made by the Church be minimized or blamed entirely on the Communists. The Communist "takeover" would be better described as the replacement of the old ecclesiastical elite with a new ecclesiastical elite, obedient to the regime. As Lucian Leuştean rightly suggests, what happened in the first years of Communism, although dramatic in some cases, was not out of the ordinary. The Church did nothing other than apply once more the Byzantine inspired principle of *symphonia*, according to which the church and the state are interconnected "and their influences overcome their strict spheres."[65] Collaboration with the new Communist regime thus followed a long tradition of the Romanian Orthodox Church allying itself as closely as possible to political power.

NOTES

1. Comisia Prezidenţială pentru Analiza Dictaturii Comuniste din România [Presidential Commission for the Analysis of the Communist Dictatorship in Romania], *Raport Final* (Bucharest: Humanitas, 2006), 130–133.

2. The name of the country was Romanian People's Republic from 1947 to 1965, when it was changed to Socialist Republic of Romania (1965–1989).

3. Lucian N. Leuştean, *Orthodoxy and the Cold War: Religion and Political Power in Romania* (London: Palgrave Macmillan, 2009), 71.

4. Cristian Vasile, *Biserica Ortodoxă Română în primul deceniu comunist* [The Romanian Orthodox Church during the First Decade of Communism] (Bucharest: Curtea Veche, 2005), 17.

5. Dennis Deletant, *Communist Terror in Romania: Gheorghiu-Dej and the Police State, 1948–1965* (London: Hurst, 1999), 90.

6. Leuştean, *Orthodoxy and the Cold War*, 79–81.

7. CNSAS D11381, Comunitatea Evreilor din România, 1943–1949 [The Jewish Community of Romania, 1943–1949], "Nota a DGSS, 16 Iunie 1948 Despre Alegerea lui Moses Rosen," 221.

8. Radu Ioanid, *Holocaustul în România: distrugerea evreilor şi romilor sub regimul Antonescu, 1940–1944* [The Holocaust in Romania: The Destruction of Jews and Roma under the Antonescu Regime, 1940–1944] (Bucharest: Hasefer, 2006), 19.

9. George Voicu, ed., *Pogromul de la Iaşi (28–30 Iunie 1941): prologul Holocaustului din Romania* (Iaşi, Romania: Polirom, 2006), 11.

10. Liviu Rotman, *Evreii din România în Perioada Comunistă, 1944–1965* [The Jews of Romania during Communism, *1944–1965*] (Iași, Romania: Polirom, 2004), 27.

11. Tuvia Friling, Radu Ioanid, and Mihai Ionescu, eds., *The Final Report of the Elie Wiesel Commission for the Study of the Holocaust in Romania* (Bucharest: Polirom, 2005), 179.

12. See Hary Kuller, *Evreii în România Anilor 1944–1949: evenimente, documente, comentarii* [The Jews in Romania 1944–1989: Events, Documents, Comments] (Bucharest: Hasefer, 2002), 48–52.

13. Rotman, *Evreii din România*, 28.

14. Kuller, *Evreii în România*, 37.

15. Liviu Rotman, *The Communist Era until 1965*, vol. 4 of *The History of the Jews in Romania* (Tel Aviv: The Goldstein-Goren Diaspora Research Center, 2005), 54.

16. CNSAS D11387, Problema Evreiască, 1943–1947 [The Jewish Problem, 1943–1947], "Proces Verbal între Centrala Evreilor, Oficiul Tutova, Eforia Judeţeană a Copilului şi Crucea Roşie, 5 Aprilie 1944," 58–59. According to this account 119 orphan Jewish children were transferred in April 1944 from the local administration to the Red Cross.

17. Rotman, *The Communist Era until 1965*, 55.

18. Rotman, *Evreii din România*, 62.

19. Ibid., 29.

20. CNSAS D11381, "Radiograma No. 2030S [no date, but from the content of the document the ceremony took place on 29 May 1946], Inspectoratul de Poliţie Oradea," 133.

21. CNSAS D8891, Federaţia Sioniştilor din România (1945–1946) [The Zionist Federation of Romania (1945–1946)], "Adresa Uniunii Democrate Polone către Ministrul Justiției, no. 15173, din 14 Februarie 1946, Minsterul Justiției, Secţia Judiciară," 164; see also, "Nota no. 9073S din 30 Martie 1946 a Direcţiei Generale a Poliţiei, Inspectoratul Regional de Poliţie Iași," 206.

22. See Victor Neumann, *Istoria evreilor din România: studii documentare şi teoretice* (Timişoara, Romania: Amarcord, 1996), 245–248.

23. Rotman, *Evreii din România*, 33–37, 83. Both Filderman and Safran left Romania in December 1947 due to the increasing pressures they faced from the Communist authorities.

24. Kuller, *Evreii în România*, 140.

25. Alexandre Safran, *Resisting the Storm, Romania 1940–1947: Memoirs* (Jerusalem: Yad Vashem, 1987), 189–206.

26. Moses Rosen and Joseph Finklestone, *Dangers, Tests and Miracles: The Remarkable Life Story of Chief Rabbi Rosen of Romania* (London: Weidenfeld & Nicolson, 1990), 11.

27. Ibid., 20.

28. Ibid., 25–26.

29. Ibid., 34.

30. Rotman, *The Communist Era until 1965*, 180.

31. Rotman, *Evreii din România*, 83.

32. Rosen and Finklestone, *Dangers, Tests and Miracles*, 51.

33. Rotman, *Evreii din România*, 83–84.

34. CNSAS D11381, "Nota a DGSS, 16 Iunie 1948 Despre Alegerea lui Moses Rosen," 221.

35. Rotman, *The Communist Era until 1965*, 163.

36. Ibid., 157–161.

37. CNSAS D8891, "DGP, DGPS, Nota 10272S din 19 Iunie 1945, Inspectoratul de Poliţie Suceava," 35.

38. Ibid., "Dosar cu Incidentul din 28 Mai 1945 în Oraşul Botoşani între Subofiţerul Feraru Mihai şi un Grup de Cetăţeni Evrei din Acel Oras, Inspectoratul de Poliţie Suceava," 39.

39. Ibid., "Adresa către Prim-Ministrul Petru Groza, no. 1122, din 26 Aprilie 1946, Federaţia Uniunilor de Comunităţi Evreeşti," 250.

40. Rotman, *The Communist Era until 1965*, 162.

41. Safran, *Resisting the Storm*, 169–170.

42. Lazăr Iacob, "Biserica și transformările sociale" [The Church and the Social Changes], in *BOR* 63, nos. 7–8 (July–August 1945): 302.

43. Ibid.

44. Leuștean, *Orthodoxy and the Cold War*, 63.

45. Vasile, *Biserica Ortodoxă Română*, 109. Tension arose, for example, when the Communists dared to bury some of their members without a religious service.

46. Ibid., 111–112.

47. Lucian Nastasă, ed., *Antisemitismul universitar în România (1919–1939): mărturii documentare* [Academic Antisemitism in Romania (1919–1939) Documentary Evidence] (Cluj-Napoca, Romania: Kriterion, 2011), 278–280.

48. "Lazăr Iacob, Profesor de Teologie, Canonist" [Lazăr Iacob, Professor of Theology, Canonist], *Dicționarul Teologilor Români*, accessed 22 February 2012, http://biserica.org/WhosWho/DTR/I/LazarIacob.html.

49. See Nicolas Zernov, *Eastern Christendom* (London: Weidenfeld & Nicolson, 1961), 44–47; see also Nicolae Iorga, *Istoria bisericii românești și a vieții religioase a Românilor* [The History of the Romanian Church and of Romanians' Religious Life] (Vălenii de Munte, Romania: Neamul Românesc, 1908), 20–22.

50. Vasile, *Biserica Ortodoxă Română*, 41–42.

51. CNSAS D56, Problema Preoțească în Vechiul Regat, 1945–1947 [The Priesthood Problem in the Old Kingdom, 1945–1947], "Nota din 26 Septembrie 1945, sursa Viator," 65.

52. Vasile, *Biserica Ortodoxă Română*, 36.

53. CNSAS D56, "Nota No 78 din 23 Februarie 1946 sursa Viator," 86.

54. Vasile, *Biserica Ortodoxă Română*, 147.

55. Vasile, *Biserica Ortodoxă Română*, 44.

56. "Supliment," *BOR* 65, nos. 1–3 (January–March 1947): 130–132.

57. Vasile, *Biserica Ortodoxă Română*, 136.

58. "Cronica Interna," *BOR* 65, nos. 4–9 (April–September 1947): 272–274.

59. Lucian Leuștean provides a good analysis of the suspect ascension to power of Justinian Marina in *Orthodoxy and the Cold War*, 61–62.

60. See CNSAS D56, "Nota din 15 Decembrie 1945, sursa Viator," 84; ibid., "Nota No. 25, din 26 Ianuarie 1946, sursa V," 99; Vasile, *Biserica Ortodoxă Română*, 48–49.

61. Vasile, *Biserica Ortodoxă Română*, 201.

62. Ibid., 151.

63. CNSAS D12088, "Inspectoratul regional de Siguranță Sibiu, no. 4604 din 26 Octombrie 1947," 8.

64. Ibid., "DGSS, Nota din 17 Februarie 1948. Strict Secret. Se va distruge prin ardere," [DGSS, Note from 17 February 1948. Strictly Secret. It will be destroyed by fire], 142.

65. Leuștean, *Orthodoxy and the Cold War*, 189.

4

CLEANSING THE PAST, REWRITING HISTORY

The Romanian Orthodox Church from Active Involvement in the
Holocaust to the Whitewashing Process

AFTER AUGUST 23, 1944, THE day Romania left Germany and joined the
Allies, the Romanian Orthodox Church found itself in an awkward position: the Soviets and the Communists, against whom the patriarch, other
members of the high hierarchy, and the journals of the Church spoke openly
before and during the war, became the new masters of the country. So it is
not surprising that a large campaign of hiding the compromising pages of
the recent past took place in 1945. This campaign also involved covering up
the Church's negative involvement in the Holocaust.

THE ROMANIAN ORTHODOX CHURCH AND THE
1945 WHITEWASHING CAMPAIGN

Under the new political circumstances and for the ways in which the Romanian Orthodox Church would deal with the past, 1945 was an important
year in church-state relations. The submission of the Orthodox Church to
the new power became visible on the same day Romania left Germany and
joined the Allies, and this submission was not enforced from outside at the
beginning. As Lucian Leuștean suggests, it probably came from fear and a
desire to please the new authorities.[1] In his pastoral letter addressed to the
Church immediately after August 23, 1944 (but not published in *BOR* until
December 1944), Patriarch Nicodim wrote, "For many years in our beloved
country we had a regime that actually limited the free expression of our
people's thoughts and sentiments." This statement contradicted entirely the
Church's actions and hopes since the 1930s. Up to that point the Church had

advocated an authoritarian state in which Orthodoxy was one of the core ingredients (Nichifor Crainic), and attacked democracy (Patriarch Miron Cristea) as the real danger to the Romanian soul. The Church had encouraged in various forms Marshal Antonescu's regime, which it saw as the realization of many of its dreams: a politically powerful Church, the destruction of Jews and of "sects," and state laws that enforced weekly worship and Orthodox ethics.

Moreover, Nicodim seized the opportunity to blame others for what had happened in Romania: "The dictatorship is alien from the soul and the ethos of Romanian people. It came to our country from foreign lands." Blaming the Germans for events in Romania in the 1930s and during the war would become a powerful tool in the whitewashing process. Nicodim said, "The country itself was forced to enter a war which the most part of our people did not understand and did not want."[2] Here again Nicodim elided facts, as on several occasions between 1941 and 1944 he himself had clearly expressed support for the war. In two articles published in the main journal of the Church (the last one in the January–March 1944 issue of *BOR*), he emphasized the difference between an offensive and a defensive war, calling the war against the USSR defensive because, as a holy war, the Romanians were defending themselves and the Church from the "Bolshevik Dragon."[3]

But the Church's willing submission to the new power was expressed when he wrote that "the modern Romanian state formed and strengthened itself with the unselfish support of our present allies. With the powerful neighbor from the East [the USSR] we always had the best political, cultural, and religious relations."[4] Yet as early as the 1920s, the Romanian Orthodox Church had led a vigorous campaign against Bolshevism, this campaign reaching its climax during the war, when the Church expressed without any reservation its hatred for "Judeo-Bolshevism." In another text published at the beginning of 1945, the patriarch especially praised the new government and the Allies for the reintegration into the Romanian territory of northern Transylvania, but said nothing about Bessarabia and northern Bukovina, which remained under Soviet rule after the war. He ended his message with an appeal for the submission of the Orthodox faithful to the king and to the new government. Then he added, "Stop the hatred and the tensions between you. Set aside the religious and nationalist hatred. Set aside any interests that would promote hatred and any vain ambitions."[5]

It is hard to say whether the patriarch really believed in his message. It is clear that even from 1945 onward the Communists imposed "harmonious" social and religious relations. They wanted to pose as a united country, without religious or ethnic dissensions, and this policy would be one of the most important points on the Communist agenda up until 1989. If the message was the patriarch's initiative, we should see the last words as a genuine step toward peace, after a long period of hatred.

Nicodim was a very interesting personality. He reluctantly accepted to be elected patriarch in 1939 because of his old age and, probably, because of the turbulent political climate at the time. Although an anti-Semite who did almost nothing to help the Jews, he was probably sincere. He believed that the Bolsheviks were the real threat to the existence of Romania and that Jews were the main creators and supporters of Bolshevism; that Antonescu and Hitler fought a holy war against the Dragon from Revelation. He defended his position until the very end of the alliance with Germany. However, he was not a cunning man, nor a perfidious one. It seems that, in October 1942 in the context of massive deportations of Jews to Transnistria, he contacted Marshal Antonescu, the king, and the queen mother at the request of Chief Rabbi Alexandre Safran. Nevertheless, according to Safran, "he did not get far with him [Antonescu]" and did not press further in favor of the Jewish community.[6]

Immediately after the patriarch's message a note bearing the stamp of the Communist propaganda machine was published: "The impulse from the Patriarch will not be in vain, as the faithful from the whole country always followed the counsel of their spiritual leaders. The Church was always present with its counsel and action at the corner points of our historic evolution and this should be especially the case today. The priests from the villages of the valleys, hills, or plains are united in work and prayer with their faithful, and the Patriarch himself is counseling and watching, giving a good example of hard and yielding work."[7] The note tried to present a picture of a hardworking Church and a fatherly patriarch living in a country where anyone should work and leave behind any tensions that would undermine the new regime. This emphasis on the collaboration between the Church and the earthly leaders throughout history shows the intentions of the Communists to use the Church for legitimacy in a country where roughly 80 percent of the population lived in rural areas. In such areas, the Church was still a stronghold.[8]

In his book about to the Romanian Orthodox Church during the first decade of Communism, Cristian Vasile mentions a letter that Alexei, the metropolitan of Leningrad, the Russian Orthodox *locum tenens* patriarch, sent to the Romanian patriarch on August 25, 1944 accusing Romanians of crimes on the Eastern Front. Although the Holocaust is not directly mentioned in the letter, many of the crimes referred to were committed against Jews.[9] Patriarch Nicodim knew that without a massive whitewashing of the past the Romanian Orthodox Church would be condemned to harassment and eventual servitude. Therefore, he tried to avoid this by covering the past, rewriting history, and trying to gain, even at the price of flattery, the mercy of the new masters.

Although the rewriting of history to suit the new political situation started as soon as August 1944, a more systematic campaign to cover up the Church's involvement in the war against the USSR and in the Holocaust became visible by the middle of 1945. Starting in June, a series of articles were published in the main journal of the Church dealing with these topics. In June 1945 Dumitru Fecioru published the article "Six Years of Patriarchate of His Holiness Nicodim."[10] Fecioru was a former Legionary priest and later, in 1949, he would appear on a list of persons who should be under surveillance.[11] Any compromising information about Patriarch Nicodim was omitted from the article, the emphasis being on his writing and especially on some translations from Russian he had done in the past. In August 1945 a pastoral letter of the Holy Synod was published in *BOR*. The Holy Synod's message blamed the Germans for the events of the war[12] and presented itself as a promoter of democracy.[13] It suddenly forgot the interwar and war period when it was the main advocate of an authoritarian state.

As in the case of Nicodim's letter, the address of the Holy Synod also introduced for the first time themes that would become very important in the Church's and the Communist regime's historiography later on. When praising the Romanian army for its behavior during the war, the Holy Synod acknowledges first that, "after shedding reluctantly much blood in the war against USSR, [it] now joined the brave Soviet armies in the war against the true adversaries of our country." The victories of the Romanian and Soviet armies after August 23, 1944, it says, were important "for the liberation of northern Transylvania from the Horthyist [an allusion to the Horthy's regime in Hungary] yoke."[14] The theme of the Horthyist yoke would be seminal for later Communist nationalism. In the last sentences of the declaration, the Orthodox faithful are asked to fully support the new government.

The campaign to conceal the Church's troubled past was beneficial for both the new regime and for the Romanian Orthodox Church. First, it allowed the Party to use the Church in transmitting the new Communist values and precluded more Soviet interference in the country's business. The Church, facing a dramatic shift of power that could result in revelations about recent history, guilt, and fear (not only a theoretical fear, but a direct fear of prosecutions, with former metropolitan of Transnistria Visarion Puiu and many other priests tried for their involvement in the war), was eager to release itself from the chains of a haunted past. Therefore, it was very likely that in the new political conditions the members of the Holy Synod, with Patriarch Nicodim first in line, welcomed and encouraged this cover-up.

The major themes of these declarations marked a turning point for the Romanian Orthodox Church, completely rearranging its position. If before August 1944 the Church had praised the Germans and the campaign against the USSR as a holy war to protect Christendom, now it blamed the Germans for what had happened, painting its previous actions as performed under German pressure. If the Church encouraged dictatorship and theocracy as early as the 1930s but mostly from 1938 to 1944, now it posed as a defender and promoter of democracy. If the Church condemned Bolshevism and the Soviet army before, now it praised them for their victories against the Germans. If the Church lamented the fate of the Russian Orthodox Church under Communism before, now it declared that it would strengthen its relationship with it.

THE FIRST DOCUMENTS ABOUT THE EVENTS OF THE HOLOCAUST IN THE OFFICIAL JOURNAL OF THE ROMANIAN ORTHODOX CHURCH

In the context of a massive rearrangement of its position in relation to the events of the war, a reassessment of the Church's attitude toward Jews was unavoidable. While the declarations of the patriarch and of the Holy Synod, as well as the article by Dumitru Fecioru, hid compromising episodes and rewrote history, they did not directly address the events of the Holocaust. This was done in two articles published in the year-end 1945 issue of *BOR*, an issue that was in its entirety dedicated to Patriarch Nicodim and that celebrated his eightieth birthday.[15] The first article was written by Bishop Antim Nica, former vice head of the Romanian Orthodox mission in Transnistria

(1941–1943). It was entitled "Retracing the Romanian Apostolate,"[16] was eighteen pages long, and did not deal directly with Patriarch Nicodim. The second article, was written by Teodor Manolache, who was not an ordained priest but who had an administrative position at the Faculty of Theology in Bucharest. It was entitled "From Love and Duty: Lesser-Known Deeds Performed by Patriarch Nicodim during the War,"[17] was seven pages long, and directly focused on Patriarch Nicodim. The relative length of the articles, especially the first, suggests their importance. The Nica article deals with two major issues: the Romanian Orthodox Church's history of Jews' conversion and its attitude toward Jews during the Holocaust. The Manolache article deals only with the Holocaust period. The articles complement each other, Manolache continuing some points raised in the Nica article and describing in more detail some of the documents brought forward by the first article. Both are seminal to the topic of the Church's position toward Holocaust memory. They created several myths that have been regularly reinforced since 1945, among them the myth of the Romanian Orthodox Church's permanent tolerance toward Jews and the myth of the Church as a savior of Jews during the Holocaust.

The conversion of Jews to Christian Orthodoxy in Romania—documents brought forward in 1945 by Bishop Antim Nica, former vice head of the Romanian Orthodox mission in Transnistria (1941–1943), to support the myth of a tolerant Church

The conversion of Jews to the Romanian Orthodox faith is one of the major themes in Antim Nica's article "Retracing the Romanian Apostolate." Fifteen out of its eighteen pages focus on this topic. In the previous issue of *BOR* Nica published a preparatory article entitled "Bishop M. S. Alexander,"[18] which describes the personality and work of Michael Solomon Alexander, "the first Anglican bishop in Jerusalem from 1841 to 1845."[19] According to Nica, Alexander was emblematic of the Protestant missionary activity among the Jews in the first part of the nineteenth century. Giving details about Alexander's conversion from Judaism to Christianity and about his first steps as a missionary among the Jews, especially in Palestine, Nica suggests that evangelizing the Jews was normal, something done by Protestants successfully during the nineteenth century.

Why this emphasis in Nica's article on the conversion of Jews? There could be two reasons. First, after March 1941, when the Romanian government forbade the conversion of Jews to any other religion, the Romanian Ortho-dox Church, although expressing disapproval of the state's interference in its business, made clear its support for these racial policies and generally re-frained from baptizing Jews.[20] This is in stark contrast with the attitude of the Roman Catholic Church and other minority Christian denominations. In this context, Nica's emphasis on the Orthodox Church's tradition of con-verting Jews was an answer to an implied condemnation. He wanted to balance the rescue actions of other Christian denominations in Romania, which had used the conversion of Jews to help them avoid deportation, by presenting the Romanian Orthodox Church as equally interested in conver-sion. The fact that Bishop Nica was aware of the politics of memory was made evident when he asked the Norwegian Lutheran Church for a letter confirming his alleged positive behavior toward Jews in Transnistria (see chapter 2). Another reason why Nica was so concerned with the mission among Jews could be related to the activity of the Romanian Orthodox mis-sion in Transnistria. The author hides the Church's deafness to the cry of hundreds of thousands of Jews killed in Transnistria and its legitimation of state policies, and presents instead a neutral, unproblematic fiction focusing on the alleged merits of Christian mission.

Even from the beginning of the article it is obvious that the historical data Bishop Nica brings forward is highly selective. The first example men-tioned is a civil law called *Îndreptarea Legii* (The Righting of the Law), is-sued by Matei Basarab, the Prince of Wallachia (1632–1654), in 1652. Nica overlooks the Govora Law, which was a Church law issued in 1640 during the reign of the same prince, but which was very anti-Semitic in some of its aspects.[21] The documents he brings forward to support the idea that the Ro-manian Orthodox Church maintained a tolerant attitude toward Jews sometimes unintentionally open a window into the intolerant attitude of the Church. For example, the 1764 Church law "Law regarding the way in which the Yids can be accepted for baptism," which Nica presents in great detail, describes the rigorous conditions for the baptism of Jews, setting out pre-catechization, catechization, and baptismal rules. In this large presenta-tion of the history of Jews' conversion by the Romanian Orthodox Church, Nica mentions other Church laws and gives details about Jewish-Christian relations in the eighteenth and nineteenth centuries, sometimes complaining about the use of some apologetic Orthodox books by the Romanian anti-Semites of that period. He also offers a figure of 1,500 Jews baptized in the nineteenth century, and although he acknowledges that the number is low, he does not offer any explanation as to why that was the case.

Speaking about the interwar period, Nica mentions a group of 200 Jews from Bucharest, who in 1937 asked for permission to be baptized en masse and to set up a Christian Orthodox church that would be a link between the Jewish and the Christian worlds. They were led by Professor H. Sanielevici, a "Jew with assimilationist tendencies who viewed the baptism of the Jews as the only solution for the cessation of anti-Semitism."[22] Without offering any rationale, Nica says, "in the end, the Church did not accept their baptism en masse, neither the setup of a separate Christian group. It accepted the baptisms on an individual basis."[23] Listing the events leading to the Second World War, Bishop Nica mentions the anti-Semitic measures against the baptism of Jews: first, the request of the Ministry of Religions for Churches to ban conversion of Jews who could not prove their Romanian citizenship. Churches were asked in this way to mirror the Goga-Cuza January 1938 law for the revision of citizenship. Second, the author deals with Decree Law 711 of March 1941 which completely forbids Jews' conversion to any religion.

Nica defends the attitude of the Romanian Orthodox Church toward the two measures on different grounds. The controversial 1938 decision of the Holy Synod, which denied Jews the right to conversion unless they brought forward documentation proving their Romanian citizenship, he explains based on the assumption that "many Jews at the time sought baptism for personal reasons."[24] When discussing the decision of 1938 Nica avoids mentioning in detail the citizenship aspect, and blames the decision entirely on the state's request, forgetting to mention that at the time Patriarch Miron Cristea was also prime-minister of Romania. He completely overlooks the Holy Synod decision of 1939, which was similar to the one of 1938 (although tougher in some aspects), and which was not requested by the state. When discussing the 1941 law that forbids the conversion of Jews to any other religion, Nica looks to Metropolitan of Transylvania Nicolae Bălan to make his case. As many later articles of the Church would do, Nica presents Metropolitan Nicolae Bălan as the representative of the Church, effectively equating Bălan's actions and the Church's. Of course, Bălan opposed state interference in the Church's business, and not the state's attack on the Jews' right to conversion (see chapter 2). Moreover, when the issue was discussed in the Holy Synod, Bălan imposed the topic on the Synod's agenda, as Nica rightly says, but the final decision made it very clear that the Church was not defending the Jews.[25] Nica suggests that the Church tried to persuade the government to withdraw the law (from March to May 1941) and as the alleged efforts were unsuccessful, he acknowledges the compliance of the Church with the state's decision.[26] He indirectly suggests that the Church did not have an alternative, which is not accurate, and here one can mention the example of the Catholic Church in Romania, which continued to baptize Jews in open disobedience of the law.

Antim Nica uses the long description of the history of Jews' conversion to the Romanian Orthodox Church as a way of proving the tolerant attitude of the Church toward Jews over time. He carefully leaves aside examples of Church laws that clearly show anti-Semitism and totally ignores the anti-Semitism promoted by the Church during the interwar period. When discussing the conversion of Jews after 1938, he boasts of Nicolae Bălan's attempt to oppose state interference in the business of the Church, but forgets to mention the Holy Synod's refusal to answer any Jewish requests for help (in most cases coming from baptized Jews).

The Holocaust as it appears in Antim Nica's and Theodor Manolache's texts. The creation of the "Church as a savior of Jews" myth

If on the first fifteen pages of his article Bishop Antim Nica focuses on the conversion of Jews and how this process proved the tolerance of the Romanian Orthodox Church toward them, on the last three pages he addresses the Holocaust period; he speaks about both converted and unconverted Jews. The general tendency of his arguments supports the whitewashed version of Church history and promotes a triumphalist theology of a Church concerned with the Jews' fate. First, he describes the sufferings of baptized Jews: "The life of baptized Jews was a heart-breaking drama, in which their faith in Christ and their feelings toward other Christians were in the crucible. Starting with 1940 they knew the whole range of sufferings, alongside other Jews, until the cessation of anti-Semitic measures in 1944."[27] According to Nica, "our Church repeatedly raised its voice and brought to the governors' attention the tragic fate of [the baptized Jews]. The documents from the Holy Synod chancellery and the isolated interventions of priests bear witness to this."[28] He mentions these two sources, but produces no evidence from them. Access to the Holy Synod archive is closed to historians, but it is very unlikely that it holds documents that could change dramatically what we already know about the Church's position during the Holocaust. After all, if they did, Nica would surely have quoted them. All the requests for help from baptized Jews to the Holy Synod during the Holocaust were rejected on a variety of grounds, none of them receiving a merciful or favorable decision. He describes state measures against the Jews culminating with their deportation "over the Dniester River" (Transnistria). He does not describe at all what happened in Transnistria. He just says, "Many of the baptized Jews were taken and deported to the camps over the Dniester River, from which only a few returned home safely."[29] Then he speaks passionately about the hardship of leaving relatives behind, the tragedy of splitting families, or the strange situation of the baptized Jews, rejected by both Christian and Jewish communities. However, he does not describe Transnistria, which he knew very well, being vice-head of the Romanian Orthodox Mission from 1941 to 1943.

Toward the end of the article Nica widens his discourse to include the Church's efforts to save all the Jews. "Facing this horrendous drama, our Church showed empathy and compassion to the whole Jewish people."[30] To support his argument Nica cannot bring forward official Church documents, so he uses two documents from the Jewish community. The first is a small excerpt from a book written in 1928 by a Jew, Jacques Pineles, who said, "The Romanian clergy have always had a noble and benevolent attitude toward Jews."[31] The narrative of the Church's tolerant attitude toward Jews, built on a book written in 1928, is irrelevant to what happened in the 1930s and during the Holocaust. Moreover, the Pineles book, *Istoria Evreilor din cele mai vechi timpuri până la Declarația Balfour* (The History of Jews from Ancient Times to the Balfour Declaration), does not deal directly with the history of the Jews in Romania, let alone with Jewish-Christian Orthodox relations. The section about the history of the Romanian Jews is only twelve pages long and, for reasons that are not entirely clear, promotes a biased narrative in which Romania's anti-Semitism of the nineteenth century is largely ignored. Pineles avoided for example any mention of the 1866 constitution, which limited citizenship to Christians, or the Berlin Treaty of 1878, which acknowledged Romania's independence on the condition that it granted citizenship to Jews. Neither does he speak about the anti-Semitism of the Romanian political and intellectual elite, or about the fact that before 1918 only about two thousand Jews received citizenship. The allegation that "The Romanian clergy have always had a noble and benevolent attitude toward

Jews," quoted by Nica, appears on page 437 of Pineles's book, in a discussion of legislation concerning Jews prior to 1859.[32] Pineles's claim is sudden and rather misplaced in that paragraph, and does not come as a result of a careful analysis of the Church's attitude toward Jews.

The second argument Nica uses to substantiate his claim of the Orthodox Church's support for "the whole Jewish community" is an article published in March 1945 in the Romanian Jewish newspaper *Neamul Evreesc* [The Jewish People]: "We [the Jews] are glad to say: the Christian Church has condemned vehemently the moral and physical degradation the horrific fascist regime applied to Jews. It is enough to mention only one example."[33] The example mentioned is a situation in which some Jews were sent, during the war, to shovel snow at the patriarchate. One of them asked to see the patriarch. Nicodim received him and, on hearing what they were doing, said, "We are not Egyptians and you are not slaves." Nica carries on quoting from Neamul Evreesc: "And at the insistences of that Jew to carry on the job, His Holiness kept quiet. He meekly looked at the man who had bowed his head and said: 'Your will be done!' It was sufficient. The Head of the Church pronounced a verdict and a creed by condemning the suffering that was bestowed upon the Jewish people, and by saying: 'We are not Egyptians and you are not slaves.'"[34]

The publication of such a complimentary article about Patriarch Nicodim in a Jewish newspaper in March 1945 is problematic and could be linked to the religious harmony initiative imposed by the new regime. The episode is fully examined in the article written by Theodor Manolache. The language Manolache uses is typical of the Communist propaganda of the day, with hyperbolic and emphatic images: "From all of these [people who heroically resisted and promoted the traditional values during the war] it is luminously distinguishing the personality of His Holiness who through his activity during the events of sad remembrance entered forever the psyche and history of the Romanian people."[35]

Manolache quotes several times from a discourse of Teodor Popescu Braniște, a lay Communist personality who emphasized the patriarch's fight against the Iron Guard and his alleged support for the Jewish community. Braniște, like Nica in his article, is unable to support his statement with any concrete evidence. The presence of Braniște in these articles suggests complicity between the Church and the state when it comes to painting over the Church's recent past.

To point out the Church's support for Jews, Teodor Manolache offers several arguments. First, he relates the episode from *Neamul Evreesc* praising the patriarch, but in comparison to Nica's article he offers more information about the context. The article from the Jewish newspaper was entitled "Give Us Our Cemetery Back. Lines for His Holiness Patriarch Nicodim." According to Manolache, in March 1945 the Jewish community wanted to retrieve the cemetery on Sevastopol Street taken by the Antonescu regime.[36] They appealed to the patriarch for help. "What made Mr. Semo to cast his hopes and prayers to the head of a Church of whom he is not a member? He gives the answer."[37] And the author quotes again the episode in which the patriarch received a Jew shoveling snow at the patriarchate and said "We are not Egyptians and you are not slaves." Manolache does not say whether the patriarch helped the Jews to retrieve their cemetery or not. His conclusion after the narration of this episode was "If there is still any Jew, or moreover any Romanian who doubts the Romanian Patriarch's sentiments and convictions during the crucible we all faced, he should read the above words and meditate with objectivity upon them!"[38] This statement reflects the fact that there was tension and there were people who, knowing the patriarch's recent anti-Semitic outbursts, were circumspect about his sudden love for Jews. Both the *Neamul Evreesc* and the Manolache articles were efforts to rehabilitate Nicodim's authority.

Manolache goes on to quote another Jewish source, Mr. S. C. Cristian, the vice president of the Iaşi Jewish community, who published a book entitled *Patru Ani de Urgie. Notele Unui Evreu din România* (Four Years of Wrath. Notes of a Jew from Romania) in the spring of 1945. Cristian accompanied Chief Rabbi Alexandre Safran in 1941 when he went to the patriarch to ask for help in stopping the deportations to Transnistria. In his book Cristian acknowledges that he was not in the room when the two religious leaders met.[39] However, he interprets a gesture made by the chief rabbi during his plea for the sake of the Jews—bowing down and kissing the patriarch's hand—to suggest that the patriarch manifested understanding and caring for their fate. In his memoir, recollecting the event, Safran makes clear that Nicodim was not sympathetic toward Romanian Jews, and that the episode itself had other meanings.[40] Moreover, Safran vehemently condemns these propagandistic articles that, after the war, tried to present the patriarch and his relationship with the chief rabbi in a positive light.[41] It should be also noted that even if Cristian's recollection of the episode creates a favorable image of Nicodim, Cristian does not say that the patriarch intervened in Jews' favor in the end.

Both Nica and Manolache totally ignore articles published by Patriarch Nicodim in the same official journal of the Church, in which he publicly expresses his hatred of Jews. Nica seems to be ready to accept some controversial aspects that Manolache bypasses; for example, the fact that the racial policies of the Romanian state started in 1938, when the prime minister of Romania was Patriarch Miron Cristea. Nica also expresses regret that the Church did not do enough to help the baptized Jews (probably an allusion to the passive attitude of the Holy Synod concerning their requests for help). But in general both articles exonerate the Church of any blame related to the Holocaust. The fiction of a tolerant Church, concerned with the fate of Jews and as a savior of Jews is built by these articles. The authors select only the favorable historical data, generally avoid discussing controversial aspects, and, where the Holocaust is concerned, cover up and rewrite history to promote this new narrative of a Jew-saving Church. This mythicized history remains the narrative of the Romanian Orthodox Church today. The arguments brought forward by Nica and Manolache were used several times by the Church during and after the fall of Communism. In 1990 an article commenting on the Holocaust published in the same journal extensively revived the arguments brought forward in the two articles published in 1945.

NOTES

1. Lucian Leuștean also analyzes the pastoral letter of the patriarch. In his opinion this change in attitude "was due to two main factors. On the one hand, in the war against Germany, Soviet troops occupied Romanian territory, and a declaration such as this letter was aimed at pleasing the Soviet authorities. On the other hand, the Pastoral letter conformed to the directives of the Soviet High Command of the Southeast European Front." See Lucian N. Leuștean, *Orthodoxy and the Cold War: Religion and Political Power in Romania* (London: Palgrave Macmillan, 2009), 58.

2. Nicodim, Patriarhul României, "Pastorala cu Ocazia Incheierii Armistițiului dintre România și Statele Aliate din 23 August 1944" [The Pastoral Letter Concerning the Signing of the Armistice between Romania and the Allies, 23 August 1944], *BOR* 62, nos. 7–12 (July–December 1944): 219.

3. Nicodim, Patriarhul României, "Cuvântul de Binecuvântare al Bisericii pentru Anul Nou 1944" [The Church's Message of Blessing for the New Year 1944], *BOR* 62, nos. 1–3 (January–March 1944): 1.

4. Nicodim, "Pastorala cu Ocazia Incheierii Armistițiului," 220.

5. Nicodim, Patriarhul României, "Indemnul IPS Patriarh Nicodim către Popor" [The Appeal of H. H. Patriarch Nicodim to the People], *BOR* 63, nos. 1–3 (January–March 1945): 88–89.

6. Alexandre Safran, *Resisting the Storm, Romania 1940–1947: Memoirs* (Jerusalem: Yad Vashem, 1987), 83.

7. Nicodim, "Indemnul IPS Patriarh Nicodim," 89.

8. Daniel Chirot, "Social Change in Communist Romania," special issue, *Social Forces* 57, no. 2 (December 1978): 474.

9. Cristian Vasile, *Biserica Ortodoxă Română în primul deceniu comunist* [The Romanian Orthodox Church during the First Decade of Communism] (Bucharest: Curtea Veche, 2005), 25–26.

10. Dumitru Fecioru, "La șase ani de patriarhat ai Înalt PS Nicodim" [Six Years of Patriarchate of His Holiness Nicodim], *BOR* 63, no. 6 (June 1945): 210–212.

11. CNSAS D8925, Problema Preoțească în Vechiul Regat, 1948–1949 [The Priesthood Problem in the Old Kingdom, 1948–1949], "Nota no. 131/14 Februarie 1949, Direcția Generală a Securității Statului," vol. 1, 217–218.

12. Sfântul Sinod al Bisericii Ortodoxe Române, "Pastorala din Partea Sinodului Bisericii Ortodoxe Române," [The Pastoral Letter of the Holy Synod of the Romanian Orthodox Church], *BOR* 63, nos. 7–8 (July–August 1945): 289.

13. Ibid., 291.

14. Ibid., 290.

15. Comitetul de Redacție [Editorial Board], "Cuvânt înainte" [Foreword], *BOR* 63, nos. 11–12 (November–December 1945): 554.

16. Episcop [Bishop] Dr. Antim Nica, "Pe urmele apostolatului românesc" [Retracing the Romanian Apostolate], *BOR* 63, nos. 11–12 (November–December 1945): 571–589.

17. Teodor N. Manolache, "Din dragoste și din simțul datoriei: fapte mai puțin cunoscute din activitatea IPS Nicodim în timpul războiului" [From Love and Duty: Lesser Known Deeds Performed by H. H. Nicodim during the War], *BOR* 63, nos. 11–12 (November–December 1945): 670–677.

18. Antim Nica, "Episcopul M. S. Alexander," *BOR* 63, no. 10 (October 1945): 412–415.

19. Ibid., 412.

20. "Supliment," *BOR* 59, nos. 11–12 (November–December 1941): 12.

21. Gheorghe I. Petre-Govora, ed., *Pravila bisericească de la Govora* (Bucharest: Academia Română, 2004), 71.

22. Nica, *Pe urmele apostolatului românesc*, 581.

23. Ibid.

24. Ibid., 582.

25. "Supliment," *BOR* 59, nos. 11–12 (November–December 1941): 12.

26. Nica, *Pe urmele apostolatului românesc*, 585. He says, "If back then baptisms could not be done."

27. Ibid.

28. Ibid., 586.

29. Ibid., 585.

30. Ibid.

31. Ibid.

32. See Jacques Pineles, *Istoria Evreilor: din cele mai vechi timpuri până la declaratia Balfour* [The History of Jews: From Ancient Times to the Balfour Declaration] (Iași, Romania: Lumea, 1935), 430–442.

33. Nica, *Pe urmele apostolatului românesc*, 586.

34. Ibid., 587.

35. Manolache, *Din dragoste și din simțul datoriei*, 671.

36. See Lya Benjamin, ed. *Problema evreiască în stenogramele Consiliului de Ministri* [The Jewish Question in the Minutes of the Council of Ministers], vol. 2 of *Evreii din România între anii 1940–1944* [The Jews of Romania, 1940–1944] (Bucharest: Hasefer, 1996), 143–147.

37. Manolache, *Din dragoste și din simțul datoriei*, 673.

38. Ibid., 674.

39. S. C. Cristian, *Patru ani de urgie: notele unui evreu din România* [Four Years of Wrath: Notes of a Jew from Romania] (Bucharest: Timpul, 1944), 76–77.

40. Safran, *Resisting the Storm*, 82–83.

41. Ibid., 164.

5

FORGETTING THE TRUTH, FORGETTING THE DEAD

The Use of the Holocaust for Political and Religious Agendas and the
Persistence of Anti-Semitism (1945–1948)

THE EFFORT OF THE ROMANIAN Orthodox Church to cover up its negative actions toward the Jewish community before and during the war could
not entirely hide the existence of religious anti-Semitism after 1945. Sometimes this anti-Semitism became virulent and threatened to endanger the
efforts of the Church and of the Communist regime to present the Orthodox Church and the Jewish community as enjoying friendly relations. At the
same time, the events of the Holocaust were used, most often out of public
view, in internal political and ecclesiastical battles for supremacy.

THE USE OF THE HOLOCAUST BY HIERARCHS OF THE ROMANIAN ORTHODOX CHURCH AND BY STATE AUTHORITIES IN POLITICAL AND RELIGIOUS DISPUTES

The entire cover-up campaign of 1945, especially the articles praising Patriarch Nicodim and discussing the Holocaust, should be seen in a larger context.
Due to increasing tensions between King Michael and the new government
backed by the Communists and led by Petru Groza, rumors began to circu-
late about the ousting of the king and his replacement with a regency, with
Patriarch Nicodim as a member.[1] The idea was not new. The former patriarch, Miron Cristea, had been one of the three members of the Regency of
1927–1930. The intention of the new regime to use the Church as a political
tool was clear, and making Nicodim a member of a regency would have legitimized the Communists in the eyes of the Orthodox faithful. The articles
praising Patriarch Nicodim published in Jewish and Orthodox journals in

1945 were an attempt to create an image that would have made it easier for the patriarch to take a political role. The rewriting of history and the reinterpretation of the events of the Holocaust to present Nicodim as interested in the fate of Jews were meant both to conceal his past and to place him in a powerful political position.

Like Patriarch Nicodim, there were others inside the Church who needed to erase their troubled past. As early as the autumn of 1944, war criminals were being brought to justice. Among them were members of the Church hierarchy, such as Visarion Puiu, the former metropolitan of Transnistria, as well as lower clergy. The reinterpretation of the events of the Holocaust to support the myth of a caring and saving Church was supposed to hide compromising facts and to prevent further prosecutions. Individuals such as Bishop Antim Nica or Dumitru Fecioru, the authors of two of the articles praising Patriarch Nicodim, had their own unpleasant secrets (Fecioru had been a member of the Iron Guard, Nica, the vice head of the now discredited Romanian Orthodox mission in Transnistria). They wanted to impress the new regime and to present themselves, the Church, and the patriarch in a favorable light.

In most postwar trials involving members of the Church's hierarchy or regular priests, the Holocaust was often an adjacent aspect and not central to the prosecution. The regular judicial procedures of clergy involved in anti-Semitism prior to the war and in events related to the Holocaust were either suspended or waiting further developments according to a political agenda. This aspect is highlighted by the March 1945 declaration of Gheorghe Burducea, the new secretary of religions, who said that the regime would help those who were compromised during the war but who now were on the "democratic" side: "We will cleanse them; we will manifest understanding toward them, but not toward those who were involved in murders and deeds punished by the penal code."[2] For the new regime, the complicity of clergy in the Holocaust, although known, was simply an opportunity for political leverage.

Most often, a dark past was used for blackmail. For example, Metropolitan Nicolae Bălan of Transylvania, one of the most influential leaders of the Church at the end of the war, was almost purged in 1945. He remained metropolitan, but his activity was constantly monitored and plans were made for his replacement in case he stepped out of line. Bălan's links to the Iron Guard were used against him in several instances. For example, in the second part of 1947 and at the beginning of 1948, in the context of the succession to the patriarchal seat, the secret police wrote a report highlighting Bălan's presence at several Iron Guard ceremonies and the burial service he held, in spite an official ban, for two Iron Guard volunteers who died in the Spanish Civil War. The information was leaked to the press and a campaign against him was launched in a Transylvanian newspaper at the beginning of 1948. This was a way of preventing Metropolitan Bălan from disrupting Communist plans of replacing Patriarch Nicodim with Justinian (see chapter 3).

During discussions about the replacement of Patriarch Nicodim, sources inside the Church considered Bishop Nicolae Popovici of Oradea as one of the best options. According to a secret service note, Justinian Marina, the future patriarch, "looked everywhere for a leaflet [pastoral] in which Bishop Nicolae, after his arrival from Transnistria . . . has allegedly spoken insulting words against the USSR."[3] Justinian wanted to use such compromising information to prevent Nicolae Popovici from voicing any claim to the patriarchal seat. It is known that Bishop Nicolae, while in Transnistria, spoke openly against Jews.[4] Most likely his anti-Bolshevik stand was also anti-Semitic. At the same time, people close to Bishop Nicolae were accused of having a Legionary past, though their anti-Semitism was not mentioned.[5] Metropolitan Tit Simedrea of Bukovina was likewise purged in 1945 and forced to retire[6] because of his links to the Iron Guard in the interwar period, and his open anti-Bolshevism during the war.[7] Although the events of the Holocaust and the actions against Jews were not always mentioned directly, these cases show the way in which events of the war were used in blackmailing campaigns in the battle for ecclesiastical supremacy.

After 1948 members of the Church hierarchy who had a problematic past often used their knowledge and expertise to help the Communist regime with some of their important agenda. For example, Metropolitan Bălan of Transylvania, whose dislike of the Greek Catholic Church was well known, became one of the main advocates of its abolishment in 1948.[8] Teodor Popescu, the rightwing theologian who, during the war, published the strongly anti-Semitic article "The Communist Anti-Christianity,"[9] prepared the paper presented by the Romanian delegation at the Pan-Orthodox Conference (1948), in which the Soviet strategy regarding the Catholic problem was discussed.[10] His case in particular highlights the lack of restraint of the Communist regime in using persons who disseminated anti-Semitic and anti-Bolshevik views during the war. For them immediate political gain was more important than these individuals' problematic past.

All these aspects point to the conclusion that after the war the events of Holocaust and the evidence of anti-Semitism promoted by clerics were used as a political leverage both by the Romanian Orthodox Church and by the Communist regime. For the regime, any misdeed committed during the Holocaust became a tool used to blackmail clergy who were not obedient to the Party. Inside the Church, blackmail was a weapon in the battle for ecclesiastical power, as in the fight for the patriarchal seat between Justinian, Nicolae Bălan, and Nicolae Popovici. In a context in which both the new regime and the Romanian Orthodox Church used the Holocaust for political gain, the historical analysis was totally ignored. Nobody was interested in impartially researching this subject. This rewriting of history and cover-up of unfavorable historical data have produced the official narrative in use today.

RELIGIOUS ANTI-SEMITISM AND INTERRELIGIOUS RELATIONS IN THE AFTERMATH OF THE HOLOCAUST; THE RELIGIOUS HARMONY AGENDA AND ITS FAILURES

In 1945 the Communists started to enforce a climate of harmony between religions in Romania. This can be deduced from the actions of religious leaders and Communist regime officials. At the end of 1945 and beginning of 1946 two meetings between the Romanian Orthodox patriarch and Andrea Cassulo, the papal nuncio to Bucharest, took place; the first at the papal nuncio's residence, the second at the Palace of the Patriarchate. In a January 1946 note signed by V (most likely the controversial source Viator),[11] the second meeting was acknowledged and the Romanian Secret Service made an observation on the note implying that the meeting was meant to promote the Catholic interest in Eastern Europe and to create an anti-Soviet front.[12] Although the secret service was apparently caught by surprise, and suggested that the meetings were politically motivated, it is more likely that they were actually part of the Communist religious harmony policy. Cristian Vasile too casts doubts on the idea that the meetings were the patriarch's attempt to create an anti-Soviet front.[13] It is true that Nicodim, as noted before, had moments of open opposition to the new regime, but he was not the type of person to provoke a full and open conflict on several fronts at the same time. He was a warrior, but not a suicidal one. The meetings were reported on in the Church's main journal;[14] they were not veiled in secrecy. Indeed, it would be safe to assume that the meetings were organized with the knowledge of the Communist regime. The way in which they were portrayed in the published news suggests the promotion of a program of harmony between the two religions rather than a secret plan to oppose the Soviets.

The meetings between Orthodox and Catholic representatives were not the only example of emphasis on the new cordial relations between religions in Romania. As noted previously, in March 1945 a Jewish newspaper published an article praising Patriarch Nicodim and the Orthodox Church for their alleged saving actions during the Holocaust.[15] The article was not only meant to whitewash Patriarch Nicodim, but also to promote a new, harmonious relationship between the two communities. It ended with a clear statement suggesting the need for a more amicable relationship between Judaism and Orthodoxy. In the same month, Constantin Burducea was installed as the secretary of religions by the Communist regime. All the representatives of religions in Romania were present at the event (including the patriarch of the Romanian Orthodox Church and the chief rabbi),[16] to suggest the new reality of a strong regime overseeing the relations between different religions in Romania.

The Communist initiative of imposing religious harmony became more obvious later in the Communist era. Starting in 1967 telegrams of congratulations between the leader of the Romanian Orthodox Church and the chief rabbi were regularly published in the main journal of the Church. The telegrams were usually introduced by a note speaking directly about the initiative: "Motivated by the sincere desire toward a dialogue with other non-Christian religions too and under the ecumenical climate, which was initiated by His Holiness Patriarch Justinian, meetings for the prosperity of our country and for the realization of a climate of trust and harmony between all peoples take place regularly. This is the context in which we should see the attention given to other religious leaders on special occasions."[17] In these congratulating letters/telegrams, all that happened before 1945 was entirely overlooked. Everything had to be bright and clean. Under the Communist regime, the program of harmony between religions was more important than Holocaust remembrance.

Despite this, religious anti-Semitism continued to exist. It is true that the enforcement of friendly relations prevented major outbursts of violence, but the roots of religious hatred were not wiped out overnight. One can point first to Patriarch Nicodim's unchanged mentality. In a letter addressed to Prime Minister Petru Groza in February 1946, the patriarch protested against the new freedom given to the "sects" (the term used by the Romanian Orthodox Church to describe emerging Evangelical denominations: Baptists, Adventists, Jehovah's Witnesses) and other religious associations. He considered this freedom as "detrimental to the country."[18] This attitude was reminiscent of his ultra-nationalist policies during the war. The protest shows that Nicodim, in spite of all the efforts to acclimate him to the new situation, was still stuck in time.

Relations between the Orthodox and Jewish communities during this period were not straightforward. There were some positive examples, such as the case of a priest preaching that the Jews were not guilty for the killing of Jesus. According to a secret police note, in July 1946, a priest from Târgu Ocna, a place with a substantial Jewish population, preached a sermon entitled: "Who bears the guilt?" His main point was that "all that has happened was because of the prophecies, hence, the guilt is no one's, and we hate each other without reason, as we are all sons of God."[19] This example is in contrast to many articles published before and during the war in which Jews were portrayed as the killers of (the Son of) God. In another example an Orthodox priest participated in the commemoration of victims of the Holocaust. According to a police report dated May 1946, the Orthodox priest Tint Iosif made a speech at a commemoration in Sighet, northern Transylvania.[20] His presence could be a sign of improved relationships between the two communities, but it could also reflect the general public interest in the Holocaust. This interest was exclusively about what had happened outside Romania.[21] Transnistria or the Holocaust that took place under Romanian administration was forgotten, the focus being instead on sensational stories, most often involving survivors of the Holocaust from northern Transylvania. The use of such examples was meant to present the Hungarians as perpetrators and the Romanians as saviors of Jews.

On the negative side, according to the secret police, in September 1946 a priest from Rădăuți wrote a letter to the patriarch with a strong anti-Semitic tone: "We escaped the Hitlerist paganism, and the Marxist, socialist, and Communist paganism and all the monstrosities which emanated from the Judaic Moloch."[22] The anti-Semitic letter may have been a reaction to acts of vandalism against Orthodox churches in Bucharest in

August 1946. According to some accounts, sacred objects were destroyed, and the vandals urinated in the altars[23] of churches.[24] A strictly secret police report from August 30, 1946 mentions that "all the faithful impute the deeds to the Communists and to the Jews. During the prayers, a Communist who was identified in the Church was almost lynched." Such incidents led to political debates, political parties blaming each other for inciting and encouraging the vandalism. The police report from August 30, 1946 says that "the General Secretary of the National Peasant Party Iuliu Maniu is gathering information that proves that the desecration of churches was done by the Communists, and especially by Communist Jews." Another police note from August 29, 1946 blames Maniu for the incidents: "The democratic citizens believe that all is a maneuver of Manists [supporters of the Peasants Party and of Iuliu Maniu] in order to compromise the Communist Party."

In this war of words, political and religious anti-Semitism resurfaced. Police reports from August and October 1946 mention in detail the comments of Major (in the notes he is presented as Colonel) Ivor Porter about the incidents. Porter was one of the secretaries (senior diplomats) at the British legation in the summer of 1946. The report from August 1946 states that, according to Porter's personal spies [sic]: "The Jewish population in the capital is involved in acts of desecration against the Orthodox churches," and that "the Christian population is very inveterate against the Jews."[25] In the October report the information is more nuanced. According to this account Porter envisaged two explanations for the events: either the desecrations were the result of an order of the rabbis, as revenge for the devastation of some synagogues during the Legionary and the Antonescu regimes, or they were organized by unknown groups in order to incite eventual anti-Semitic actions. The report quotes Porter as saying "In Romania there is a strong anti-Semitic current." It also mentions the declaration of a Yugoslav Communist leader who said that "the Communist Party in Romania has a specific characteristic, unseen in any other Communist party in the world—it is anti-Semitic."[26]

There is a visible change of tone between the earlier report and the later one, especially where Major Porter is concerned. While in the first report the Communist agents imply that Porter blamed the Jews for the incidents, the latter one makes clear that the British diplomat did not have a precise answer about who desecrated the churches. Although more nuanced, the second report still assumed that Porter believed the incidents could have been organized by Jews.

Reports in October 1946 show that the incidents in Bucharest were not unique. In Pitești, Galați, and Brașov churches were desecrated, but in all cases the reason was looting.[27] In a gendarmerie report sent to the police prefecture in November 1946 the desecrations in Bucharest are confirmed— two cases took place in March 1946, another one in September 1946. According to the report, the vandals could not be identified.[28] On October 30, 1946 the police prefecture made clear its intention to "identify and arrest the bearers of tendentious and alarmist rumors."[29] It is likely that after the first incidents of desecration, whose reasons and authors could hardly be identified, a spiral of violence developed for several months. As many political and religious actors became involved and blamed each other for the attacks, it was most likely that the later incidents did not have a sole responsible actor.

It is obvious that the Communist authorities initially tried to blame the Jews for the incidents, but made clear in the October and November reports that there was no evidence to suggest that Jews were involved in the desecration of Orthodox churches. Moreover, they seem to imply that some aspects were exaggerated in unverified and tendentious rumors. Major Porter's declarations are important in several respects. First, they confirm what the Communist authorities, due to the religious harmony agenda, were reluctant to say: that after the war tensions between the Jewish and Orthodox communities persisted. The incidents, although most likely not provoked by Jews, and the way they were dealt with, were a clear expression of deep-seated religious anti-Semitism. Second, Porter's declaration confirms that in Romania a strong anti-Semitic current was still alive after the war, a claim supported by other documents as well. Third, Ivor Porter himself may have been an anti-Semite. The ease with which he blames the Jews in the first report, and the assumption he makes about a rabbinical order to desecrate Orthodox churches in the second report, without any evidence, may suggest this.

THE TRIALS OF ORTHODOX CLERGY, AND THE RELIGIOUS AND POLITICAL IMPLICATIONS FOR HOLOCAUST REMEMBRANCE

Soon after Romania signed an agreement with the Allied forces (September 12, 1944), the Romanian actions on the Eastern Front from 1941 to 1944 came under scrutiny. As early as January 1945 legislation was put in place to define the terms "war criminal" and "war profiteer," and in April 1945 people's tribunals were established to deal with the trials.[30] In May 1945 the first group of war criminals were sentenced for their actions on the Eastern Front, some of them involved in crimes against the Jewish population in Bessarabia, Bukovina, and Transnistria; among them Generals Nicolae Macici and Constantin Teodorescu, and Colonel Cornel Calotescu. Although initially the thirty-nine defendants were sentenced to death, their sentences were commuted to life imprisonment.[31] The most notable and well-publicized trial was that of Marshal Antonescu and his close political circle, which took place in May 1946.

Even during the first phase of investigations, which started as early as October 1944, priests were among those brought to justice. The vast majority of them were accused of having links to the Iron Guard. It must be said that prosecution of priests who were involved in violent actions such as political assassinations, pogroms, street turbulence, and incitement to hatred was not a new development. In 1938, at the start of King Carol II's dictatorship, Iron Guard members (among them priests—the best-known case being that of Ilie Imbrescu),[32] including the leader Corneliu Codreanu, were imprisoned. For a short period after the abdication of King Carol II, the Iron Guard was in power (September 6, 1940–January 22, 1941). In January 1941 the Guard was ousted after an attempted putsch, and Ion Antonescu remained the sole leader of the country. Ion Antonescu's regime brought to justice priests and other persons closely related to the Church involved in the Iron Guard Rebellion of January 1941, some of them prosecuted for their direct participation in the Bucharest pogrom in which 120 Jews were killed.[33]

After the war, a consistent number of priests appear in lists of persons tried for war crimes. Based on the large number of priests accused of being Legionary during trials, some historians emphasize the political dimension of these condemnations.[34] We should not forget, though, the large involvement of the Romanian Orthodox Church in the Iron Guard and other far-right parties before and during the war. Although in various documents about persons brought to justice priests are often mentioned,[35] it is hard to tell exactly how many were arrested between 1945 and 1948. Paul Caravia suggests that as many as four thousand were imprisoned during the entire Communist era,[36] but that figure is not supported by other research. According to the National Institute for the Study of Totalitarianism, mentioned by Cristian Vasile in his book, 1,725 priests were arrested between 1944 and 1989.[37]

The trials of clergy linked to the Iron Guard usually did not single out the persecution of Jews. As noted previously, for the Communist authorities affiliation with the Legion and the political dimensions of it were more important. The case of a priest from Târgu-Mureş who during the Legionary Rebellion of January 1941 "took over through the use of terror the business of a Jew,"[38] is a rare occasion when Jewish suffering at the hands of priests was brought forward in such trials. There were other situations where, although the Jews were not mentioned directly, the trial transcripts imply priests' actions against Jews. For example Father Epaminonda Grigore, from Constanta County, was condemned for killing several people in September 1940.[39] As this happened at the beginning of the Legionary State, when outbursts of violence against Jews were common, it might be possible that Father Grigore's victims were Jewish. Many of the condemned legionary priests thought the Jews were responsible for their imprisonment, which shows that in most cases, although mention of anti-Semitism as a motive was avoided during trials, it still played an important role.[40] Most of the Iron Guard priests were imprisoned in Aiud, in Transylvania, and Georgeta Pană, in her study on this topic, produces evidence that they continued to harbor anti-Semitic feelings in prison long after the war.[41]

A file compiled by the Romanian section of the Congresul Congress Mondial Evreiesc (CME, Jewish World Council) about war criminals who were directly involved in the massacre of Jews mentions several priests. The list entitled "A Table with War Criminals Reported to the People's Tribunal through the Juridical Bureau" contains 684 names; twelve of them were priests. According to this file, priests' involvement in the destruction of Jews varied (see chapter 2 for details). Attempts to find further documents in the CNSAS about these priests have been unsuccessful. Father Arbore Ion, who appears on the CME list, is also on a list of persons imprisoned in Aiud, but his file could not be found in the CNSAS archive. In other cases because the CME list does not contain full details, like the date of birth or the name of the defendant's parents, it is difficult to compare the lists. For example Father Constantin Teodorescu is mentioned as imprisoned in Aiud, but on the CME list the first name is not mentioned (the entry states only the surname: Teodorescu, priest). Given this, it is difficult to say whether they are one and the same person. In another case, a priest called Sofianu Ignat is mentioned in Aiud, while on the CME file there is a priest named Safian.

The location of the two persons coincides, but again it is difficult to say whether they are one and the same.[42] Regardless, some of the priests on the CME list were most likely imprisoned for their crimes against Jews.

Another file suggesting the involvement of a priest in the murder of Jews is that of Petre Pandrea. The informative file, which can be found at the CNSAS and USHMM, was created at the beginning of the 1960s by the Securitate. They were keeping under surveillance anyone who had previously been imprisoned or was suspected of being a Legionary. In 1945 Pandrea was condemned to life imprisonment (or according to other notes in the file, to fifteen years)[43] with hard labor. He successfully hid from authorities until 1951, when he was discovered and arrested, but in 1955 he was pardoned.[44] In most documents, he is presented as a primary school teacher. But in two places, at the beginning and end of his file, he is described as a priest-teacher.[45] He studied theology, probably in a seminary, and it is not clear whether he ever served as a priest. According to the documents, during the war he was a gendarmerie lieutenant, chief of a garrison in Mostovoi, in Transnistria. In this capacity he "actively participated in the plundering and execution of Jews from the ghettos."[46]

As mentioned previously, as far as priests were concerned, the Communist authorities were more eager to prove their links with the Iron Guard than their anti-Semitic actions. For the Communist prosecutors, at least in the first set of trials, the Holocaust was not a major topic. Sometimes even the identity of the Jews was hidden. The best example about the way in which the events of the Holocaust were downplayed is the trial of Visarion Puiu, former metropolitan of Transnistria.[47] Puiu left Romania on August 10, 1944, and for almost two years wandered through different concentration and displaced persons (DP) camps. He settled in Italy, in a Catholic monastery, from 1946 to 1948 and in 1949, with documents from the Comité Intergovernemental pour les Réfugiés from Switzerland, moved to Paris, where he lived until his death in 1964. Visarion Puiu was condemned to death in absentia in February 1946. The way in which Puiu came to the attention of Communist prosecutors is symptomatic of their priorities. Although lists of people involved in war crimes on the Eastern Front started to be compiled in October 1944, Puiu's name did not appear until the end of January 1945, and his name was last on that list. It is clear that he became a major target for Communist authorities only after the Radio Donau broadcast, on December 14, 1944, in which the setting up of a Romanian Iron Guard government in exile was announced, and Puiu's name was mentioned as the religions secretary.

Visarion Puiu was prosecuted primarily because of his association with the Iron Guard and his actions in exile, and only secondarily because of his actions in Transnistria. In the condemnation ruling, the main charge against him was that "he [had] placed himself in the service of Hitlerism and left the national territory [for] the enemy's territory and from there attacked the country." Then the charges went into more detail: "The defendant, former Metropolitan of Bukovina, from December 1, 1942 to December 1, 1943, encouraged from his position, the terror actions in Bessarabia and Transnistria." This charge was based on a report Puiu had written to the Romanian patriarchate one month after his seating as metropolitan of Transnistria, in which he spoke about "the urgent and surgical measures" a new administration had to take in order to complete its conquest. However, the charges switched immediately to Puiu's collaboration with the Iron Guard government in exile. According to this, the former metropolitan became the bishop of the Romanian Orthodox Church in Germany "through a decree signed by Horia Sima [the leader of the Iron Guard], in his position as head of the traitor government in Germany."[48]

While it is clear that Puiu's actions in Transnistria were tangential to the main accusation against him, the reference to that territory shows that the court knew about Puiu's encouragement of state policies. The reference to Jews and their suffering is largely overlooked, although the prosecutor seemed to be referring to it when quoting the metropolitan's declaration about surgical measures taken by the civil and military administration. On January 30, 1947, Visarion Puiu wrote a letter addressed to the prime president of the Romanian Cassation Court, in which he discussed the charges to which he had been found guilty. When it comes to Transnistria, he points out that, as a Church representative (not a military or civil administrator), he could not have patronized the actions of "terror which had allegedly taken place under the supervision of the civilian or military authorities." Moreover, he pretended to have known nothing about such actions: "Had I heard such rumors, I would have notified the King immediately."[49] Antim Nica, the vice head of the Romanian Orthodox mission in Transnistria, in his article "Retracing the Romanian Apostolate," makes it clear that the Orthodox administration knew about the fate of the Jews.[50] Jean Ancel, in his book *Transnistria, 1941–1942: The Romanian Mass Murder Campaigns* implicitly blames Visarion Puiu for his complicity in the destruction of Jews.[51] For example, in July 1943, in the middle of Puiu's mandate as metropolitan of Transnistria, Jewish men, women, and children were used as slave laborers, under the supervision of the gendarmerie, for road works in preparation for the upcoming inauguration of the Balta cathedral. Most of them died of hunger and exhaustion, or were executed.[52]

In his letter to the president of the Romanian Cassation Court, Visarion Puiu went even further and defended the actions of the Antonescu regime in Transnistria. In his view, "in military and public order circumstances [the authorities] can act [as] police . . . and even [take] surgical actions against elements that were proven to be rebellious and full of other grave transgressions."[53] Considering that during the war Romanian propaganda portrayed the hundreds of thousands of Jews who were deported and killed in Transnistria as Bolsheviks, rebels, and enemies of the state, Puiu's declaration suggests that even as late as 1947 he believed the state's actions against Jews were justified.

The prosecution of Visarion Puiu and his letter of defense are extremely relevant. Although neither of these documents directly mentions the Holocaust, the event is implicit. In 1955, in order to diminish his influence in Romanian Orthodox circles abroad, the Communist authorities started making efforts for the return of the former metropolitan. They even issued a pardon in order to lure him back. In the end Visarin Puiu remained and died in France, but the attitude of the Romanian Communist authorities in his case shows eloquently the way in which the Holocaust was used or not according to the political agenda of the regime. In other cases, the information about Church hierarchy's involvement in events before or during the Holocaust was either cleansed or used in blackmailing campaigns away from the public eye.

A TIME OF CHANGE: COVER UP, FRIENDLY RELATIONS, AND THE MISUSE OF THE HOLOCAUST (1945–1948)

In the first years after the Second World War both the Romanian Orthodox Church and the Jewish community faced circumstances that were radically different from their situation prior to the war. The Romanian Orthodox Church had to collaborate with a regime against which it had spoken openly before August 1944. This collaboration, although enforced in various ways by the new authorities, should not be confused with a Communist takeover of the Church. The transformations faced by the Church in the first years of Communism should instead be seen as the replacement of an old and reluctant elite with a new elite that, driven by opportunism and desire for ecclesiastical power, chose to collaborate with the new regime.

Moreover, although tensions between some members of the old elite and the new regime existed, the Jewish problem and the Holocaust were not at the root of these tensions. People such as Patriarch Nicodim, Metropolitan Bălan, Metropolitan Irineu Mihălcescu, and Bishop Nicolae of Oradea, who before August 1944 made strong anti-Semitic declarations, were silent on this topic after the war. They went on with their lives as if nothing had happened, probably content with the cover-up campaign of 1945. In some Romanian historiography not enough attention is paid to the grey zones in the life of the Orthodox Church in the first years of the Communist regime, areas in which the same members of the hierarchy persecuted for their refusal to swear allegiance to the new regime were happy that the same regime helped them hide their troubled past.[54]

The desire of the Church to erase its negative past became visible from the moment Romania joined the Allies in August 1944. The pastoral letters of Patriarch Nicodim (August 1944), and of the Holy Synod (July 1945), and the articles dedicated to Patriarch Nicodim (December 1945) signaled turning points in the discourse of the Church. All those documents attempted to exonerate the Church of any blame related to the Holocaust and to the war. In the articles directly discussing the Holocaust (December 1945), a fiction of a tolerant Church, concerned with the fate of the Jews and even of the Church as a savior of Jews was built. The authors picked only favorable historical data, generally avoided discussing controversial aspects, and where the Holocaust period was concerned whitewashed, covered up, and rewrote history to promote this new narrative.

Anti-Semitism, including the anti-Semitism of the Romanian Orthodox Church, did not die in Romania at the end of the war. The religious harmony initiative that was increasingly imposed after 1945, which tried to sanitize the relationship between the Jewish and the Christian Orthodox communities, could not entirely hide the problems that continued to exist. The attacks on Orthodox churches in 1946, which caused religious anti-Semitism to resurface, present a clear example. In addition, the outspoken critique of the Orthodox Church by Chief Rabbi Alexandre Safran in the immediate postwar years threatened the agenda of the Communist authorities. Safran ignored, for example, Patriarch Nicodim's irritation that his name was not included on the chief rabbi's list of personalities who helped the Jewish community during the war.[55] The omission of the patriarch is suggestive of the (non)contribution of the Romanian Orthodox Church to the rescue efforts. The former chief rabbi also condemned Nicodim and other members of Church hierarchy for their biased and insulting way of equating Communists and Jews. Numerous Church officials pleaded with the chief rabbi to intervene with the Communist authorities in their favor, as if the chief rabbi were the leader of the Communists.[56] In fact, in his memoir Safran gives evidence to the contrary, speaking about the troubles he had with the Communists of Jewish descent.[57] Safran even provides examples in which Nicodim openly insulted the Jews after the war and condemns any attempt by the Orthodox Church to use the chief rabbi's image. Safran also spoke against the propagandistic messages that pretended relations between the patriarch and the chief rabbi were excellent.[58] This public condemnation of the Romanian Orthodox Church and of the patriarch for their attitude before and after the Holocaust was in great contrast with the forgetfulness promoted by the later leadership of the Jewish community.

While Safran, who had experienced firsthand the anti-Semitism of the Church, openly condemned it, later Jewish leadership accepted the Communist initiative of religious harmony, to the detriment of Holocaust memory. For the leadership installed in 1948, harmony with the Romanian Orthodox Church was more important than a correct assessment of the Church's attitude during the Holocaust. This has had significant consequences for Church's Holocaust memory up to the present day.

NOTES

1. Cristian Vasile, *Biserica Ortodoxă Română în primul deceniu comunist* [The Romanian Orthodox Church during the First Decade of Communism] (Bucharest: Curtea Veche, 2005), 70.

2. Vasile, *Biserica Ortodoxă Română*, 63.

3. Ibid., 153. For Metropolitan Bălan, see 58 and 155.

4. Jean Ancel, *Transnistria, 1941–1942: The Romanian Mass Murder Campaigns* (Tel Aviv: Tel Aviv University, 2003), 1:476.

5. Vasile, *Biserica Ortodoxă Română*, 154–155.

6. Ibid., 58.

7. Tit Simedrea, "Cuvântarea IPSS Tit Simedrea Mitropolitul Bucovinei cu prilejul deschiderii adunării eparhiale" [The Speech of His Holiness Tit Simedrea, the Metropolitan of Bucovina at the Opening of the Church Assembly], *Cuvântul Preoțesc* 9, no. 5 (May 1942): 1–3.

8. Vasile, *Biserica Ortodoxă Română*, 155.

9. Teodor Popescu, "Anticreștinismul communist" [The Communist Anti-Christianity], *BOR* 60, nos. 1–4 (January–April 1942): 13–50.

10. Vasile, *Biserica Ortodoxă Română*, 203.

11. It was usual for secret agents to sometimes use only the initial of their code name. Although we do not know exactly who Viator was, it is very likely that he was close to, if not even a member of, the Orthodox Church's hierarchy. For more details, see Vasile, *Biserica Ortodoxă Română*, 61–62, 119.

12. CNSAS D14673, Culte și Secte dupa 23 August 1944 [Religions and Sects after 23 August 1944], "Nota din 20 Ianuarie 1946, sursa V si M," 174–176. The first meeting, at the Nuncio's palace, is also acknowledged on 162.

13. Vasile, *Biserica Ortodoxă Română*, 98.

14. Comitetul de Redacție [Editorial Board], "Cronica interna, un dejun interconfesional," *BOR* 64, nos. 1–3 (January–March 1946): 156.

15. See Teodor N. Manolache, "Din dragoste și din simțul datoriei: fapte mai puțin cunoscute din activitatea IPS Nicodim în timpul războiului" [From Love and Duty: Lesser-Known Deeds Performed by HH Nicodim during the War], *BOR* 63, nos. 11–12 (November–December 1945): 670–677.

16. Vasile, *Biserica Ortodoxă Română*, 55.

17. "Schimb de telegrame între Prea Fericitul Părinte Iustinian Patriarhul Bisericii Ortodoxe Române și Eminența Sa, Dr. Moses Rosen, Șef Rabinul Cultului Mozaic din România" [Exchange of Telegrams between His Holiness Iustinian, the Patriarch of the Romanian Orthodox Church and His Eminency, Dr. Moses Rosen, the Chief Rabbi of the Jewish Community (Mosaic Religion) of Romania], *BOR* 92, nos. 5–6 (May–June 1974): 560.

18. CNSAS D56, Problema Preoțească în Vechiul Regat, 1945–1947 [The Priesthood Problem in the Old Kingdom, 1945–1947], "Nota 84 din 9 Februarie 1946, sursa V," 82.

19. Ibid., "MAI, DGP, Inspectoratul de Poliție Iași, No. 5477S din 26 Iulie 1946," 126.

20. CNSAS D11381, Comunitatea Evreilor din România, 1943–1949 [The Jewish Community of Romania, 1943–1949], "Radiograma no. 2030S [no date, but from the content of the document it seems likely that the ceremony took place on 29 May 1946], Inspectoratul de Poliție Oradea," 133.

21. See, for example, CNSAS D14480, Procesul de la Nuremberg. Criminalii de Război Hitleriști [The Nuremberg Trial. The Hitlerists War Criminals], "Timpul, No. 3007 din 6 Decembrie 1945, 'Procesul de la Nuremberg: Crimele împotriva Păcii Săvârșite de Conducătorii Naziști,'" 13. See also ibid., "Jurnalul de Dimineață, No. 343 din 17 Ianuarie 1946: 'Titlu Nr. 50.865 dela Auschwitz s-a Sinucis in Capitală'" [Number 50.865 from Auschwitz Committed Suicide in the Capital], 31.

22. CNSAS D56, "Nota a Inspectoratului Regional de Poliție Suceava, no. 10859S din 29 Decembrie 1946 către DGP București," 204–205.

23. In Orthodox churches the altar is a room located at the east end of a church, usually behind an iconostasis (altar screen).

24. CNSAS D56, "Corpul Detectivilor, Referat no. 6321 din 3 Octombrie 1946 adresat Ministerului de Interne referitor la Profanarea Bisericilor Creștine: Nota no. 23408 DGP, Arhiva Siguranței din 29 August 1946," 156–168.

25. Ibid., 162–166.

26. Ibid., 168.

27. See, for example, CNSAS D56., "Nota No. 4694S din 19 Octombrie 1946 Inspectoratul Regional de Poliție Pitești" and "Nota No. 12829 din 23 Octombrie 1946 Inspectoratul Regional de Poliție Galați," 170; 175.

28. Ibid., "Nota no. 40858 a Inspectoratului General al Jandarmeriei din 9 Noiembrie 1946, către DGP," 188.

29. Ibid., "Nota no. 20496S din 30 Octombrie 1946 a Prefecturii Poliției Capitalei," 180.

30. Keith Hitchins, *Rumania 1866–1947* (Oxford: Clarendon, 1994), 529.

31. Dennis Deletant, *Communist Terror in Romania: Gheorghiu-Dej and the Police State, 1948–1965* (London: Hurst, 1999), 75.

32. See Ilie Imbrescu, *Biserica și Mișcarea Legionară* [The Church and the Legionary Movement] (Bucharest: Cartea Românească, 1940). The Orthodox priest Ilie Imbrescu was arrested along with other Iron Guard members in 1938. The book presents his versions of events and condemns the Holy Synod and Patriarch Miron Cristea, who was the prime minister of the country during most of Imbrescu's imprisonment, for their silence at his plea for help.

33. Here the case of Valerian Trifa, future Bishop of the Romanian Orthodox Episcopate of America is interesting. At the time of the Legionary Rebellion he was the president of the National Union of Romanian Christian Students. He was condemned in absentia after the events, by the Antonescu regime, to life imprisonment and labor. See Radu Ioanid, "The Pogrom of Bucharest, 21–23 January 1941," *Holocaust and Genocide Studies* 6, no. 4 (1991): 379.

34. Vasile, *Biserica Ortodoxă Română*, 232–233.

35. See, for example, CNSAS D8175, "Nota de Fruntași Legionari Ramași Nearestați, 29 Noiembrie 1944," 57. In this list of twenty-two persons who should be brought to justice, at point 9 we can find priest Pălăghiță Stefan, from Bucharest. At 58–66 another table with persons who should be arrested mentions priest Bestea (no first name) "an Iron Guard commandant," 64.

36. Paul Caravia, *The Imprisoned Church: Romania 1944–1989* (Bucharest: The National Institute for the Study of Totalitarianism, 1999), 21.

37. See Vasile, *Biserica Ortodoxă Română*, 12.

38. CNSAS D13273, Preoți Operați 1945 [Priests Filed in 1945], "Nota a Inspectoratului de Jandarmi Mures," 47.

39. Gina Pană, "Inchisoarea legionară Aiud," *Holocaustul, Studii și Cercetări* 1, no. 1 (2009): 21–27.

40. Vasile, *Biserica Ortodoxă Română*, 223.

41. Pană, "Inchisoarea Legionara Aiud," 22.

42. See CNSAS D8750, Tabelele Nominale cu Rudele și Membrii de Familie, Criminali de Război, Intocmite de DGSS și Organe din Subordine în 1952 [Nominal Tables with Relatives and Family Members, War Criminals, Compiled by DGSS and Auxiliary Agencies in 1952], "Tabel cu cei intemnițați." For Arbore Ion, see 24; for Teodorescu Constantin, see 82; for Sofianu Ignat, see 99.

43. CNSAS I261884, Pandrea Dumitru, "MAI, Referat privind trecerea în evidență a numitului Pandrea Dumitru," 1.

44. Ibid., "Nota din 16 Iunie 1960," 4.

45. Ibid., see 1 and 20.

46. Ibid., "MAI, Dir. Regională Brașov, Oraș Făgăraș, 20.04.1962, Hotărâre de trecere în evidență," 20.

47. For a complete analysis of this case, see Ion Popa, "Visarion Puiu, the Former Romanian Orthodox Metropolitan (Archbishop) of Transnistria—A Historical Study on His Life and Activity before, during and after the Holocaust (1935–1964)," *Holocaust. Study and Research* 6, no. 1 (2013): 182–203.

48. CNSAS, DIE 142, Privitor la Visarion Puiu, "Scrisoare Adresată Primului Președinte al Curții de Casație [Letter Addressed to the First President of the Romanian High Court], 30 Ianuarie 1947," sent from Brescia Region, Italy, 6.

49. Ibid., "Scrisoare Adresată Primului Președinte al Curții de Casație," 7.

50. Antim Nica, "Pe urmele apostolatului românesc" [Retracing the Romanian Apostolate], *BOR* 63, nos. 11–12 (November–December 1945): 571–589.

51. Ancel, *Transnistria*, 1:490, 1:496–497.

52. Ibid., 1:504–505.

53. CNSAS, DIE 142, "Scrisoare Adresată Primului Președinte al Curții de Casație," 8–9.

54. See, for example, the Rugul Aprins case as well as that of Nichifor Crainic, in the otherwise excellently written and balanced book by Cristian Vasile, *Biserica Ortodoxă Română*, 157–188. The mention of Nichifor Crainic appears on 172. A more biased approach can be found in Adrian-Nicolae Petcu, ed., *Partidul, Securitatea și cultele, 1945–1989* [Party, Securitate, and Religions, 1945–1989] (Bucharest: Nemira, 2005); see especially the chapter "Slujitorii Altarului și Mișcarea Legionară. Studiu de Caz: Preotul Ilie Imbrescu" [The Priests and the Legionary Movement. Case Study: Priest Ilie Imbrescu], 17–117. The same can be said about the collaborative article written by several Romanian historians on the *Final Report of the Presidential Commission for the Analysis of Communist Dictatorship* in which individuals or organizations known for their rightwing anti-Semitism are defended and rehabilitated: George-Eugen Enache, Adrian-Nicolae Petcu, Ionuț-Alexandru Tudorie, and Paul Brusanovski, "Biserica Ortodoxă Română în anii regimului comunist. Observații pe marginea capitolului dedicat cultelor din *Raportul Final al Comisiei Prezidențiale pentru analiza dictaturii comuniste*" [The Romanian Orthodox Church during the Communist Regime. Observations Regarding the Religions Chapter from the *Final Report of the Presidential Commission for the Analysis of the Communist Dictatorship*], *Studii Teologice*, series 3, vol. 5, no. 2 (April–June 2009): 21–22.

55. Alexandre Safran, *Resisting the Storm, Romania 1940–1947: Memoirs* (Jerusalem: Yad Vashem, 1987), 163–164.

56. Ibid., 165–166.

57. Ibid., 161, 208.

58. Ibid., 164.

6

BEHIND RELIGIOUS HARMONY

The Romanian Orthodox Church and the Jewish Community
during the Communist Era (1948–1989)

THE PERIOD OF 1945–1948 REPRESENTED the definitive ascension to power of the Communist regime in Romania. In 1945 the Romanian Orthodox Church constructed a fictional history for itself in which any links with the Antonescu regime and the far right were hidden. This campaign reached a climax toward the end of 1945 when, in two articles celebrating Patriarch Nicodim, any negative involvement of the Church in the Holocaust was whitewashed. The articles went so far as to suggest that the Church acted to save Jews during the Holocaust, in spite of significant evidence to the contrary. After 1948, the Romanian Orthodox Church and the Jewish community tried their best to follow the policy of harmonious relations imposed by the new regime. The anti-Zionist policy of the Romanian Communist authorities, the official attitude toward the new state of Israel, and reactions to the Second Vatican Council's Nostra Aetate declaration were important factors in shaping Jewish-Orthodox relations and Holocaust memory.

THE ROMANIAN COMMUNIST AUTHORITIES' ATTITUDE TOWARD ISRAEL, THE JEWISH COMMUNITY OF ROMANIA, AND THE HOLOCAUST

After 1948 the political anti-Semitism of the Romanian state became more obvious. This trend could be seen especially in the way in which the Slansky trial[1] in Czechoslovakia was reported in Romania and, following the Soviet model, in the increasing elimination of Jewish politicians from the state apparatus.[2] The Slansky trial was followed with interest by the Romanian Communist Party, in which several Jewish Communists held high-ranking positions. There is a direct link between the trial and the elimination of these politicians, including Ana Pauker, who was regarded for several years as one of the most important Communist politicians in Eastern Europe. She was the minister of Foreign Affairs (1947–1952), the first woman in the world to hold this position, and one of the most important leaders in Romania, alongside Gheorghiu Dej and Teohari Georgescu. Her public role created discontent in many circles, including inside the Romanian Orthodox Church, and she was often the target of virulent anti-Semitism.[3]

Grassroots anti-Semitism was not as visible as it had been before 1948 but it still persisted. In 1951 several police reports describe the desecration of Jewish cemeteries in Cluj and Iași.[4] According to Liviu Rotman, until 1965 there were several instances in which anti-Semitism was deliberately promoted by the Communist authorities in order to divert attention from other economic or social problems.[5] Political anti-Semitism and anti-Zionism were also doubled by a process in which the Communist regime branded the leaders of the Jewish community of the interwar and war period (mostly Wilhelm Filderman and Alexandre Safran) as traitors.[6]

The Romanian Communist authorities' position toward Israel varied over time. While initially they presented the creation of the state in 1948 as a victory for socialism,[7] this narrative was soon replaced by one in which Israel was portrayed as the creation of imperialists to the detriment of Arabs. But after the death of Gheorghiu Dej in 1965 and the ascension to power of Nicolae Ceaușescu, the tone changed again. Documents about the meeting of the Warsaw Pact's leaders discussing the situation created by the Six-Day War reveal that Ceaușescu (1965–1989) opposed Brezhnev in branding Israel "the aggressor state" and condemned the Arab and Soviet language that called for its destruction. He believed that Israel had a right to existence.[8] This was the first major display of Ceaușescu's desire to create a strong Romanian Communism, independent from the Soviet Union. Other signs followed, as when Romania refused to invade Czechoslovakia during the Prague Spring of 1968 and Ceaușescu created a dictatorship inspired by the North Korean model, which he implemented in the last part of his life. Soon after 1967, as a clear sign of its stand, Romania elevated its relations with Israel from the rank of consulate to that of embassy, Romania being the only country in the Communist block to maintain diplomatic relations with Israel after the Six-Day War.

According to secret documents released by the Israel State Archive in November 2012, Ceaușescu played a mediator role in the peace talks between Israel and Egypt that led to the November 1977 visit of the Egyptian President Anwar El Sadat to Israel. The visit, which was the first of an Arab leader, paved the way for the September 1978 Camp David Accords.[9] Ceaușescu's stand in the Israeli-Arab conflict followed a middle ground: on the one hand, he fully recognized the right to existence of the state of Israel and condemned anyone opposed to it. On the other hand, he openly supported the PLO and Yasser Arafat, and asked Israel to withdraw from the territories occupied after 1967. According to Ofer Aderet, who quotes Israeli secret documents released in 2012, Menachem Begin, the Israeli prime minister, informed his government in 1977 of what Ceaușescu told him:

> We should recognize the PLO, hold negotiations with [Yasser] Arafat— Arafat is a good person—Ceaușescu has spoken to him and there are people who are a lot worse in the PLO—Arafat is prepared to recognize the State of Israel. . . . He [Ceaușescu] demanded withdrawal to the 1967 borders. . . . He said: If the Israeli policy continues, that is, according to what he said, non-agreement to a withdrawal to the lines of June 4, 1967, non-recognition of a Palestinian state, non-conducting of negotiations with the PLO—he is concerned, and he said this anxiously, that anti-Jewish feelings will arise in many parts of the world.[10]

In the late 1970s and the 1980s Ceaușescu continued to play a mediator role in what he envisaged as the peace process between the Arabs and the Israelis. His attempt at a balanced approach suffered periodic setbacks; toward the end of his rule, his leaning toward the Arab cause became more obvious.[11] It should be noted that the unique position of Romania as the only Communist country to maintain diplomatic relations with Israel was influenced by the fact that it acted as a gateway for the emigration of Jews, starting in the 1970s. Bucharest was the only city in Communist Europe to have direct flights to Israel.

The Holocaust was avoided in public discourse in the first twenty years after the war. Toward the end of the 1960s several books, including a censored version of *The Murderers Among Us* by Simon Wiesenthal, were published in Romania.[12] The emphasis was entirely on what the Nazis did, the Romanian involvement having been forgotten in what Michael Shafir brands as "the state-organized forgetting of the Holocaust."[13] In secret service documents, the involvement of some Romanians of Hungarian origin in the Holocaust (especially those who took part in the killing process in Auschwitz) is mentioned immediately after the war,[14] but details were not available to the general public. In 1978 an aggressive campaign of denying Romanian participation in the Holocaust was launched. The centerpiece of this propaganda was *Zile însîngerate la Iaşi: 28--30 iunie 1941* (Bloody Days in Iaşi: 28–30 June 1941), written by Aurel Karețki and Maria Covaci.[15]. The book, which grossly downplayed the number of Jews killed in the Iaşi pogrom and denied any Romanian wrongdoing, was commented on in several articles published in historical journals with a large circulation.[16]

In the later 1970s Ceauşescu revived the 1945 cover-up for several reasons. First, he needed a whitewashed history for the new national Communism, which portrayed Romanians as always having been hospitable, tolerant, and in harmonious relations with ethnic and religious minorities. In addition, most importantly, he needed it to shore up his relationship with Israel and to keep his desired role as a mediator in the Israeli-Arab conflict. If Romanians' murderous acts against Jews were to come out, his entire foreign agenda would be compromised. While the Jewish community of Romania was forced to promote this narrative, which denied Romanian involvement in the Holocaust, the state of Israel did not push, during the Ceauşescu regime, for full exposure. In the opening speech marking the start of his mission, Yosef Govrin, the Israeli ambassador to Romania (1985–1990), acknowledged the Holocaust in Romania but said nothing about Romanian involvement. The speech praised those "anti-fascist fighters" who saved Jews; the same language and imagery were used in the Communist propaganda.[17] It is very likely that Govrin's speech was censored in order to be align with the regime's view on this topic. Even after the fall of Ceauşescu, some Israeli politicians, such as former president Shimon Perez, continued to take a conciliatory approach that minimized the role of Romanians in the Holocaust, although why is unclear.

The fact that the whitewashing campaign was more aggressively promoted from 1978 onward shows that Romania was still connected to the larger European and international stage. That year the American TV drama *The Holocaust* became popular in Western Germany and reignited debates about its past. It is likely that Ceauşescu's campaign was a way of forestalling debate about Romanian involvement in the Holocaust. He balanced the cover-up, which involved history cleansing and mythmaking, with positive gestures toward the Jewish community and Israel. One such gesture was his 1978 approval of the creation of the Museum of Jewish Culture and Civilization in Bucharest.

The Romanian Orthodox Church and the Jewish community of Romania faced different challenges during the Communist era. The Jewish community strived to secure safe travel to Israel of those who wanted to emigrate. The policy of religious harmony ensured that excesses of anti-Semitism were generally kept under control. In Communist ideology anti-Semitism did not exist, as it contradicted the model of a perfect society. The Romanian Orthodox Church continued to be used in Communist plans, most importantly as a means of legitimizing Communist rule. During the Dej era (1947–1965), as well as the Ceaușescu era (1965–1989), the Romanian Orthodox Church became one of the cornerstones of Communist nationalist legitimacy.

The Jewish community of Romania during the Communist regime

The most striking aspect of the Romanian Jewish community between 1948 and 1989 is its significant decrease in number. As mentioned in chapter 5, there were about 400,000 Jews living in Romania in 1947.[18] Continued anti-Semitism, the reluctance of one regime after another to repair the injustices of the war and the Holocaust, the precarious living conditions, and distrust of the state made Romanian Jews eager to emigrate. There were cases of emigration to Palestine before 1948,[19] but massive immigration took place only after the creation of the state of Israel. The analysis made by Radu Ioanid reveals two periods of massive exodus. The first wave of emigration took place between 1949 and 1951, when roughly 116,500 Jews left Romania for Israel.[20] The Romanian Communist authorities, following the Soviet example, hoped that the emigrants would create a Communist outpost in Israel.[21] When this did not happen, they stopped for several years, and only small numbers of Jews were able to leave Romania between 1952 and 1958.

Allowing emigration could also have been motivated by the anti-Semitism of the Communist regime, which wanted to get rid of those it considered dangerous for the country. On the one hand, the Jews were unhappy with the economic policies of the Communists, especially with monetary reform and collectivization. Documents from the Romanian archives testify to the open rebellion against such measures in places with substantial Jewish populations.[22] This open rebellion can be easily understood considering that in less than a decade the Romanian Jews twice had their property seized by the state. In some cases Jews who were still waiting for the return of property taken during the Antonescu regime saw their hopes shattered by the new regime's policies. The fact that Jews were overrepresented in sectors of the Romanian economy such as small industry and trade worsened the situation. On the other hand, the first wave of emigration should be understood in the context of Communist authorities' increasingly anti-Zionist policies. Archival documents reveal that in northern and eastern Romania Zionism was strong. Between 1948 and 1955 the Communist authorities declared war on Zionist organizations, arresting their leaders, many of whom died in Communist prisons.[23]

The second period of large-scale emigration took place between 1958 and 1966 when approximately 106,200 Jews left Romania for Israel. It should be noted that this occurred at the start of a more relaxed internal attitude on the part of the Communist authorities, after the departure of the Soviet army and its tough response to the 1956 uprisings in Hungary and Poland. But research shows that the most important factor in the policy change was external developments. Toward the end of the 1950s Romania used the chief rabbi and his links with the West in its effort to join international organizations. While working with the Romanian authorities, Moses Rosen drew attention to the Jewish population's need to emigrate to Israel.[24] The second major wave of emigration also marked the beginning of financial and economic deals between the two states.[25] Israel agreed to pay cash and commercial and economic goods in exchange for any Jew leaving Romania. Some wealthy Jewish families paid too. This trade—humans in exchange for foreign currency—was taken a step further during the Ceaușescu era, most of the money entering the secret accounts of the Ceaușescu family, according to Mihai Pacepa, the former vice head of the Romanian Foreign Secret Service.[26] After 1966, the number of Jews leaving Romania remained steady, between 1,000 and 3,000 each year.[27] The vast majority of these went to Israel, with smaller numbers going to France, the United States, Canada, Germany, and Great Britain. By the end of the Communist era the number of Jews living in Romania had dropped to 20,000.

Those Jews who did not emigrate continued to face precarious conditions. Moreover, the nationalization of property and monetary reform affected them deeply. Secret police documents acknowledge that the monetary reform of 1952 "left Jewish citizens without money. They cannot pay their passport taxes, the fiscal taxes, baggage fees, etc. . . . The Jewish citizens cannot sell their goods as no one has money to buy them."[28] Another document describes what Rabbi David Safran, Moses Rosen's contender for the office of chief rabbi, believed about the Jewish situation under the new regime. He complains that "the Jews are in great suffering, they are more persecuted than other minorities." As an example, he says that "rabbis are forced to read in synagogues insults toward the state of Israel and toward the faith of the forefathers."[29] This was especially the case in the 1950s, when many Jews, because of harassment by the Communist authorities, had to change their names if they wanted a professional career.

The relationship between the Jewish community and the new regime was complex. The chief rabbi, who was also the president of the Federation of Jewish Communities of Romania, although elected with the support of the Communist regime and generally following its policies, exercised a degree of independence. His attitude toward the regime seems to have been very similar to Patriarch Justinian's. On the one hand, he complied with major policies, such as silence about the involvement of the Romanians in the Holocaust and participation in the religious harmony initiative. On the other hand, he promoted policies that kept a healthy sense of independence, such as forging the emigration plan and the creation of the Jewish Museum. Moreover, during the Ceaușescu era he was successful in securing the right to religious education for Jewish children as well as freedom of worship.[30]

The Romanian Orthodox Church during the Communist regime

Between 1948 and 1989 three patriarchs of the Romanian Orthodox Church succeeded to power. Justinian (1948–1977) was imposed by the regime and collaborated with it on major projects, especially the "defense of peace" program, the canonization of Romanian saints, monasteries' reform, and the development of national Communism. However, Justinian was not entirely obedient, which created confusion and consternation in the Party. For example, he successfully intervened for the liberation of priests imprisoned after 1945,[31] openly opposed education reform, which involved the abolition of religious education classes in schools,[32] and, in 1949, refused to publish a laudatory article about the new Religions Law.[33] These examples raised concerns among some of the members of the political elite, but the fact that Justinian was seen as a friend of Gheorghiu Dej, the leader of the country, was sufficient to silence any discontent.

When Dej died and Ceauşescu became the general secretary of the Communist Party, Justinian's dislike of Ceauşescu became apparent. For example, in all the issues of *BOR* from 1965 to 1972, there is no instance of Justinian publicly congratulating Ceauşescu, while his telegrams of congratulation to other leaders of the Communist Party, such as Chivu Stoica and Ştefan Voitec, were regularly published. The first telegram congratulating Ceauşescu appeared in 1973, when it became increasingly obvious that he was developing a strong cult of personality and that his leadership would be uncontested.[34] But Justinian acted too late and Ceauşescu did not forget his long silence. In 1977 Justinian died in suspect circumstances.[35] It may be that he shared the fate of Nicodim, in whose elimination he himself allegedly played a role.

Iustin Moisescu, the next patriarch, is presented in the *Final Report of the Presidential Commission for the Analysis of Communist Dictatorship* as being a "collaborator of the Securitate."[36] A secret service document from 1948 mentions Moisescu's strong links with Communist circles, stating that "from a political point of view he has been on the staff of the PMR [Romanian Workers' Party, that is, the Communist Party] in the last two years. . . . Prof. I. Moisescu is important among the main Romanian theologians and is considered, from a political point of view, well integrated on the line of popular democracy."[37] During his time in office the Church went along with the Ceauşescu regime in promoting the new "national Communism" and the Cultural Revolution. At the same time an increasing return to the interwar Orthodox nationalism became visible.

In 1986 Moisescu died and was replaced by Teoctist Arăpaşu. Teoctist's ascension to power is interesting. He was born in 1915 in Botoşani County, in Bukovina, a place with a large Jewish population. He became a monk in 1935 and in 1940 he began his theological studies at the University of Bucharest, from which he graduated in 1945. According to some (controversial) documents, the young Teoctist, an admirer of the Iron Guard, was involved in the Bucharest pogrom (January 1941), taking active part in the looting and violence against Jews. After the war, his ecclesiastical ascension was often mentioned in the main journal of the Church. Usually this open promotion had a political significance, suggesting the full support of the regime. In contrast to Justinian, who was coopted and suddenly promoted by the regime, Teoctist was raised to become a Communist patriarch. He continued the policies of his predecessor: legitimation of the new nationalism and silence about the demolition of churches. Patriarch Teoctist went along with these plans without raising any concerns. As a culmination of his willing submission, in December 1989, just a few days before the fall of Ceaușescu, the patriarch expressed unconditional support for the dictator in a telegram and condemned the popular revolt then going on in Timișoara.[38]

The Romanian Orthodox Church took full advantage of the abolition of the Greek Catholic Church[39] and supported without reservation the main programs of the Communist regime, including the Defense of Peace program initiated by the Soviets in 1948,[40] which Ceaușescu revived in the last years of his reign. The Defense of Peace campaign promoted the Soviet propaganda that split the world into enemies of peace, represented by the American and European "imperialists," and defenders of peace, represented by the Communist countries. Sometimes a latent anti-Semitism could be sensed in some of the details of this campaign.

Many priests were imprisoned during the Communism regime. How many there were is not entirely known; Paul Caravia suggests that the number could be as high as four thousand over the entire Communist era, although his book details (most often very vaguely) about only twenty-five hundred priests and other ecclesiastical personnel.[41] Most of these were imprisoned immediately after the war. Despite the narrative developed after 1989, which considered any imprisoned priest to have been a victim of Communist injustice, some of them were probably rightly sentenced for their affiliation with extreme rightwing movements and parties, such as the Iron Guard and the National Christian Defense League, and for their participation in the Holocaust.

Behind religious harmony: Jewish-Orthodox relations during the Communist era and the problem of Holocaust remembrance

The Communist policy of religious harmony, which started as early as 1945, became more evident after 1948. Skipping through the issues of the main journals of the Church during the Communist period, one aspect becomes obvious: the effort to present the Jewish and the Christian Orthodox communities as enjoying a friendly relationship. During Justinian's tenure as patriarch regular telegrams of congratulations between the leaders of the

Romanian Orthodox Church and the Jewish community were sent (and published).[42] New Year telegrams, telegrams celebrating the birthday of one or the other of the leaders, and celebratory articles appeared regularly, written in the typical style of Communist propaganda.[43] During the tenure of Iustin Moisescu as patriarch (1977–1986) these kinds of documents ceased to appear. They reemerged when Teoctist became patriarch in 1986.[44] This may mean that the religious harmony policy was gladly embraced by Justinian and Teoctist, but not by Iustin.

The Holocaust is never mentioned in these exchanges of letters, telegrams, and celebratory articles. In the July–August 1968 issue of the Romanian Orthodox Church's main journal an article entitled "Celebrating 20 years since the Election of His Eminency Dr. Moses Rosen as the Chief Rabbi of the Jewish Community" was published. In it the history before 1948 is entirely ignored. Moses Rosen is praised for his "contribution to the reconstruction of the Jewish community destroyed by the Second World War," but there is no mention of the Holocaust or of the Romanian/Orthodox involvement in the destruction of the Jewish community. The good relations between the Jewish and the Orthodox communities, shaped and developed by Rosen and Justinian, are praised, as are the Communist authorities for encouraging a climate of good will between religions.

In all the issues of the main journals of the Romanian Orthodox Church published during the Communist era, there appears to be only one instance in which Moses Rosen mentions the Holocaust in the context of Jewish-Orthodox relations, and even that mention is minimal. The context is the death of Patriarch Justinian in 1977. In his speech, the chief rabbi pays respect to Patriarch Justinian who "not only was a shepherd to the Orthodox Church, but he was to all of us, the co-inhabitant religions of the fatherland, a father and a wise mentor." Toward the middle of his message Moses Rosen says, "After many and hard years in which hatred and enmity between religions have been sown, Patriarch Justinian has built a new climate of nobility and brotherhood in the churches' relations."[45] This veiled mention of events prior to 1948, which had been entirely avoided before, can be best understood in the context of increasing knowledge of the Holocaust leading to the events of 1978.

In Church journals the message of tolerance is often visible. For example in 1949 in *Studii Teologice* the article "The Missionary Role of the Romanian

Orthodox Church" states that "the differentiation between individuals and the racial discriminations are abolished. Saint Paul clearly says: 'there is no Jew, nor Greek.'"[46] However, this tolerance was not without limits. First, any mention of the Church's mistakes and intolerance in the past is entirely overlooked; the narrative of the Church as a permanent promoter of peace and harmony is emphasized instead. Second, although anti-Semitism is officially condemned in the Church's journals, there are instances in which Jews are indirectly attacked. Take, for example, an article written in 1949 by future patriarch Iustin Moisescu, entitled "The National Problem and Its Democratic Resolution in the People's Republic of Romania: the Role of the Church in the Fight against Chauvinism, Anti-Semitism and Antisovietism." Although the title suggests a clear condemnation of anti-Semitism, Moisescu indirectly blames the Jews for the situation before the war. In a section discussing nationalism, he quotes the Political Bureau of the Communist Party: "In this case, the middle class, which in a feudal form was obedient to imperialism and hooked up with the bourgeoisie of the co-inhabitant minorities, has always promoted a policy of oppression, denationalization, and hatred spread through press campaigns and other propaganda tools."[47] This was not only an attack on the old regime's middle class, but also on the bourgeoisie of the co-inhabitant minorities, the Jews being one of the most visible before the war. The reference to the press could be another indirect reference to the "Jewish press,"[48] which was condemned before the war for its denationalizing message. This was one of the few instances where articles that largely promoted the harmony narrative slipped into the old intolerance and nationalism.

The fact that religious harmony was just a façade is also suggested by other developments. Secret service documents in the Romanian archives reveal that in 1949 an enquiry carried out by the Communist authorities mentions the existence of anti-Semitic verses in several Orthodox religious liturgical songs: the Prohod (the Good Friday Lamentation), Octoih, and Triod. According to secret cables, examples included

> Octoih, part 1, page 23: "The lawless blasphemy of the Yids, killers of God, has come to an end." On page 322: "The Yids, our Redeemer, on the cross nailed You." On page 326: "The lawless people with nails nailed You."
> Triod: "The Assembly of the killers of God, the Yids lawless people, in madness shout to Pilate: Crucify Christ!"[49]

The Good Friday song was modified after this enquiry, many verses being entirely removed (especially those portraying Jews as the killers of God). For example the fifty-first verse of the second stage of the song replaced "Jews" with "Pharisees":

O, Jews (Pharisees in the modified version)
Be at least ashamed of the ones who were resurrected from death
by the Life Giver, the one who, full of malice you killed.[50]

Teodor Popescu, the theology professor who in 1942 published the article "Communist Anti-Christianity," expressed again after the war his prejudice against Jews. His unchanged anti-Semitic stand, although less virulent, is evident in an article published in *Studii Teologice* in 1950. In it he condemns the Jews for not being capable of accepting Jesus as the Messiah: "This was the great scandal and their tragedy: not being able to believe in Jesus Christ as Messiah, to wait for a political liberator instead of a soul re-deemer, to have denounced Him as an agitator and to have judged Him as an heretic and blasphemer."[51]

In 1951, when the Communists introduced education reform and banned Saturday afternoon religious education classes taught by the Orthodox Church, Patriarch Justinian reacted by vehemently attacking the Zion-ists.[52] This outburst could not have been directed only against Zionist lead-ers, as most of them were by that time imprisoned or dead. By "Zionists" the patriarch meant the Communist Jews (and maybe the entire Jewish com-munity), whom he considered responsible for the reform. He could openly speak about his frustration against Jews because the general policy of the Communist Party at the time was one of anti-Semitic attacks against Zion-ism and against Jewish Communists.

The position of Ana Pauker as one of the three main leaders of the coun-try before 1952 was also an occasion for anti-Semitic outbursts inside the Romanian Orthodox Church. In 1949 a conflict erupted between the new patriarch, Justinian, and Bishop Emilian Antal, the protégé of the former patriarch Nicodim. Antal tried to present Justinian in an unfavorable light, saying that he had deliberately delayed transmitting to the churches some economic messages of the Communist authorities. Justinian replied by making public an anonymous letter he alleged to have been written by Antal. The letter, addressed to Justinian, blamed the patriarch for the killing of the metropolitan of Moldova, Irineu Mihălcescu. The anonymous author then attacked Ana Pauker: "How is it possible for you to have such a lack of dignity and to keep at the head of the country a Jewish bitch of the lowest rank [*o putoare ovreică de ultimă speță*] . . . for you to see the crime you do by allowing a kike bitch [*putoare jidoavcă*] at the head of the country."[53] The letter also openly discusses the idea of Ana Pauker being burnt alive and makes "jokes" such as "Madam, please, when will Ana Pauker be burnt, because we would like to see how she is burnt alive; we heard that the saints are not crying, they only pray to God."[54] To the "Jewish bitch of the lowest rank" insult, the letter adds another one: "the beastly bitch."

It is impossible to tell who the author of that letter was, but this is relatively unimportant. Truly important is that inside the Church there were individuals, some of them clearly members of the hierarchy, who continued to hold, express, and disseminate virulent anti-Semitism packed with vitriolic language in which the image of burning, probably a direct allusion to the fate of Jews during the Holocaust, was promoted without remorse.

The real attitude of the Romanian Orthodox Church toward the Jewish community can also be deduced from articles published between 1964 and 1972 in the journal of the Romanian Orthodox patriarchate, *Ortodoxia* (see chapter 7). Tensions between the Romanian Orthodox Church and the Jewish community are also suggested by the increasing promotion of a strong Orthodox nationalism in the pages of the main journal of the Church in the 1980s. In this way, the prominent figures of interwar rightwing Orthodox nationalism were gradually rehabilitated. Through this rehabilitation, the Church indirectly set the stage for the return of anti-Semitism. It must be said that before 1989 the rehabilitation of rightwing interwar Orthodox figures generally avoided expressions of anti-Semitism, but anti-Semitism was in the air. It was just awaiting the proper conditions to be unleashed.

When it came to remembrance of the Holocaust, the Communist regime increasingly developed a kind of amnesia, which was largely reflected in *BOR*. According to this narrative, Romanians were victims of Nazi policies. The Holocaust did happen, but only in Poland and at the hands of the Nazis and Hungarians. Any Romanian involvement in the Holocaust was denied and Romanians were presented as a tolerant and hospitable people.[55] The Iron Guard was seen as a German agency and the Jewish identity of the victims was replaced with Communists, co-inhabiting nationalities, and "combatants of the anti-Hitlerist resistance."[56] While this attack on the memory of the Holocaust (that is, the Romanian and Orthodox involvement in the Holocaust) was made through different mediums, the leaders of the Jewish community continued to promote religious harmony without any public mention of the Orthodox Church's active involvement in the destruction of Romanian Jewry. It should be acknowledged, however, that in a totalitarian regime it was difficult (if not impossible) to raise objections to the official narrative promoted by the regime.

NOTES

1. In 1952 Joseph Stalin turned to a more open anti-Semitic policy in the Soviet Union. Moscow doctors (predominantly Jews) were accused of conspiring to assassinate Soviet leaders in what would be known as "The Doctor's Plot." In this context, political anti-Semitism spread to other Communist countries. On November 20, 1952, Rudolf Slansky, General Secretary of the Communist Party of Czechoslovakia, and thirteen other leading party members (eleven of them Jews), were accused of participating in a Trotskyite-Titoite-Zionist conspiracy and convicted. Eleven of them, including Slansky, were hanged in Prague on December 3, and three were sentenced to life imprisonment.

2. See CNSAS D13029, Procesul Complotist Antistatal în Frunte cu Rudolf Slansky [The Trial of the Anti-State Plot Headed by Rudolf Slansky], vol. 1, 1–28.

3. CNSAS D8925, Problema Preoțească în Vechiul Regat, 1948–1949 [The Priesthood Problem in the Old Kingdom, 1948–1949], "Nota No 64/163, 22 Ianuarie 1949, sursa Velican," 154–155.

4. CNSAS D164, Problema Evreiască, Anii 1948–1957 [The Jewish Problem, 1948–1957], "Referat no 353/12 Noiembrie 1951," 28, and "DGSS No 353/7.563 din 6 Iunie 1951," 91.

5. Liviu Rotman, The Communist Era until 1965, vol. 4 of The History of the Jews in Romania (Tel Aviv: The Goldstein-Goren Diaspora Research Center, 2005), 163.

6. CNSAS D8743, Sinteza Privind Cercetările Efectuate în Problema Sionistă, 1952 [Synthesis Regarding the Inquiries into the Zionist Problem, 1952], 5.

7. See CNSAS D8889, Fond Documentar Privind Sioniștii, 1948 [Documentary File Regarding the Zionists, 1948], "Document al Comitetului Democratic Evreesc, București, Comitetul Central din 1 Iunie 1948," 2.

8. Yosef Govrin, Israeli-Romanian Relations at the End of the Ceaușescu Era: As Seen by Israel's Ambassador to Romania (London: Frank Cass, 2002), 4–5.

9. See Ofer Aderet, "Behind the Scenes of Anwar Sadat's Historic Visit to Jerusalem," Haaretz, 27 November 2012, http://www.haaretz.com/israel-news/behind-the-scenes-of -anwar-sadat-s-historic-visit-to-jerusalem.premium-1.480957.

10. Ibid.

11. Ceaușescu's links with major dictators in the Arab world, such as Saddam Hussein and Muammar Gaddafi, increased toward his final days. He acknowledged the PLO in 1988. His last external visit was to Iran in December 1989. See Jacob Abadi, "Israel and the Balkan States," Middle Eastern Studies 32, no. 4 (October 1996): 307.

12. Simon Wiesenthal, Asasinii printre noi [The Murderers Among Us] (Bucharest: Editura Politică, 1969).

13. Michael Shafir, "Romania's Torturous Road to Facing Collaboration," in Collaboration with the Nazis. Public Discourse after the Holocaust, ed. Roni Stauber (London: Routledge, 2011), 253.

14. CNSAS D169, *Problema Evreiască pe Anul 1952* [The Jewish Problem, Year 1952], "Nota No 351/1 Septembrie 1952," 83.

15. Aurel Kareţki and Maria Covaci, *Zile însîngerate la Iaşi: 28–30 iunie 1941* [Bloody Days in Iaşi: 28-30 June 1941] (Bucharest: Editura Politică, 1978).

16. See Cosmina Guşu, "Reflectarea Holocaustului în revista Magazin Istoric," [The Holocaust as it Appears in 'The Historical Magazine' Review], *Holocaustul. Studii şi Cercetări* 1, no. 1 (2009): 151–160.

17. Govrin, *Israeli–Romanian Relations*, 25.

18. Hary Kuller, *Evreii în România Anilor 1944–1949: evenimente, documente, comentarii* [The Jews in Romania, 1944–1949: Events, Documents, Comments] (Bucharest: Hasefer, 2002), 35–37.

19. See Radu Ioanid, *The Ransom of the Jews: The Story of the Extraordinary Secret Bargain between Romania and Israel* (Chicago: Ivan R. Dee, 2005), 28. See also documents about the collaboration between Andrea Cassulo, papal nuncio to Romania, and Angelo Roncalli, papal nuncio to Turkey and Greece and their efforts to help Jewish immigrants, including orphan children, reach Palestine in 1944 and 1945, in the International Raoul Wallenberg Foundation and Casa Argentina en Israel Tierra Santa, eds., *John XXIII—"The Good Pope,"* 2009, accessed 10 December 2014, http://www.raoulwallenberg.net/wp-content/files_mf/1310655046 ebookroncalli-ENGLISHcorrected.pdf.

20. Rotman, *The Communist Era until 1965*, 23.

21. Ioanid, *The Ransom of the Jews*, 30.

22. CNSAS D12208, *Activitatea Sionistă a Unor Organizatii Evreieşti din România. Starea de Spirit a Populaţiei Evreieşti, Emigrarea în Palestina, Tezaurul unor Organizaţii Sioniste, 1936–1964* [The Zionist Activity of Some Jewish Organizations from Romania. The Morale of the Jewish Population, Immigration to Palestine, the Treasury of Some Zionist Organizations, 1936–1964], "Raport al Sublocotenent de Securitate Lungu Dumitru, 15 April 1950," 74. According to this report 300 to 400 Jews publicly confronted the police in Iaşi, discontent with the immigration process. According to another Iaşi police document, 26 April 1950, 82, the Jews shouted at the police, among other things, "If you do not give us bread, we want to leave!"

23. For a better understanding of Zionism in Romania, see Rotman, *Evreii din România în perioada comunistă* (Iaşi, Romania: Polirom, 2004), the chapter "O relaţie problematică: sionism şi communism" [A Problematic Relationship: Zionism and Communism], 133–145.

24. Rotman, *The Communist Era until 1965*, 49.

25. Ioanid, *The Ransom of the Jews*, especially the chapter "Barter," 68–92.

26. Ibid., 182. According to Ion Mihai Pacepa, the former deputy chief of the Romanian Foreign Secret Service who defected to the United States in 1978, around $500 million entered the accounts of the Ceauşescu family via this route.

27. See Rotman, *The Communist Era until 1965*, 23.

28. CNSAS D169, "DGSS Regionala Bucureşti, no. 35/46771 din 7 Februarie 1952," 3.

29. Ibid., "DGSS Regionala Bucureşti, no. 35/87.121 din 28 Octombrie 1952," 150.

30. See the speech of former Israeli President Chaim Hertzog in Moses Rosen, *Chief Rabbi of Romania Dr. Moses Rosen on His Eightieth Birthday Anniversary* (Bucharest: Hasefer, 1992), 3.

31. Cristian Vasile, *Biserica Ortodoxă Română în primul deceniu comunist* [The Romanian Orthodox Church during the First Decade of Communism] (Bucharest: Curtea Veche, 2005), 239–240.

32. Ibid., 222.

33. CNSAS D68, Nunciatura Papală, 1948–1949, "Strict Secret, Dosar A. S. Justinian Marina, Patriarch, 24 Februarie 1949," 463.

34. Justinian, Patriarhul României, "Telegrama de Felicitare Cu Prilejul Celei de-a 55-a Aniversări a Zilei de Naștere a Domnului Nicolae Ceaușescu, Președitele Consiliului de Stat al RS Romania" [The Congratulatory Telegram to Mister Nicolae Ceaușescu, the President of the Romanian RS's (Socialist Republic) State Council, at His 55th Birthday Celebration], BOR 92, nos. 1–2 (January–February 1973): 9.

35. See Ioan Dură, "Ierarhi ai Bisericii Ortodoxe Române indepărtați din scaun și trimiși în recluziune monastică de către autoritățile comuniste în anii 1944–1981" [Clergy of the Romanian Orthodox Church Sacked and Sent into Monasteries by Communist Authorities from 1944 to 1981], BOR 120, nos. 110–112 (October–December 2002): 305–306.

36. See Comisia Prezidențială pentru Analiza Dictaturii Comuniste din România [Presidential Commission for the Analysis of the Communist Dictatorship in Romania], Raport Final (Bucharest: Humanitas, 2006), 467.

37. CNSAS D14673, Culte și Secte după 23 August 1944 [Religions and Sects after 23 August 1944], "Nota despre Iustin Moisescu, nesemnată, 23 July 1948," 15–16.

38. See Carol Harsan, "Cumpăna Patriarhului," România Liberă, 2 August 2007, http://www.romanialibera.ro/exclusiv-rl/investigatii/Cumpăna-patriarhului-102585.html.

39. Comisia Prezidențială pentru Analiza Dictaturii Comuniste din România, Raport Final, 463–465.

40. See Sfântul Sinod al Bisericii Ortodoxe Române, "Biserica Ortodoxă Română și apărarea păcii. Pastorala Sfântului Sinod către clerul și credincioșii ortodocși și către toți creștinii din Republica Populară Română" [The Romanian Orthodox Church and the Defense of Peace. Holy Synod's Pastoral Letter to Orthodox Clergy and Faithful of the Popular Republic of Romania], BOR 67, nos. 3–6 (March–June 1949): 164–166.

41. Paul Caravia, The Imprisoned Church: Romania 1944–1989 (Bucharest: National Institute for the Study of Totalitarianism, 1999), 21.

42. Moses Rosen, "Mesajul Eminenței Sale Dr. Moses Rosen șef rabinul cultului mozaic din România" [The Message of His Eminency Dr. Moses Rosen, the Chief Rabbi of the Jewish Community (Mosaic religion) of Romania], BOR 86, no. 6 (June 1968): 540–541; "Schimb de telegrame între Prea Fericitul Părinte Iustinian, Patriarhul Bisericii Ortodoxe Române și Eminența Sa, Dr. Moses Rosen, șef rabinul cultului mozaic din România" [Exchange of Telegrams between His Holiness Iustinian, the Patriarch of the Romanian Orthodox Church and His Eminency, Dr. Moses Rosen, the Chief Rabbi of the Jewish Community (Mosaic Religion) of Romania], BOR 92, nos. 5–6 (May–June 1974): 560.

43. See "Schimb de Telegrame," BOR 92, nos. 7–8 (July–August 1974): 855.

44. See Comitetul de Redacție [Editorial Board], "Participarea Prea Fericitului Patriarh Teoctist la aniversarea Eminenței Sale Dl. Șef Rabin Moses Rosen" [The Participation of His Holiness Patriarch Teoctist at the Anniversary of His Eminency Mister Chief Rabbi Moses Rosen], BOR 106, nos. 7–8 (July–August 1988): 25. It should be noted that previously Moses Rosen was introduced as "His Eminency Dr. Moses Rosen, the Chief Rabbi of the Jewish community" here is introduced as "Mister Chief Rabbi Moses Rosen."

45. Comitetul de Redacție [Editorial Board], "Excelenta sa Dr. Moses Rosen, Șef Rabinul Cultului Mozaic din România, Președintele Federației Comunităților Evreiești din România a Adus Omagiul Său Personalității Patriarhului Justinian" [His Excellency Dr. Moses Rosen, the Chief Rabbi of the Jewish Community (Mosaic Religion) of Romania, the President of the Federation of Jewish Communities of Romania Has Paid Homage to the Personality of Patriarch Justinian], BOR 96, no. 4 (April 1977): 250–251.

46. Petru Răzuș, "Rolul Social și Misionar al Bisericii Ortodoxe Române" [The Social and Missionary Role of the Romanian Orthodox Church], *Studii Teologice*, series 2, vol. 1, nos. 7–8 (September–October 1949): 504.

47. Ghe. I. Moisescu, "Problema natională și rezolvarea ei democratică în republica populară Română. Rolul Bisericii în lupta contra șovinismului, antisemitismului și antisovietismului" [The National Problem and Its Democratic Resolution in the People's Republic of Romania: the Role of the Church in the Fight against Chauvinism, Anti-Semitism and Antisovietism], *Studii Teologice*, series 2, vol. 1, nos. 7–8 (September–October 1949): 670.

48. During the interwar period, Romanian daily newspapers such as "Dimineața" and "Adevărul," were portrayed by right-wing nationalists in conspiratorial tones. They were seen as tools in advancing Jewish interests in society. See Tuvia Friling, Radu Ioanid, and Mihai Ionescu, eds., *The Final Report of the Elie Wiesel Commission for the Study of the Holocaust in Romania* (Bucharest: Polirom, 2005), 40–41.

49. CNSAS D8925, "Nota No 1/15135S din 16 Decembrie 1948 Direcția Poliției de Siguranță, Direcția Regională a Securității Poporului Suceava," vol. 1, 16.

50. Dinu C. "Prohodul Domnului CENZURAT!" [The Good Friday Lamentation Song CENSORED!], Creștin Ortodox Forum, accessed 21 June 2012, http://www.crestinortodox .ro/forum/showthread.php?t=8641.

51. Teodor M. Popescu, "Privire istorică asupra schismelor, ereziilor și sectelor" [Historical Overview of Schisms, Heresies, and Sects], *Studii Teologice,* series 2, vol. 2, nos. 7–8 (1950): 353–354.

52. Vasile, *Biserica Ortodoxă Română*, 222–223.

53. CNSAS D8925, "Nota No 64/163, 22 Ianuarie 1949, sursa Velican," 154–155.

54. Ibid.

55. Comitetul de Redacție [Editorial Board], "23 August 1944–23 August 1964. A Douăzecea Aniversare a Eliberării Romîniei" [The Twentieth Anniversary of Romania's Liberation], *Studii Teologice*, series 2, vol. 16, nos. 7–8 (September–October 1964): 403–407.

56. Gușu, *Reflectarea Holocaustului în revista Magazin Istoric*, 154–155.

7

THE ROMANIAN ORTHODOX CHURCH, HOLOCAUST MEMORY, AND ANTI-SEMITISM DURING THE COMMUNIST ERA (1948–1989)

ALTHOUGH THE HOLOCAUST WAS NOT a major item on the agenda of the Romanian Orthodox Church from 1948 to 1989, the topic was mentioned explicitly and implicitly in several situations. In this, the Church mirrored the state's attitude toward the events of the war. For about twenty years the subject was entirely ignored in the Church's journals. A relative openness to discussing some aspects of the Holocaust, which became visible in Romanian society at the end of the 1960s through the publication of books dealing exclusively with Nazi atrocities, was reflected in the journals of the Church by a series of articles on the Nostra Aetate declaration. This Second Vatican Council document, which expressed the Catholic view on non-Christian religions (including on Judaism), was commented on in articles published in the theological journal *Ortodoxia*. Although the Holocaust itself was not mentioned, these articles echoed the cover-up of 1945 and presented the Romanian Orthodox Church as always tolerant and hospitable toward minorities in general and toward Jews in particular. In the late 1970s and 1980s, the Communist narrative that denied any Romanian involvement in the Holocaust was reflected in the journals of the Church too. Moreover, the revival of Orthodox nationalism led to the rehabilitation of rightwing, anti-Semitic figures such as Patriarch Miron Cristea, Octavian Goga, Teodor Popescu, and Metropolitan Nicolae Bălan. The reinforcement of the whitewashing narrative in the late 1960s, the rehabilitation of rightwing anti-Semitic personalities in the late 1970s and 1980s, and the return to the Orthodox nationalism of the interwar period are all important in understanding the attitude of the Romanian Orthodox Church toward Holocaust memory. They constitute the basis on which the Church positioned itself with regard to the Holocaust at the end of the Communist era.

THE ROMANIAN ORTHODOX CHURCH, THE COMMUNIST REGIME, AND THE MEMORY OF THE HOLOCAUST IN THE CASE OF VALERIAN TRIFA, THE FORMER ROMANIAN ORTHODOX BISHOP OF AMERICA

Immediately after the Second World War, both the Romanian Orthodox Church and the Communist authorities used the events of the Holocaust for political or ecclesiastical gain. They were hidden or brought to light according to the political and religious agendas of different individuals and institutions.

The most eloquent case before 1948 was that of Visarion Puiu, the former metropolitan of Transnistria (see chapter 5), who was condemned to death in absentia in 1946. Although his involvement in legitimizing state policies in Transnistria was acknowledged in the final ruling, this was just an offshoot of the main charge against him. In 1950 the Holy Synod of the Romanian Orthodox Church defrocked Puiu.[1] As in the case of his condemnation, this decision was not a result of sensitivity toward Holocaust memory. It was driven by political reasons, namely by Puiu's increasing influence in the Orthodox diaspora. After two years of wandering through displaced persons camps in Germany and Austria, and a period of settlement in Italy with the help of the Catholic Church, Puiu arrived in 1949 in France, where he became the bishop of the Romanian Orthodox Diocese of Western Europe.[2] But the Communist authorities were most worried about his influence in deciding the fate of the Romanian Orthodox Church in America.

Andrei Moldovan, who had been the secretary of the Romanian Episcopate of America, was appointed bishop with the help of the Romanian Communist authorities in 1951, replacing Policarp Moruşcă. A large number of the episcopate's laymen rejected Moldovan's authority. Instead, they elected, in 1951, Valerian Trifa as the new bishop.[3] Trifa was helped in his ecclesiastical ascension by the Russian Orthodox Church Outside Russia (ROCOR), a dissident Orthodox Church that did not acknowledge Soviet authority.[4]

The relationship between Visarion Puiu and Valerian Trifa is interesting. We do not have details about their encounter before the end of the Second World War. After the war, they could be found together in several locations.[5] By some accounts Trifa was Visarion Puiu's secretary in Italy and Paris (the period from 1946 to 1949).[6] Trifa arrived in the United States in 1950 under the Displaced Persons Act. Documents in the Romanian archives and at the USHMM do not make it clear whether Puiu intended Trifa to be his right hand in America. For unknown reasons, an open conflict between the two erupted in 1955. In a 1956 letter to the Romanian Orthodox faithful of America, Puiu condemned Trifa's links with the "Russian aberration of the samosfeats"[7] but, more importantly, he made a direct reference to Trifa's past as an Iron Guard member.[8] Given Puiu's cunning character, it is likely that he introduced that reference as a way of compromising Trifa's image. He knew how damaging such revelations could be, because he experienced this himself when he wanted to leave Switzerland for France in 1948.[9]

Valerian (birth name: Viorel) Trifa became involved in the Iron Guard at an early age. As a student he took part in the Târgu-Mureş meeting of Legionary Orthodox students (1936) that decided on the creation of death squads. Their aim was the annihilation of the political and intellectual elite whom the Guard considered undesirable. In 1938 Trifa fled to Nazi Germany to avoid King Carol II's policy against Guard leaders. He returned to Romania on the eve of the Legion's ascension to power in September 1940. In January 1941, during the Legionary Rebellion, Valerian Trifa was the president of the National Union of Christian Students. In this capacity he was directly involved in acts of aggression against Jews during the Bucharest pogrom.[10] He was condemned to life imprisonment and labor by the Antonescu government, but, like other Iron Guard leaders, escaped to Germany. In Germany he was imprisoned in several concentration camps as an "honorary guest" benefiting from special treatment from the Nazi authorities.

Details about Trifa's past started to surface soon after he became bishop of the Romanian Orthodox Episcopate in America (Visarion Puiu's letter is such an example). Several Romanian Jewish organizations in America pressed for full disclosure of his history.[11] The main figure in this campaign was a Jewish physician born in Romania, Charles Kramer. In the beginning, this campaign was small, but as time went by it grew stronger and many institutions in Romania and America became involved. In 1962 Chief Rabbi Moses Rosen publicly attacked Trifa in a series of speeches made at meetings with Romanian Jewish diaspora communities.[12] The campaign to unveil Trifa's involvement in violent actions against Jews grew even stronger at the beginning of the 1970s. The unveiling involved the publication of articles, including some in the *New York Times*,[13] in which the past of Trifa was revealed, and several radio broadcasts at radio stations in Washington and New York.[14]

According to documents available at the CNSAS, the campaign was openly supported by the Romanian Foreign Affairs Secret Service (Direcţia de Informaţii Externe, DIE) starting in 1971, in the context of rumors about the bad health of Archbishop Irineu (ROCOR), and about the possibility of Trifa succeeding him as archbishop of all the Orthodox Christians in America.[15] Although the secret cables sometimes exaggerate the role of the Romanian secret service in Trifa's uncovering (it is obvious, for example, that DIE often claimed credit for the actions of the Romanian Jewish community in America) it is clear that it still played an important role. In one instance, for example, Charles Kramer asked DIE to provide him with official documents from Romania regarding Trifa's condemnations in 1941 and 1946.[16] He used those documents in his enquiries at the Department of Naturalization and in letters he wrote to several US congressmen. As a result, a Congressional commission was formed to investigate the case.

According to the DIE cables, in 1972 several US congressmen declared their surprise that a former assassin could be accepted as a bishop in America.[17] In 1975 the US Department of Justice opened a case against Trifa, the core argument being that he had entered the United States under false pretenses, hiding his Iron Guard affiliation. In October 1976, a group of members of the Concerned Jewish Youth organization occupied the headquarters of the National Council of Churches as a protest against the refusal of the organization to oust Trifa.[18] The archbishop was expelled from the body in November, after the council stated that, with respect to Nazi atrocities, "we cannot allow any doubt about a complete repudiation."[19]

Trifa's case also involved the Israeli authorities. According to some accounts, an Israeli prosecutor asked for Trifa's extradition so that Israel could try him for crimes against humanity. In 1983, the Justice Department's Office of Special Investigations negotiated with the Israeli government for the extradition "but the efforts failed, apparently because the Israelis did not feel they could build a sufficient war crimes case against him."[20]

In 1980 Trifa renounced his US citizenship under mounting public pressure about the way in which he got the citizenship in the first place and in the context of revelations about his extreme rightwing, anti-Semitic past.

In 1984 he was deported and took refuge in Portugal, where he died in 1987. Trifa's arrival in the United States in 1950, his sudden ascension to ecclesiastical power, and his prestige in the first years of his religious career (in 1955 Bishop Trifa gave the opening prayer before the US Senate) are still veiled in secrecy. Communist authorities alleged that he was helped at the beginning by the CIA[21] (sometimes they confuse the CIA with the FBI in their notes),[22] which is not entirely improbable considering the role played by the CIA in hiding and rehabilitating persons linked with the Nazi regime in the context of the Cold War.[23]

This is another excellent example of the way in which the Romanian Communist authorities related to the Holocaust. The events of the war were important only when they could be used for political gain. The Communist authorities did not disclose information about Valerian Trifa for the sake of historical truth, but because they wanted to get rid of him and to consolidate the power of the bishop they supported. With respect to the attitude of the Romanian Orthodox Church, according to some accounts Bartolomeu Anania and Nicolae Corneanu, both bishops of the Orthodox Church, were involved in the plans of the secret service to expose Trifa.[24] However, officially the Church did not play any role in the process. This could be explained by the fact that Trifa was never a priest in Romania, so the Church had no jurisdiction. It should be noted however, that in 1990, when the Holy Synod decided to rehabilitate Visarion Puiu, they also rehabilitated Valerian Trifa (see chapter 9).

DOCUMENTS OF THE ROMANIAN ORTHODOX CHURCH REGARDING THE HOLOCAUST AND JUDAISM, INCLUDING ORTHODOX COMMENTARIES ON THE NOSTRA AETATE DECLARATION

The main articles dealing with the attitude of the Romanian Orthodox Church toward Jews during the Holocaust were published in 1945. For several years after 1945, any mention of the events of the Second World War in the journals of the Church was avoided. Even when the Church participated in external meetings of the World Council of Churches (WCC) in which declarations on anti-Semitism were discussed, although the participation in the meetings was acknowledged (such as the meeting in Delhi, 1961), the documents relating to anti-Semitism were only vaguely mentioned.[25] The situation changed in 1964 when an article discussing the debates of the Second Vatican Council on the declaration on the non-Christian religions, the

Nostra Aetate (In Our Time), was published in *Ortodoxia*, the journal of the patriarchate. In the next eight years, several articles discussing this topic and the Orthodox Church's attitude toward non-Christian religions were published in the same journal. It must be said that during this entire period *BOR*, the main journal of the Church, was completely silent on this subject. The publication of these articles in *Ortodoxia* also coincides with a general cultural relaxation. Still, the publication in a journal reserved to clerics and theologians suggests that the topic was not for everyone.

The articles in question were about Judaism and Jewish-Christian relations, and did not deal directly with the Holocaust. However, the events of the war were in the background. They generally built on the narratives promoted in the first years after the war. The myth of a tolerant Church, first promoted in 1945 to conceal the Church's involvement in the Holocaust, had acquired full maturity by the 1960s. The revision of history that was necessary in 1945 to hide the Church's participation in the Shoah was not even mentioned in the articles. The fiction of a loving Church, which had always had harmonious relations with all non-Christian religions in Romania, was the uncontested narrative by the end of 1960s and was promoted without hesitation.

A first article looking generally at the proceedings of the Second Vatican Council was published in December 1964.[26] It mentions the difficulties of drafting a final version of the Nostra Aetate, which had to be revised several times. Special attention is given to the word "deicide," which was eliminated in the final declaration.[27] The thirty-two-page article tackles the Nostra Aetate in only two or three pages.

In 1967 Professor Emilian Vasilescu published a ten-page article entitled "Declarations Regarding the Non-Christian Religions" in *Ortodoxia*. Vasilescu presents the context in which the document was issued and some previous declarations of Pope Paul VI. He points out that the Nostra Aetate was conceived of as an independent document and included religions other than Judaism. The author discusses very briefly the prologue and the first three parts of the declaration, which address other religions, then goes into greater detail about the fourth part, which refers to Jews. Vasilescu says that "the content itself of this part of the declaration [the part referring to Judaism] would deserve to be published here in its entirety, especially in its initial form, in which the anti-Semitism and the deicide accusation were more clearly condemned."[28] He only briefly comments on the first paragraphs, which discuss the Jewish heritage in the Christian faith, then quotes the next paragraphs in their entirety, including the recommendations to avoid blaming the entire Jewish people for the death of Jesus and promoting the idea that the Jews were cast off or cursed. Vasilescu next discusses the reactions of the Jewish world, including Israel and the diaspora, and the reactions of the Arab countries. He also details the reactions of various Orthodox Churches. The large amount of text he dedicates to quoting Orthodox Christian comments offers us a window into the less well-known territory of Eastern/Greek Orthodox reactions to the Second Vatican Council document.

First, the author quotes the Greek Orthodox patriarch of Jerusalem, Benedict, who said that the Nostra Aetate is "alien to the Oriental Church. . . . We publicly declare that Our Church has nothing to do with this declaration." Benedict emphasized that the Orthodox Churches did not have delegates to the Second Vatican Council, and that they "will continue to remain faithful to the Four Gospels." Vasilescu describes the march of two thousand Christians in Aleppo protesting the Nostra Aetate. "The demonstrators, carrying banners vehemently condemning any attempt to exonerate the Jews for the crucifixion of Jesus . . . addressed a message to the Pope asking for the retraction of the declaration to avoid it being used for political purposes." Mar Ignatie Jacob, the patriarch of the Old Oriental Church of Antioch, also criticized the document: "The entire Jewish nation was responsible [for the crucifixion of Jesus], and, in consequence, the Vatican is in contradiction with the Holy Scripture. This is unacceptable."

Chiril the Fourth of Alexandria, the patriarch of the Coptic Orthodox Church, "gave instructions that Sunday sermons preached in the Coptic churches of Africa should condemn the Council's declaration. The Patriarch also asked the preachers to mention the texts from the New Testament that impute the guilt of Jesus' crucifixion to the Jews and to mention the idea that 'all those who support the rehabilitation of Jews should be considered accomplices to this murder.'" At the patriarch's initiative, a conference of the Coptic Orthodox Churches of Ethiopia, Sudan, Jordan, and the United Arab Emirates took place on February 18, 1965. The conference formulated a declaration in seven points condemning the Second Vatican Council's Nostra Aetate:

> The Bible states clearly that the Jews crucified Our Lord Jesus Christ so they bear the responsibility of His crucifixion, as they said and repeated in front of Pontius Pilate. . . . This act was not only the responsibility of a small group

of Jews. Clemency toward the sinners is not exercised by making them blameless of their sins, but by showing them the road to penitence and faith so that their sins can be forgiven. . . . To affirm a historical and dogmatic fact does not mean contradicting the Christian teaching of love, brotherhood, tolerance toward all human beings.[29]

According to Vasilescu, the Coptic conference also declared itself in line with the position of Mar Ignatie Jacob, the patriarch of the Old Oriental Church of Antioch, who condemned the entire Jewish nation for Jesus' crucifixion.

The only exception to this clear trend of Orthodox Churches vehemently and publicly condemning the Catholic Nostra Aetate was the Non-Chalcedonian Oriental Churches' position, made public after a meeting in Addis Ababa, January 15–18, 1965. According to Vasilescu, they refused to comment on the Nostra Aetate. He also presents Protestant reactions quoting Protestant pastors who further condemned anti-Semitism or expressed regret that the word "deicide" was not directly included in the final declaration.[30]

Following the political trend of the Communist regime, Vasilescu speculates heavily on the political connotations of the Nostra Aetate, especially on the Israeli-Arab conflict. At the end, he points out that an Orthodox official reaction to the Second Vatican Council's document was necessary, and for several years he and other theologians returned to the topic. It should also be noted that Vasilescu's gentle comparison between the vehement condemnation by most Orthodox Churches of the Nostra Aetate and a more moderate approach to the Jewish-Christian relations as revealed in the Catholic and Protestant commentaries, would be replaced by an increasingly intolerant approach in later articles.

These articles discussing the relations between Christians and non-Christians generally promoted two narratives: that of the tolerant Orthodox Church and that of an intolerant Catholic Church. For example, in an article published in September 1968 N. Vîlcu had no reservations about citing evidence that implicitly presented the Catholics in a negative light, such as this quote from Cardinal Richard James Cushing (Boston): "The Catholics did not behave in a proper way toward the Jews. They are guilty of indifference, and sometimes of crimes. We have to ask them forgiveness for our transgressions."[31] The repentance shown in Cardinal Cushing's statement and the acknowledgement of past misdeeds were used as tools in the

Orthodox Church's discourse against the Catholics. This trend followed the Communist agenda against the Catholic Church. Toward the end, Vîlcu brought forward what he called the Eastern Orthodox theological response to the Nostra Aetate. He wrote that "the Orthodox theology states its point of view toward the Non-Christian religions based on the Christian Revelation's canon, without denying though the value of these religions. . . . The Orthodox Church is not ready to compromise in any way the uniqueness and the definitive character of the Christian Revelation without denying, by this, what is valuable in other religions."[32] The Orthodox Church, in the author's view, was skeptical about the Catholic declaration on non-Christian religions, which he suspects of promoting proselytism. As with the Orthodox view on other religions, the author takes a confusing approach. He defends the Christian Orthodox revelation as unique and definitive, but because the interreligious dialogue doors have to be kept open, he acknowledges the value of other religions.

The same dilemma is visible in later articles when the swing between promoting the myth of a historically tolerant Church and the increasingly visible theological intolerance of the Orthodox Church toward non-Christian religions becomes more visible.[33] Even Emilian Vasilescu, who had a more balanced approach to this topic at the beginning, hardened his discourse. This is obvious in his article "Preoccupations in the Theology of the Romanian Orthodox Church about the non-Christian Religions" published in *Ortodoxia* in 1971. The myth of tolerance developed after the Second World War is extended here to the entire Byzantine world. According to Vasilescu, the Byzantine emperors did not persecute the Jews, but tried to convert them to Christianity through other means. He says that the Crusaders introduced anti-Semitism in Byzantium and that the anti-Semitism was political, not religious. He forgets the writings of the Eastern Orthodox fathers, some of them extremely anti-Semitic. Speaking about Romania, the only example of intolerance he mentions is the persecution of Armenians in 1551; he does not mention at all the interwar or the Holocaust period. Instead, he follows the trend of the Orthodox theology at the time and attacks the Catholics as intolerant.[34] He sees things in black and white. For him the West was intolerant, while the East was the land of harmony and tolerance: "Therefore, we believe that the Orthodox Church does not deserve the accusations that are generally brought against Christianity, against 'Christian civilization,' by the non-Christian religions for the acts of intolerance done, throughout centuries, by the Western part of Christianity. The Orthodox Church generally, and the Romanian Orthodox Church especially, have given numberless proofs of tolerance, if it is to use this inappropriate concept brought to us from the West."[35] This statement shows that the tolerance narrative implemented in 1945 had taken roots, and the rewriting of history were effective. In the twenty-five years since the publication of the first articles covering up the involvement of the Church in the Holocaust, any controversial aspect had been forgotten and the myth of a tolerant, loving, and harmonious East was promoted without any doubt.

The last article in the series dedicated to the topic of the Orthodox Church's theological position toward non-Christian religions written after the Second Vatican Council and published in *Ortodoxia* was entitled "The Redemption Work of God [*Iconomia*] in the view of the Orthodox Church." It was published in 1972. Although it mentions the interreligious dialogue, the text deals mostly with relations inside Christianity, pointing out the ways in which other denominations (Catholic, Lutheran, and Anglican particularly) could be part of the grace that springs from the Orthodox Church. As in previous articles, the approach adopted here is one of glorification of the Orthodox dogma, portrayed as the definite and unique truth, and of the Orthodox Church, the "Ark of the Covenant and the administrator of God's grace."[36] This last article is important because it offers a theological basis for a triumphalist view of the Church not only in relation to other non-Christian religions, but in relation to other Christian denominations.

The theological approach to Judaism, although it did not publicly express anti-Semitism, clearly promoted, behind its slogans of harmony and tolerance, disregard toward Judaism and a position of Orthodox superiority. In the articles published in *Ortodoxia* the Jews are often placed in the same category as the heretics. This position is also expressed several times in *Studii Teologice*, where Jews are depicted as heretics for whom prayers were needed in order for them to come to repentance and to the knowledge of truth.[37] In other places Jews are openly condemned for not accepting Jesus as the Messiah, although the tone is not as harsh as it was before and during the war.[38]

The myth of tolerance promoted in *Ortodoxia* can also be seen in *Studii Teologice* and in *BOR*. In 1953, an article entitled "Christianity and Patriotism," claims that "in the history of Orthodox Christianity's development one cannot see any racial persecutions, exterminations, and pogroms, common to all peoples possessed by the nationalist chauvinism."[39] In October 1980, Mircea Păcurariu published in *BOR* an article entitled "The Romanian Orthodox Church, the Servant of Peace in the History of the Romanian People." In it he brings together several myths developed under national Communism: the myth of Romanians' hospitality and goodness, the myth of the Church as never having advocated discrimination toward other religions, and the myth of the Romanian Orthodox Church as consistently tolerant. In the article, Păcurariu directly mentions the Jews as the beneficiaries of the Church's goodness and tolerance. A special section discussing the contribution of the Orthodox Church to the peace process in the twentieth century uses several themes of the 1945 whitewashing narrative. Any compromising information is ignored and the Church is presented as a brave defender of peace.[40]

In 1981 and 1982 *BOR* published two articles in which two far-right anti-Semitic personalities, Octavian Goga[41] and Metropolitan Nicolae Bălan,[42] are presented in a very favorable light. This was part of a large program of rehabilitation of the interwar far-right Orthodox nationalists. Goga's political activity, including anti-Semitic measures, is overlooked. The article about Metropolitan Bălan of Transylvania was written by Mircea Păcurariu, the author of one of the articles mentioned above. While in the previous article, Păcurariu avoided any mention of the Holocaust, in his portrayal of Bălan, he takes the opportunity to present the former metropolitan of Transylvania as a patriot and a savior of Jews: "We should mention the fact that during the war Metropolitan Nicolae, alongside other hierarchs, among them Patriarch Nicodim, raised their voice[s] against the persecution of Jews."[43] This important claim is not supported by any evidence: no concrete actions, no rescue efforts. Moreover, in the same vein as the 1945 cover-up campaign, any compromising information, including these individuals' anti-Semitism or links to the Iron Guard, is completely obliterated.

The myth of the Romanian Orthodox Church's favorable attitude toward Jews appeared one more time before the fall of Communism, in an article published in *BOR* in 1987 written by Bishop Vasile Târgovișteanu, the vice patriarch. The article marks the climax of the new Orthodox national Communism. Communist themes such as the harmony between the co-inhabitant nationalities/religions and the defense of peace are mixed with the myths of the Orthodox Church's tolerance toward all religions in Romania throughout history and its continuity on the Romanian territory since the time of the Dacians and Romans. The Communist language, full of hyperbolic imagery, can be seen even in the first sentence: "In the history of the world, the Romanian people excel as one of the most eloquent examples of stability and uninterrupted continuity in the geographic area of its birth and becoming."[44] The 1938 constitution is mentioned in the same sentence with the constitution of 1923 as "providing without discrimination equal political, national, economic, social, cultural, and confessional rights to all citizens of the country, no matter their ethnic, racial, or religious background." There is no mention at all of the revoking of citizenship and other discriminatory actions against Jews put in place in 1938 while Patriarch Miron Cristea was prime minister. While previous articles entirely overlooked Cristea's period, this one tries to whitewash it.

In hundreds of issues of the Church's central and regional journals, this is the first article in which the word "Holocaust" is directly mentioned in a Church journal: "During the holocaust [sic], which took place in the context of the Second World War, the Romanian people revealed its humanism and solidarity with the Jewish population threatened with extermination by the fascist menace. Despite many interventions and pressures of the Nazis on the Romanian government, the Romanians continued to treat the Jews with much humanness, giving them permission in many cases even to emigrate to Israel."[45]

The Communist discourse that denied any Romanian involvement in the Holocaust is obvious here. The false history presents Romanians as humane toward and concerned with the fate of Jews. The entire blame is laid on the Nazis (not the Germans). In the next paragraph Hitler's anti-Semitic policies in Eastern Europe are clearly mentioned, with a special attention given to the wearing of the yellow star. Neither here, nor in the rest of the article does the author mention the extermination process and the death camps, let alone the situation in Transnistria. Speaking about the implementation of the law imposing the wearing of the yellow star in Romania, the author acknowledges that after a few months the Romanian government abolished it "as is revealed in the documents exhibited at the Museum of the History of the Jewish Community of Romania."[46] Toward the end, the author mentions the Holocaust in Hungary, praising the Romanians for offering shelter to the Hungarian Jews. He does not give details about the way in which the Hungarian Jews perished or concrete details about how the Romanians helped the Hungarian Jews.

The articles published in the journals of the Romanian Orthodox Church during the Communist era carried forward the deceptive narrative of 1945 denying any Romanian and Orthodox involvement in the Holocaust. They presented the Church as always tolerant and hospitable toward minorities in general and Jews in particular. In the 1980s, in the context of increasing interest in the Holocaust, the Church again used elements of the 1945 campaign, which based on several positive (and in some case controversial) examples promoted the fiction of a Church that saved the Jews during the war. In parallel with this covering up of negative involvement in the Holocaust, a theological intolerance toward Judaism became visible in the articles commenting on the Nostra Aetate. This dualistic attitude toward Judaism and the Holocaust would become more relevant after the fall of Ceaușescu.

THE ROMANIAN ORTHODOX CHURCH AND NATIONAL COMMUNISM: REDISCOVERING THE INTERWAR ORTHODOX NATIONALISM AND THE EFFECT ON HOLOCAUST REMEMBRANCE

One of the first major Communist projects that reignited Orthodox nationalism was the canonization of several Romanian saints. This program was a means of emphasizing local Communism, of promoting Romanian identity in a country that was trying to shake off the yoke of Soviet influence. The process of sanctification started in 1950 and was finalized in 1955, the year in which the Soviet troops started to withdraw from Romania and two years after Stalin's death. The process was not easy and was at every step accompanied by the pretense that the USSR and the Russian Orthodox Church themselves were interested in the promotion of Romanian saints.

In 1954 the idea of Romanian saints' canonization and the advance of the new Orthodox nationalism acquired new strength. That year marked 450 years since the death of Stephen the Great, one of the most representative rulers in Romanian history, both for his political achievements in his war against the Ottomans and for his Orthodox ethos. The July 1954 issue of *BOR* was entirely dedicated to "450 years since the death of Stephen the Great." For the first time Stephen was called "the Great" and "the Saint."[47] Interestingly enough, Stephen would be canonized by the Church only after 1989, but the incipient steps in this process were made as early as 1954. Moreover, the idea of Stephen's celebration was a Communist state decision.[48] In 1954 the regime wanted to make a good impression on the Romanian people, as Stephen was a beloved historical figure among many Romanians.

Nevertheless, the Communists' avidity for popularity empowered Orthodox nationalism and their 1954 decision would have important effects in the years to come.

A second major step in the use of the Romanian Orthodox Church in the new nationalist narrative was the visit of Communist leaders, led by Nicolae Ceaușescu, the new general secretary of the Communist Party, to the Dealu Monastery in 1967. The event had a twofold importance. First, it marked an important step in the development of the myth of the medieval ruler Michael the Brave, who united Wallachia, Moldova, and Transylvania for few months in 1600–1601 in order to create an anti-Ottoman front. He was killed shortly after this endeavor and his head was buried at the Dealu Monastery, situated approximately eighty kilometers north of Bucharest. The new Communist narrative saw Michael as a great visionary who was the first to create a national and unitary Romania. Second, the event was important because it took place at an Orthodox monastery in the presence of the patriarch and other religious leaders. In his speech in front of the Communist leaders of the country, Patriarch Justinian made clear that the Romanian Orthodox Church was the national church.[49] The episode bears significant similarities to the case of Stephen the Great, when Communist authorities traveled to Putna in 1954 to give their approval for the process. The 1967 moment was important because it marked the beginning of Ceaușescu's use of the Church to lend legitimacy to his nationalism and his cultural revolution.

The myth of tolerance was increasingly promoted after 1965. The Jews were especially mentioned as benefiting from the Romanians' goodness and hospitability. This anachronistic and false narrative was pushed forward in parallel with the rehabilitation of many interwar nationalists. For example, in an article published in 1965 in *BOR*, Nicolae Iorga was commemorated and praised.[50] Killed by the Iron Guard, Iorga was known for his right-wing nationalism and anti-Semitism. Later rehabilitations were more telling about the return to the interwar rightwing nationalism. By 1981 even Octavian Goga, the promoter of the "Romania for Romanians" program, was praised in articles in *BOR*.[51] As prime minister (December 1937 through February 1938) Goga had passed the first major anti-Semitic laws in Romania. His anti-Semitism is not mentioned, the emphasis being placed on his literary activity. Although his political activity is neglected, his nationalist/religious poetry is revered and praised. Controversial persons, some of them clear promoters of anti-Semitism, such as former metropolitan of

Transylvania Nicolae Bălan,[52] the writer Alexandru Brătescu-Voinesti[53] (whose article "Communism" published in 1938, promoting strong anti-Semitism, is mentioned in chapter 1), Teodor Popescu,[54] and former Patriarch Miron Cristea,[55] were in stages rediscovered by the journals of the Church.

The Church's history was used to show the harmony between the medieval rulers and the Church, the implicit suggestion being that the collaboration of the Church with the authorities should be replicated by the Orthodox faithful. As the Orthodox faithful of the medieval age followed, respected, and even shed its blood for whoever was backed by the Church, the people living under Communist rule were taught to trust the authorities, whom the Orthodox Church legitimized. The Church's organization, ecclesiastical structure, and journals were all used to promote this new narrative, which was a mixture of Orthodox nationalism with Communist ideology. In this context the rehabilitation of interwar promoters of Orthodox nationalism was not an accident. Romanian national Communism during the Ceaușescu era slipped back to the fascist elements of the interwar and its use of rightwing prewar Orthodox nationalism is one of the clearest examples. This is why Romanian nationalism, especially since 1967, could be called an "Orthodox national Communism." The fact that the Church was placed at the heart of this Communist nationalist resurgence increased its prestige greatly.

The complicity between the Church and the Communist state when it came to the creation of a new nationalism is of great significance for Holocaust remembrance. A Church that returned to prewar nationalism, that instead of addressing such nationalism as the key factor for its problematic attitude toward Jews before and during the war had been rediscovering it and promoting it, would be less willing to acknowledge its mistakes and role in the Holocaust. The Communists were content with this turn of events as the Church's collaboration secured them much-needed validation in the eyes of the public. Without outright expressions of anti-Semitism, the Church was returning to its interwar rightwing nationalism. The dangers of the latent anti-Semitism that grew alongside the increasing rediscovery and rehabilitation of interwar Orthodox nationalist personalities would become obvious in the first years after the collapse of Communism. Although surprising for many, the outburst of anti-Semitism in 1990s' Romania did not come out of the blue. The ground for that outburst was prepared tacitly in the last decades of Ceaușescu's rule.

The relationship between the Romanian Orthodox Church and the Jewish community continued the tradition of religious harmony developed since 1945. This had a major effect on the memory of the Holocaust. For the sake of harmonious relations and under the pressure from the Communist regime, the Jewish community avoided any mention of the problematic involvement of the Church in the Holocaust. While the Romanian Orthodox Church contributed to the development of these amicable relations by refraining from open displays of anti-Semitism, it fostered an intolerant theology in which Orthodoxy was presented in a triumphalist way as the "Ark of the Covenant of God," the only way to salvation. At the same time it continued to promote the 1945 myth that the Church had been a savior of Jews and hid any compromising aspects about its involvement in the destruction of Romanian Jewry. Despite the efforts of the Communist authorities to present the two communities as enjoying friendly relations, tensions continued to exist. Cases such as the inquiry into the anti-Semitism of some verses of the Good Friday Lamentation, Patriarch Justinian's fury against the Zionists, and the letter about Ana Pauker that was disseminated in Orthodox circles are all examples supporting this argument.

NOTES

1. Dumitru Stavrache, *Mitropolitul Visarion Puiu: documente din pribegie (1944–1963)* [Metropolitan Visarion Puiu: Documents from Wandering] (Paşcani, Romania: Moldopress, 2002), 22–23.

2. See Ion Popa, "Visarion Puiu, the Former Romanian Orthodox Metropolitan (Archbishop) of Transnistria—a Historical Study on His Life and Activity before, during and after the Holocaust (1935–1964)" *Holocaust. Study & Research* 6, no. 1 (2013): 182–203.

3. Gerald J. Bobango, *The Romanian Orthodox Episcopate of America: The First Half Century, 1929–1979* (Jackson, MI: Romanian-American Heritage Center, 1979), 196–198.

4. CNSAS, DIE 142, Privitor la Visarion Puiu, "O lămurire pe intelesul tuturor românilor ortodocşi din SUA," letter written by Visarion Puiu and sent by DIE from France on 17 May 1956, 180–181.

5. CNSAS D14673, Culte şi Secte după 23 August 1944 [Religions and Sects after 23 August 1944], "Nota, sursa 'Mihai', 7 Noiembrie 1945," 267.

6. Stefano Pitrelli, Giovanni Del Vecchio, "Storia e memoria/I fascicoli dei lager nazisti. Non aprite l'Olocausto. L'archivio della Shoah resta chiuso: l'Italia non ha ancora ratificato gli accordi," *L'Espresso*, 1 June 2007, https://groups.google.com/forum/#!topic/skypeful-blog/ezudVFebVqk.

7. The samosfeats were a dissident Ukrainian Orthodox group in the diaspora. See Sorin Petcu, *Samosfeaţii*, March 2009, http://www.ortodoxia.de/html/samosfeatii.html.

8. CNSAS, DIE 142, "O Lămurire pe intelesul tuturor Românilor Ortodocşi din SUA," 180–181.

9. See Popa, "Visarion Puiu," 198.

10. Radu Ioanid, "The Pogrom of Bucharest, 21–23 January 1941," *Holocaust and Genocide Studies* 6, no. 4 (1991): 377; see also CNSAS D10419, Procesul Masacrului de la Iași [The Trial of the Iași Massacre], 7.

11. CNSAS, DIE 82, Privitor la Valerian Trifa, "Nota din 14.05.1972, Urgent," 37.

12. Ibid., "The Romanian Orthodox Episcopate of America, Office of the Bishop, November 26, 1973. Informative Bulletin: The Visit of Nicolae Ceaușescu to the USA," 196–199.

13. Ibid., "Telegrama Fulger, 17.12.1973," 190; see also Raphael Blumenthal, "Bishop under Inquiry on Atrocity Link," *New York Times*, 26 December 1973, http://select.nytimes.com/gst/abstract.html?res=9E0DE7D71731E63BBC4E51DFB4678388669EDE&scp=18&sq=trifa&st=p.

14. CNSAS, DIE 82, "Nota din 23.01.1973," 148.

15. Ibid., "Nota din 29.04.1972," 67.

16. Ibid., "Nota No 585/N, 114/C din 27.04.1972, Urgent," 36.

17. Ibid., 67.

18. George Dugan, "Jews Occupy Building and Urge Ouster of Prelate," *New York Times*, 15 October 1976, http://select.nytimes.com/gst/abstract.html?res=9E06EFDE173CE336A057 56C1A9669D946790D6CF&scp=28&sq=trifa&st=p; see also George Dugan, "Rumanian Prelate Denounced by Jews," *New York Times*, 9 October 1976, http://select.nytimes.com/gst/abstract.html?res=9E00EEDB1F3AE03BBC4153DFB667838D669EDE&scp=5&sq=trifa&st=p.

19. Kenneth Briggs, "Rumania Archbishop Loses Council Seat," *New York Times*, 5 February 1977, http://select.nytimes.com/gst/abstract.html?res=9F06E1DA103BE334BC4D53D FB466838C669EDE&scp=26&sq=trifa&st=p.

20. See Ari Goldman, "Valerian Trifa, an Archbishop with a Fascist Past, Dies at 72," *New York Times*, 29 January 1987, http://www.nytimes.com/1987/01/29/obituaries/valerian-trifa-an-archbishop-with-a-fascist-past-dies-at-72.html?scp=1&sq=trifa&st=nyt.

21. CNSAS, DIE 82, "Raport No 113/0024433 Privind pe Viorel [Valerian] Trifa, 21 Octombrie 1971, Strict Secret," 21.

22. Ibid., "Nota cu Privire la Activitatea lui 'LUNGU', 14.10.1972, Strict Secret," 1.

23. See Gerald Steinacher, *Nazis on the Run: How Hitler's Henchmen Fled Justice* (New York: Oxford University Press, 2011), 159–161.

24. See Claudiu Pădurean, "Spovedania de sub Patrafirul Securității" [Confession in the Securitate Confessional], *România Liberă*, 20 October 2006, http://www.romanialibera.ro /actualitate/locale/spovedania-de-sub-patrafirul-Securității-53169.html.

25. See Comitetul de Redacție [Editorial Board], "Partea Oficială. Lucrarile Sfântului Sinod din 16-17 Decembrie" [Official Part. The Proceedings of the Holy Synod from 16–17 December], *BOR* 80, nos. 1–2 (January–February 1962): 176; see also the vague reference to the document on anti-Semitism in Alexandru Ionescu, "Lucrările Celei de-a Treia Adunări Generale a Consiliului Mondial al Bisericilor" [The Proceedings of the Third General Assembly of the World Council of Churches], *BOR* 80, nos. 3–4 (March–April 1962): 293.

26. Barbu, Gr. Ionescu, "A Treia Sesiune a Conciliului al II-lea de la Vatican" [The Third Session of the Second Vatican Council], *Ortodoxia* 16, no. 4 (October–December 1964): 471–503.

27. Ibid., 482.

28. Emilian Vasilescu, "Declarații asupra Religiilor Necreștine" [Declarations on Non-Christian Religions], *Ortodoxia* 19, no. 1 (January–March 1967): 138.

29. Ibid., 140.

30. Ibid., 141, 142.

31. N. Vîlcu, "Romano-Catolicismul şi religiile necreştine după documentele conciliului al II-lea de la Vatican" [Roman-Catholicism and the Non-Christian Religions According to the Documents of the Second Vatican Council], *Ortodoxia* 20, no. 3 (July–September 1968): 396.

32. Ibid., 404–405.

33. Corneliu Sîrbu, "Poziţii principale ale Ortodoxiei faţă de celelate religii" [The Main Considerations of Orthodoxy toward Other Religions], *Ortodoxia* 21, no. 4 (October–December 1969): 510.

34. Emilian Vasilescu, "Preocupări în teologia ortodoxă română în legătură cu religiile necreştine" [Considerations in Romanian Orthodox Theology Regarding Non-Christian Religions], *Ortodoxia* 23, no. 1 (January–March 1971): 34.

35. Ibid., 36.

36. Comisia InterOrtodoxă Pregatitoare a Sfântului şi Marelui Sinod, "Iconomia în Biserica Ortodoxă" The Redemption Work of God [Iconomia] in the view of the Orthodox Church], *Ortodoxia* 24, no. 2 (April–June 1972): 289.

37. Ioan Ghe. Chirvasie, "Pentru cei păcătoşi se roaga biserica" [For the Sinners, the Church Is Praying], *Studii Teologice,* series 2, vol. 10, nos. 9–10 (November–December 1958): 561–562.

38. Teodor Popescu, "Privire istorică asupra schismelor, ereziilor şi sectelor," [Historical Overview on Schisms, Heresies and Sects], *Studii Teologice* series 2, vol. 2, nos. 7–8 (September–October 1950): 353–354.

39. Diac. M. Chialda, "Creştinism şi patriotism" [Christianity and Patriotism], *Studii Teologice,* series 2, vol. 5, nos. 1–2 (January–February 1953): 68.

40. Mircea Păcurariu, "Biserica Ortodoxă Română, slujitoare a păcii în istoria poporului român" [The Romanian Orthodox Church, a Servant of Peace in the History of the Romanian People], *BOR* 98, nos. 9–10 (September–October 1980): 120–147.

41. Gheorghe Cunescu, "Octavian Goga—la centenarul naşterii poetului" [Octavian Goga - A Centenary since the Poet's Birth], *BOR* 99, nos. 3–4 (March–April 1981): 323–334.

42. Mircea Păcurariu, "Mitropolitul Nicolae Bălan al Ardealului. La 100 de ani de la naştere" [Metropolitan Bălan of Transylvania. One Hundred Years since His Birth], *BOR* 100, nos. 5–6 (May–June 1982): 494–518.

43. Ibid., 511.

44. Bishop/Vice Patriarch Vasile Targovisteanu, "Spiritul de colaborare şi frăţietate dintre poporul român şi naţionalităţile conlocuitoare" [The Spirit of Collaboration and Brotherhood between the Romanian People and the Co-Inhabitant Nationalities], *BOR* 105, nos. 5–6 (May–June 1987): 5.

45. Ibid., 9, 10.

46. Ibid., 10

47. See the collection of articles under the title "Stefan cel Mare şi Sfânt, Binecredincios Domn şi Apărător al Dreptei Credinţe" [Stephen the Great and the Saint, Faithful Ruler and Defender of the True Religion], *BOR* 72, no. 7 (July 1954): 700–740.

48. "450 de ani de la moartea lui Stefan cel Mare. Expunerea Acad. Prof. Constantinescu-Iaşi în Sedinţa Comemorativă de la Ateneul R.P.R" [450 Years since the Death of Stephen the Great. The Speech of Academician Professor Constantinescu-Iaşi at the Commemorative Meeting Held at the R.P.R Athenaeum], *BOR* 72, no. 7 (July 1954): 697.

49. "Vizita conducătorilor de partid şi de stat la Mănăstirea Dealu," [The Visit of the Party and State Leaders to the Dealu Monastery], *BOR* 85, nos. 5–6 (May–June 1967): 517–521.

50. Nicolae Stefănescu, "Nicolae Iorga istoric al Bisericii Ortodoxe Române. 23 de Ani de la Tragica Sa Moarte" [Nicolae Iorga, Historian of the Romanian Orthodox Church. 23 Years since His Tragic Death], *BOR* 83, no. 11–12 (November–December 1965): 1010–1032.

51. Cunescu, *Octavian Goga*, 323–334.

52. See Păcurariu, "Mitropolitul Nicolae Bălan al Ardealului," 494–518.

53. Alexandru Bratescu-Voinești's short text "Puiul" became part of the secondary-level curricula in Romania in the 1980s.

54. In 1979–1980, several articles written by Teodor Popescu were published in the main journal of the Church.

55. Nicolae, Mitropolitul Banatului [the Metropolitan of Banat], "Primul Patriarh al Bisericii Ortodoxe Române" [The First Patriarch of the Romanian Orthodox Church], *BOR* 94, nos. 1–2 (January–February 1976): 164–167. It should be noted that the article does not mention Cristea's name in the title. His anti-Semitism and other controversial aspects of his political career were kept quiet.

8

NATIONALISM, ANTI-SEMITISM, AND THE ROMANIAN ORTHODOX CHURCH AFTER 1989

Understanding the Context of Holocaust Memory's Reemergence in Postcommunist Romania

THE FALL OF THE CEAUŞESCU regime in December 1989 sparked a major change in the building of Holocaust memory in Romania. If before 1989 the Romanian involvement in the Shoah was entirely denied, after 1989 scholars inside and outside Romania challenged this myth. The Holocaust debate that followed led to the creation, in 2003, of the Elie Wiesel International Commission on the Holocaust in Romania. How the commission came into existence is suggestive of the debates that took place in Romania after the fall of Communism and of the role of international politics.

In 2003, Ion Iliescu, the president of Romania, educated in Moscow and a member of the Communist apparatus prior to 1989, declared to an Israeli newspaper that it was impossible to accuse the Romanian people and Romanian society of the crimes committed on Antonescu's orders.[1] This statement fit what other Romanian officials, such as the culture minister Răzvan Teodorescu, said: that there had been no Holocaust in Romania.[2] Teodorescu's declaration generated a strong reaction from the state of Israel, which recalled its ambassador in protest and called for the creation of a commission to study the Holocaust in Romania. At a time when Romania was attempting to join the European Union and NATO, and facing this international pressure, Iliescu agreed to create the Elie Wiesel Commission. The *Final Report* of the commission was issued at the end of 2004 and was publicly accepted by the Romanian president and government. It concluded that there had been clear Romanian involvement in the Holocaust and that between 280,000 and 380,000 Romanian and Ukrainian Jews died in territories under Romanian control, most of them in Transnistria.[3] Ion Antonescu's policies against Jews were also analyzed and highlighted.

The Holocaust debate that has taken place in Romania since 1990 has placed many individuals and institutions involved in the destruction of Romanian Jewry under scrutiny, but the Romanian Orthodox Church has successfully avoided formal investigation. This was due to several factors, such as the lack of knowledge about the actions of the Church during the Holocaust and the Church's promotion of the cover-up developed since 1945. Contrary to the experience of Western Christian institutions after the Holocaust, the Romanian Orthodox Church's whitewashing effort was not challenged from within. At the same time, the unchanged amicable relations between the Romanian Orthodox Church, the Romanian Jewish community, and the state of Israel helped the Church avoid a proper analysis of its actions during the war.

The reemergence of Holocaust memory in postcommunist Romania was decisively influenced by nationalism and by the revival of anti-Semitism. The post-1989 position of the Church toward its wartime past was paradoxical: on the one hand, it promoted similar elements of Orthodox nationalism that were at the basis of the Holocaust in Romania and, on the other hand, it presented itself as a savior of Jews during the Second World War.

THE ROMANIAN ORTHODOX CHURCH AND THE JEWISH COMMUNITY OF ROMANIA AFTER THE FALL OF COMMUNISM

The Romanian Orthodox Church and the Jewish community experienced different challenges after the fall of Ceaușescu. The Romanian Orthodox Church emerged from the Communist era with its prestige untouched. It generally avoided any scrutiny about its collaboration with the Communist regime and became increasingly vocal in the social, political, and educational life of the country. The Jewish community, on the other hand, although marked by its decrease in number as a consequence of the massive emigrations in the 1950s and 1960s, fought bravely to establish a proper Holocaust memory, in which the Romanian involvement in the Shoah had to be acknowledged. It was precisely as a result of these efforts that the Elie Wiesel Commission was created and its *Final Report* was publicly acknowledged in 2004. The two religious communities' friendly relations have had a great impact on the attitude of the Romanian Orthodox Church toward Holocaust memory.

The Romanian Orthodox Church after the fall of Communism

For many years after the fall of Communism, the Romanian Orthodox Church was first in polls researching which institution Romanians trusted the most. The figures were outstanding, with all major polls suggesting that between 80 percent and 90 percent of the population believed the Orthodox Church was the most trusted Romanian institution.[4] These numbers have fallen, but according to 2013 figures, 66 percent of the population still has faith in the Church. Patriarch Teoctist, who was elected in 1986, headed the Romanian Orthodox Church until 2007. His silence in relation to the demolition of Orthodox churches in the 1980s, and his open support for Ceaușescu during the violent protests in Timișoara in December 1989[5] (events that extended in the following week to Bucharest, leading to the Communist leader's fleeing and his eventual execution on December 25, 1989), led to his retirement immediately after the dictator's fall. For three months the Romanian Orthodox Church was led by a patriarchal deputy comprised of three metropolitans, one bishop, and one vice bishop.[6] In April 1990, for reasons that are not entirely clear, Teoctist returned as patriarch, remaining in that position until his death.[7] This had great consequences for the Church's position on its Communist past and on the Holocaust. In 2007, after Teoctist's death, Daniel, the metropolitan of Moldova, was elected as the new patriarch.

After the fall of Communism there was a boom of new churches being built and the attendance of religious services grew in comparison to the Communist period, although not as much as expected. According to the polls conducted after 1990 more than 85 percent of Romanians believe in God (some more recent polls even put forward an astonishing figure of 98 percent),[8] but only 19 percent attend weekly services.[9] Priests continued to be paid by the state.[10] A 1992 decision of the Holy Synod asked the state to continue with this practice, which dates back to the creation of modern Romania, and the state complied.[11] The state also finances other Church projects. Since 2007, fierce debates took place in the Romanian and international media over plans to build one of the largest cathedrals in Eastern Europe. The Romanian People's Salvation Cathedral, which is to be built in the center of Bucharest, will cost an estimate of 500 million euros (1 billion according to *Le Figaro*).[12] According to a law passed by the lower chamber of the Romanian parliament in 2007, the government would pay half of the final bill of the construction.[13]

In the context of dire economic conditions, many organizations have objected to the cathedral being paid from the state budget, contending that the Church is wealthy enough to support itself, but no decision on this issue has been made as of this writing.[14] The Orthodox Church has retrieved many of its properties confiscated during the Communist era, has a strong media presence (radio and television) throughout Romania, and in many regions of the country local archbishoprics own or have assets in successful businesses.

The Romanian Orthodox Church has used its prestige to consolidate its strong position in politics and society. From the important sessions of the Romanian Parliament to ceremonies in small villages, such as the opening of the school academic year, Church representatives are active participants in these events. The Church also regained the right, taken away during the Communist era, to hold religious education classes in public schools and has been often consulted on political decisions in matters such as abortion, homosexuality, sexual education, and legalization of prostitution.[15] Often the Church's position on such problems expresses its conservatism.[16]

Although the Holy Synod has decided several times since the fall of Communism, especially in election campaigns, that the Church should stay out of politics,[17] in reality it often does just the opposite. As during the interwar period, lower clergy and theology students tend to back whatever political party suits them.[18] This was especially the case during the 2000s, with the grassroots support given to Gheoghe Becali's New Generation Party (Partidul Noua Generatie, PNG), a rightwing, anti-Semitic political organization. On the other hand, members of the Church hierarchy have often openly supported various political organizations and/or personalities. The 2014 presidential elections and the controversies surrounding the support of the Church for Victor Ponta, the Social Democratic Party candidate, are discussed in the introduction of this book.

In many cases members of the Church hierarchy tried to use their links with political parties to promote their position inside the Church. For example, the links of Archbishop Teodosie of Constanta with leaders of the Social Democratic Party, and his use of these links to promote his ecclesiastical career have been much debated in local and national media.[19] As during the interwar period, the postcommunist years have seen a marked distinction between the lower clergy and the leadership of the Romanian Orthodox Church. For example, while the leadership of the Church and the Holy Synod have refrained from openly promoting anti-Semitism, at the local level many monks and clergy have promoted and encouraged it.

Since 1990 the Romanian Orthodox Church has displayed two clear tendencies, visible in the official declarations of the hierarchy and in the articles published in the journals of the Church. First, the Church has presented itself as a victim of Communism, hiding the compromising collaboration of its hierarchy with the old regime. The second major feature has been its emphasis on and promotion of Orthodox nationalism. Both these tendencies were visible in the declaration of the Holy Synod issued a few days after the fall of Ceaușescu. The declaration emphasized the victimization narrative: "Given the regime of limited liberties imposed by the dictatorship and terror upon the entire people, our Church was subject to pressures and limitations. . . . We are determined to rebuild the sanctuaries of our ancestral history, churches and monasteries, victims of Ceaușescu's bulldozers."[20] The declaration presented the Church as a victim of Ceaușescu's regime but did not mention the fact that the demolition of churches was done with the accord of the Church leadership. The nationalist message, which grew constantly in the 1990s and 2000s, was highlighted when the Synod said, "Although we were not able to overcome them [the limitations imposed by the Communist regime], with perseverance and patience we strived to keep alive our people's consciousness [conștiință de neam] and to promote, as far as we could, its immortal values."[21] By this declaration, the Holy Synod reminded its faithful that the Church continued to be, even in the hard circumstances of Communism, the keeper of the people's conscience, the core of national identity.

The Jewish community of Romania after the fall of Communism

The Jewish community started, immediately after the fall of Ceaușescu, a sustained process of unveiling the events of the Holocaust. This suggests that the narrative it supported during the Communist era was imposed from the outside and that, as soon as the political conditions allowed it, the Jewish community began to repair the damage. In the first years of the 1990s, the Hasefer Publishing House (under the jurisdiction of the Federation of Jewish Communities) published dozens of books and archival material analyzing the involvement of the Romanians in the Holocaust. Its activity generated an important academic debate and was one of the significant factors that led to the Elie Wiesel Commission's *Final Report* in 2004. Especially notable here is the activity of Lya Benjamin, who, through her books and published archival material, was one of the driving historians inside Romania fighting this battle.

Moses Rosen continued to be the chief rabbi and the president of the Federation of Jewish Communities of Romania (Federația Comunităților Evreiești din România, FCER) until he died in 1994. The fact that the campaign of publication of materials analyzing the Romanian involvement in the Holocaust started under his leadership shows that, after 1989, he grasped the opportunity to address the past and that his silence during the Communist regime was generated by the political context rather than by unwillingness. The memoir he published in 1990 shows that his stand on the Holocaust, at the time, was still significantly influenced by the Communist narrative. For example, he believed that Antonescu deported the Jews just to impress Hitler, and that he "did not, like Hitler, set out to kill Jews."[22] Rosen also seemed to have little knowledge about the involvement of Romanians in the Iași pogrom and about the involvement of the Church in legitimizing state policies.[23]

In 1994, after the death of Moses Rosen, Nicolae Cajal, an internationally reputed scientist and physician, was elected president of the FCER. Cajal was the vice president of the Romanian Academy from 1990 to 1994 and was a member of prestigious international organizations such as the British Royal Society of Medicine and the New York Academy of Sciences. After 1994 the post of the chief rabbi was held by several foreign rabbis, among them Menachem Hacohen. Since 2012 Rafael Shaffer has served as chief rabbi of Romania. Born in Arad (western Romania), he emigrated to Israel with his family at the beginning of the 1970s.[24] In 2005 Dr. Aurel Vainer, a reputed economist and honorary member of the Romanian Academy of Sciences, was chosen as the president of the FCER.[25]

Because most of the Jews who survived the war left Romania during Communism, there was no major wave of emigration after 1989. According to some accounts 20,000 Jews were in Romania in 1990.[26] More than half of them chose to emigrate in the coming years, the approximately 9,000 who remained adapting to the new situation. Some of them became important historians, linguists, artists, and politicians in the new Romania, their achievements being sometimes outstanding. Other Jews came back to Romania and started successful businesses.

According to the official declaration of the FCER, the main goals of the institution are to promote the involvement of all Jews from Romania in the community's activities; to secure the continuity of religious services; to preserve, maintain, and modernize the historic and sacred patrimony of the community; to continue the publication of local and central Jewish journals; to support the Hasefer Publishing House; to promote good relations with the Jews whose roots are in Romania; and to fight anti-Semitism and Holocaust denial.[27] After 1989, the Jewish Community of Romania became a guardian of the correct memorialization of the Holocaust, a mission facilitated after 2005 by the creation of the Elie Wiesel National Institute for the Study of Holocaust in Romania (Institutul Național Pentru Studierea Holocaustului din România Elie Wiesel, INSHREW).[28]

NATIONALISM, ANTI-SEMITISM, AND THE ROMANIAN ORTHODOX CHURCH AFTER 1989

Immediately after the fall of Communism a wave of strong nationalism swept through Romania. This resurgence of rightwing nationalism was not a surprise. The basis for its reemergence was laid by the late Ceaușescu era, which rediscovered and rehabilitated interwar Romanian nationalists.[29] It seems that Ceaușescu even intended to fully rehabilitate Ion Antonescu, and a statue of him was to be erected in front of the People's Palace in Bucharest.[30] The anti-Semitism of such figures, although not mentioned directly, was in the air, awaiting the proper moment to be rediscovered and unleashed.

Katherine Verdery, in her excellent analysis of post-Ceaușescu Romania, suggests a link between interwar and the postcommunist nationalism. She argues that the effectiveness of the nationalism promoted in Eastern Europe after the First World War did not die out with the emergence of Communism. It remodeled and reinvented itself, retaining most of its initial elements.[31] The national idea from the interwar period was kept alive "despite the Party's formal disapproval of it."[32] Verdery also highlights the effectiveness of the us–them dichotomy in the nationalistic discourse of 1990s Romania, pointing out that "the pervasive us–them split precluded legitimation, but it also did far more: it formed people's very identities." She also suggests that after 1989, the enemy represented by Communism had to be replaced by something else. "As a group of east European social scientists visiting Washington in fall 1991 told their host, 'We had to find a new enemy.' That enemy, I suggest, became 'the other others'—other nationalities who existed in greater or smaller numbers in every one of these states."[33]

The nationalism of the 1990s was well prefigured in the events of the year 1990. The new national day of postcommunist Romania was voted as December 1, a celebration of December 1, 1918 when Greater Romania was created. This return to the narrative of the "glorious" Greater Romania of the interwar period also meant, to some extent, a return to the interwar attitude toward minorities. This involved not only tensions between the Romanians and Hungarians, the largest minority in the country, which led to the clashes in Târgu Mureș in March 1990,[34] but also tensions between the majority Orthodox and the minority religions in Romania throughout the 1990s. The failings of the Romanian state to create a climate of legal protection and reciprocal respect was continuously mentioned in US State Department reports,[35] as well as in the reports of European institutions.[36]

Far-right parties like the Greater Romania Party (Partidul România Mare, PRM) or the New Generation Party (Partidul Noua Generație, PNG) gained increasing support from the public. Overtly anti-Semitic, these parties clashed several times with the Jewish community and INSHREW over their stand on the Holocaust. Although Vadim Tudor, the leader of the PRM, mixed religion with politics in his messages, there was no clear support of the Romanian Orthodox Church for his party. The same thing cannot be said about the PNG. Its leader, Gheorghe Becali, the owner of one the most successful football clubs in Romania, Steaua Bucharest, portrayed himself as a true Orthodox, used religious language extensively, and spent large amounts of money on building new churches and repairing Romanian monasteries on Mount Athos. PNG openly promoted the Iron Guard ideology, with an emphasis on extreme nationalism and Orthodox Christianity. Although PNG has not been as active on the Romanian political scene as it once was, the movement created by Becali furthered the formation of ultra-conservative Orthodox groups. They are often called the Orthodoxists, and are very active on the internet and in the social media sphere.[37] One of their best-known online journals, Rost, is a platform for anti-Semitism and Holocaust denial, both often openly promoted, an aspect that has triggered the special attention of INSHREW.[38]

Far-right parties and the Orthodoxists promote anti-Semitism that goes hand in hand with the denial of the Holocaust, or with comparative trivialization. Most often this discourse minimizes the number of victims of the Holocaust and/or compares it with the "greater" number of victims of Communism in what Michael Shafir brands "competitive martyrology."[39] The Judeo-Bolshevik propaganda has again resurfaced. The presence of Jews in the early Romanian Communist apparatus has also been discussed, the general discourse of such groups being that Communism, with all its ills, was brought to Romania by the Jews.[40] Influential anti-Semitic books such as *Mein Kampf* and *The Protocols of the Elders of Zion* have been published in Romania by Holocaust deniers.[41] Access to new technology also means that this propaganda can be spread more easily, an aspect noted in some research.[42]

The Romanian Orthodox Church has been no stranger to these developments. On the contrary, as soon as Communism collapsed the Church reinforced the nationalist message. In the first issue of the main journal of the Church, immediately after the fall of Ceaușescu, the nationalist themes promoted in the last years of the Communist rule were emphasized.[43] In a careful research of all the issues of the Church's journals before and after 1989, one is struck by the continuity of this nationalist discourse. Strong language, reminiscent of the interwar extreme nationalist Orthodox propaganda, has been disseminated in articles published in these journals. This language speaks of a war against the Romanian people, the danger to the very existence of the Romanian people represented by the "Magyar Greek Catholics" (although most of the Greek Catholics were ethnic Romanians, the interwar and war prejudice that saw any Catholic as a Hungarian, resurfaced during this period), or by the sects. Dumitru Stăniloae, who has been held in high regard by the Church[44] and who became a member of the Romanian Academy in 1992, published an article in the first issue of *BOR* after the fall of Ceaușescu highlighting the link between Orthodoxy and Romanian ethnicity (a concept harking back to the interwar debate about Românianism): "This is how the difference of faith produces an abolition of the unity of the people, of its fundamental spirituality. When the historical contexts produce the amalgamation of other peoples with the main people, this brings about an abolition of the spiritual identity of the people itself. This could lead to the destruction of the Romanian people."[45]

On close reading, it is obvious that this quotation contains the major traces of the ideology that was responsible for the Holocaust in Romania. Stăniloae identifies Orthodoxy with the very essence of what it is to be a

Romanian, but he does not stop there. He speaks in terms of annihilation of the Romanian people by the others, and by "others" he means other ethnic and religious groups. He also brings forward concepts like "the unity of the people" and "the identity of the people," which would allegedly be destroyed by allowing an amalgamation with others. The article primarily targets the Greek Catholics, the main adversaries of the Romanian Orthodox Church at the beginning of the 1990s, but Stăniloae's declaration shows a larger tendency of enmity toward anyone who was not Orthodox. At the end he declares: "Let us not lose this unity as nobody knows what political hardships the future will bring! And if we lose even this unity, with what else will be able to sustain our existence as a special people?"[46]

Stăniloae was revered on the pages of *BOR*.[47] Nevertheless, he was not the only theologian with a strong nationalist discourse promoted in the main journal of the Church. In the first part of the 1990s, editions of Church journals opened with articles written by well-known anti-Semites like Nichifor Crainic[48] and Teodor Popescu.[49] The selection of articles highlights the attitude of the Church at the time: emphasis on Orthodoxy as the basis of Românianism, but avoidance of direct expressions of anti-Semitism.

The process of canonization also suggests the nationalism of the Romanian Orthodox Church after 1989. This process started in 1950 in the context of the Communist authorities' decision to promote national Communism. Several saints were canonized in 1955. Although the name of Stephen the Great was considered for canonization in the 1950s, the proposal did not come to fruition. After 1989 the Orthodox Church restarted the process. Stephen was proposed for canonization in 1992 alongside the medieval monk Daniil Sihastrul and the medieval ruler Constantin Brancoveanu.[50] The proposals were approved in June 1992. The ceremonies organized to celebrate Stephen's canonization were an occasion to reiterate the message that Romania was an Orthodox country, and the link between Stephen, the nation, and the Church were emphasized.[51]

Although the Orthodox Church played an essential role in the extreme nationalism of the 1990s, it kept away from openly promoting anti-Semitism. This has several explanations, which are more carefully looked at in chapter 9. The Church continued the tradition of good relations with the Jewish community and with the state of Israel; its open involvement in the promotion of anti-Semitism would have put these relations at risk. The avoidance of direct expressions of anti-Semitism can also be explained in terms of the

Orthodox Church's position on Holocaust memory. After the fall of Communism the Church continued to present itself as always tolerant toward Jews and to hide its involvement in the Holocaust; open promotion of anti-Semitism would have compromised this image and awakened the dark monsters of the past.

STRUGGLING WITH HOLOCAUST DENIAL: THE POLITICAL AND ACADEMIC DEBATE ON THE ROMANIAN INVOLVEMENT IN THE HOLOCAUST

Holocaust memory reemerged in postcommunist Romania in a very complex context, defined by a strong nationalism that continued the nationalist narrative developed under Communism. Almost all political parties espoused this nationalism in one form or another and used it for political gain. As Randolph Braham points out, after "many years, in Romania, as elsewhere in the former Soviet bloc nations, the Holocaust sunk in the Orwellian black hole of history." It reemerged during the worsening of Hungarian-Romanian relations and the rehabilitation of marshal Ion Antonescu.[52]

After 1989, a battle between those defending Antonescu, and those condemning him as a war criminal took place in academic circles. Although Romanian involvement and the role of Ion Antonescu in the Holocaust were politically acknowledged in 2004, the *Final Report* of the Elie Wiesel International Commission on the Holocaust in Romania failed to generate a wide debate. Alexandru Florian, the director of INSHREW, attributes this phenomenon to the fact that Romanian society was reluctant to acknowledge the mistakes of the past, especially in the context of more than fourteen years of non-involvement propaganda since 1990.[53] As late as 2007, three years after the issuance of the *Final Report*, some modern European history professors in Constanta still denied Romanian involvement, the role of Antonescu, or even the number of Jewish victims of the Holocaust. Many Romanians still did not know the involvement of their country in the Holocaust; according to a survey done by INSHREW in 2007, 54 percent of the respondents said that the Holocaust was an "extermination of the Jews by the Germans," and only 28 percent said that the event took place in Romania. Eleven percent said that Ion Antonescu was responsible for the Holocaust in Romania, while 79 percent thought that responsibility lay with the Nazi government. Only 6 percent declared themselves interested in the topic of the Holocaust, about 22 percent knew that there was a Holocaust memorial day in Romania, and only 10 people knew which day it was.[54] The results to the same survey were not significantly different in 2010. Sixty-one percent said that the Holocaust was the "extermination of the Jews by the Germans" and 32 percent that the Holocaust took place in Romania. Knowledge about Ion Antonescu's role seemed to have increased: 52 percent said that Antonescu was responsible for the Holocaust in Romania. But 92 percent still believed that responsibly for the Holocaust in Romania was shared by the Nazi government too.[55]

In postcommunist Romania public expressions of anti-Semitism and Holocaust denial became more visible and aggressive. The desecration of Jewish cemeteries was a common experience throughout the 1990s and it was noted regularly in international reports.[56] Even after the publication of the *Final Report* in 2004, international reports mentioned Jewish cemeteries being vandalized and public expressions of anti-Semitism.[57] The promotion of Holocaust denial did not end in 2004. As Alexandru Florian demonstrates in an article published in 2009, Holocaust denial and anti-Semitism remained widespread in the Romanian media.[58] Scandals about high-ranking officials or important institutions that denied the Romanian involvement in the Holocaust continued to make headlines. In 2011, Dan Sova, a Romanian Socialist MP, who would later become the minister for infrastructure projects (2012–2014), said in a TV interview that there was no Holocaust in Romania and that only a few dozen people were killed in the Iași pogrom.[59] In 2010 the Romanian Central Bank decided to issue special coins commemorating the five patriarchs of the Romanian Orthodox Church, despite protests from USHMM and INSHREW.[60] On February 14, 2013, the Romanian Academy was involved in a great scandal as, at one of its public meetings, the entire audience applauded at the end of a speech during which the Romanian involvement in the Holocaust was denied.[61]

In such a context, the position of the Romanian Orthodox Church is of extreme importance. The way in which the Church relates to Judaism, anti-Semitism, and the events of the Holocaust can have far-reaching effects in Romanian society. Its prestige among the populace and its political influence could be factors in helping society to become more aware of these problems and in starting a process of healing. As a religious institution, which puts the seeking of truth, the confession of guilt, and the concept of renewal at the core of its teachings, the Church could become the main driving force for true reconciliation with the past and for mutual ethnic and religious respect in Romania.

NOTES

1. See Ha'aretz staff and Associated Press, "Romanian President Backtracks on Holocaust Remarks," *Ha'aretz*, 27 July 2003, http://www.haaretz.com/print-edition/news/romanian -president-backtracks-on-holocaust-remarks-1.95414.

2. Michael Shafir, "Romania's Torturous Road to Facing Collaboration," in *Collaboration with the Nazis: Public Discourse after the Holocaust*, ed. Roni Stauber (London: Routledge, 2011), 267.

3. Tuvia Friling, Radu Ioanid, and Mihai Ionescu, eds., *The Final Report of the Elie Wiesel Commission for the Study of the Holocaust in Romania* (Bucharest: Polirom, 2005), 179.

4. Gabriel Bejan, "De ce scade încrederea Românilor în Biserică?" [Why Is the Romanians' Trust in the Church Going Down?], *România Liberă*, 18 April 2012, http://www .romanialibera.ro/opinii/editorial/de-ce-scade-increderea-romanilor-in-biserica-261025 .html.

5. See Harsan, "Cumpăna patriarhului," *România Liberă*, 2 August 2007. See also Michael Bourdeaux, "Patriarch Teoctist, Ceaușescu-supporting Head of the Romanian Church Who Survived the Dictator's Downfall," *The Guardian*, 6 August 2007, http://www.theguardian .com/news/2007/aug/07/guardianobituaries.religion.

6. Comitetul de Redacție [Editorial Board], "Sedințele extraordinare ale Sfântului Sinod," *BOR* 108, nos. 1–2 (January–February 1990): 7.

7. Comitetul de Redacție [Editorial Board], "Comunicat," *BOR* 108, nos. 3–4 (March–April 1990): 3.

8. David Moller, "Credem în Dumnezeu?" [Do We Believe in God?], *Readers Digest Romania*, http://www.erd.ro/credem_in_dumnezeu.

9. US Department of State, "Romania—International Religious Freedom Report 2005," http://www.state.gov/j/drl/rls/irf/2005/51575.htm.

10. See ibid., on specific budget figures.

11. See "Supliment," *BOR* 110, nos. 1–3 (January–March 1992): 191.

12. Arielle Thedrel, "Les projets pharaoniques de l'Église Orthodoxe à Bucarest," *Le Figaro*, 1 February 2008, http://www.lefigaro.fr/international/2008/02/01/01003-20080201ARTFIG 00478-les-projets-pharaoniques-de-l-eglise-orthodoxe-a-bucarest.php.

13. Cristina Dobreanu, "Catedrala bugetului neamului" [People's Budget Cathedral], *România Liberă*, 13 December 2007, http://www.romanialibera.ro/actualitate/eveniment /catedrala-bugetului-neamului-113550.html.

14. ASUR [Asociația Umanistă din România - The Romanian Humanist Association], "Apel către Parlament: Opriți finanțarea de către Stat a cultelor religioase și redirecționati aceste fonduri către Educație, Cercetare și Sănătate!" [Appeal to the Parliament: Stop State Subsidies for Religions and Re-direct These Funds toward Education, Research and Health], online petition signed by twenty-two NGOs and published on 5 February 2013, http://www .asur.ro/apel-catre-parlament-3/?lang=en.

15. Lavina Stan and Lucian Turcescu, *Religion and Politics in Post-Communist Romania* (New York: Oxford University Press, 2007), 171–193.

16. Sorin Cosma, "Homosexualitatea—patimă de necinste" [Homosexuality—Shameful Vice], *BOR* 122, nos. 1–4 (January–April 2004): 171–182.

17. See, for example, the formal decision of the Holy Synod for the elections of 1996, 2004, and 2008 in "Partea Oficiala," *BOR* 114, nos. 1–6 (January–June 1996): 384–386; "Partea Oficiala," *BOR* 122, nos. 1–4 (January–April 2004): 330, 339–341; "Partea Oficiala," *BOR* 126, nos. 3–6 (March–June 2008): 398–400.

18. Stan and Turcescu, *Religion and Politics*, 119–143.

19. Mihai Rotaru, "Lumină din Lumină la Neptun," *Ziua de Constanța*, 8 May 2002, http://www.ziuaconstanta.ro/stiri/eveniment/lumina-din-lumina-la-neptun-583.html.

20. Sfântul Sinod, "Mesajul Bisericii Ortodoxe Române," *BOR* 107, nos. 11–12 (November–December 1989): 3.

21. Ibid.

22. Moses Rosen and Joseph Finklestone, *Dangers, Tests and Miracles: The Remarkable Life Story of Chief Rabbi Rosen of Romania* (London: Weidenfeld & Nicolson, 1990), 31.

23. Ibid., 32.

24. Dilema, "Rafael Schaffer," Festival Dilema Veche, 2 August 2016, http://festival.dilema veche.ro/2016/08/02/rafael-shaffer/.

25. Federația Comunităților Evreiești din România (FCER- The Federation of Jewish Communities of Romania), "Prezentare Generală," https://www.jewishfed.ro/index.php /despre-noi-mainmenu-127/14-prezentarea-fcer/18-4-prezentare-generala?showall=.

26. Jacob Abadi, "Israel and the Balkan States," *Middle Eastern Studies* 32, no. 4 (October 1996): 309.

27. FCER, "Obiective Generale," https://www.jewishfed.ro/index.php/despre-noi -mainmenu-127/14-prezentarea-fcer/27-obiective-generale.

28. "Cine Suntem. Istoricul Institutului" [Who We Are. Brief History of the Institute], INSHREW, http://www.inshr-ew.ro/ro/despre-noi/cine-suntem/istoricul-institutului.html.

29. Michael Shafir, *Between Denial and "Comparative Trivialization": Holocaust Negationism in Post-Communist East Central Europe* (Jerusalem: Hebrew University of Jerusalem, 2002), 50.

30. Shafir, "Romania's Torturous Road," 252.

31. Katherine Verdery, "Nationalism and National Sentiment in Post-socialist Romania," *Slavic Review* 52, no. 2 (Summer 1993): 181.

32. Ibid., 184.

33. Ibid., 193.

34. See *Human Rights World Report 1990*, Romania section, http://www.hrw.org/reports /1990/WR90/HELSINKI.BOU-02.htm.

35. See, for example, US State Department, *Romania Human Rights Practices 1993*, http:// dosfan.lib.uic.edu/ERC/democracy/1993_hrp_report/93hrp_report_eur/Romania.html.

36. See, for example, European Commission, "Regular report from the Commission on Romania's progress towards accession 1998," Bulletin of the European Union Supplement 9 (1998), 17 December 1998, http://aei.pitt.edu/44598/, 10–12.

37. Paul Shapiro, "What Is in the Air?" *Holocaustul. Studii si Cercetări* 1, no. 2 (2009): 159.

38. Alexandru Florian, "Teme antisemitie și de negare a Holocaustului în media din România anului 2007" [Anti-Semitic and Holocaust Denial Themes Used in Romanian Media during 2007], *Holocaustul. Studii si Cercetări* 1, no. 2 (2009): 121, 133.

39. Shafir, "Romania's Torturous Road," 254.

40. Verdery, *Nationalism and National Sentiment*, 196.

41. *Mein Kampf* was published several times after 1990 and is available on extreme right-wing websites. *The Protocols* was published by Ion Coja in 2004. See Ion Coja, *Protocoalele kogaionului: teze și ipoteze, consemnate și autentificate de Ion Coja Pentru a se înțelege și evalua corect contenciosul româno-evreiesc, inclusiv—așa numindu-l unii—holocaustul din România*

[The Protocols of Zion: Thesis and Hypothesis, Recorded and Authenticated by Ion Coja for a Good Understanding of the Jewish-Romanian Discord, Including the So-Called Holocaust in Romania] (Bucharest: Țara Noastră, 2004).

42. Mihai Dinu Gheorghiu, William Totok, Elena-Irina Macovei, and Simona Sinzianu, "Naționalism, rasism, antisemitism și xenofobie pe platformele electronice ale unor publicații românești difuzate pe internet" [Nationalism, Racism, Anti-Semitism and Xenophobia on the Internet Electronic Platforms of Romanian Publications], *Holocaustul. Studii si Cercetări* 1, no. 2 (2009): 139–154.

43. Patriarch Teoctist, "Cuvânt înainte" [Foreword], in *Autocefalie, Patriarhie, Slujire Sfântă. Momente Aniversare în Biserica Ortodoxă Română* [Autoceaphaly, Patriarchate, Sacred Service. Aniversary Moments in the Life of the Romanian Orthodox Church] (Bucharest: Editura Institutului Biblic si de Misiune, 1995), 5.

44. See, for example, Gheorghe F. Anghelescu and Cristian Untea, *Father Dumitru Stăniloae: A Worthy Disciple of the Classical Patristics: Bio-bibliography* (Bucharest: Editura Enciclopedică, 2009).

45. Dumitru Stăniloae, "Unitatea spirituală a neamului nostru și Libertatea" [Our Nation's Spiritual Unity and Freedom], *BOR* 108, nos. 1–2 (January–February 1990): 49.

46. Ibid.

47. Gheorghe Drăgulin, "Recunoașterea Supremă în Țară a Valorii Unui Filosof și Teolog Creștin" [The Supreme Recognition in the Country of the Value of a Christian Philosopher and Theologian] *BOR* 108, nos. 5–6 (May–June 1990): 28–30.

48. Nichifor Crainic, "Ortodoxia—Concepția Noastră de Viață" [Orthodoxy—Our Life Mind-set], *Studii Teologice,* series 2, vol. 45, nos. 3–4 (May–August 1993): 3–12.

49. Teodor Popescu, "Vitalitatea Bisericii Ortodoxe" [The Vitality of the Orthodox Church], *Studii Teologice,* series 2, vol. 47, nos. 1–3 (January–June 1995): 3–41; Teodor Popescu, "Ce reprezintă azi Biserica Ortodoxă?" [What Represents Today the Orthodox Church?], *Studii Teologice,* series 2, vol. 47, nos. 4–6 (July–December 1995): 3–25.

50. "Partea Oficială," *BOR* 110, nos. 1–3 (January–March 1992): 197.

51. Comitetul de Redacție [Editorial Board], "Slujbele Solemne de la Mănăstirea Putna" [The Solemn Liturgies at Putna Monastery], *BOR* 110, nos. 7–10 (July–October 1992): 86–87.

52. Randolph L. Braham, "A TV Documentary on Rescue during the Holocaust. A Case of History Cleansing in Romania," *Eastern European Quarterly* 28, no. 2 (June 1994): 193.

53. Alexandru Florian, "Evreii din România în Timpul Celui de-al Doilea Război Mondial, o Problema de Cultură și Conștiință Civica" [The Jews of Romania during the Second World War, An Issue of Civic Culture and Consciousness], *Holocaust. Studii si Cercetări* 1, no. 1 (2009): 139.

54. "Sondaj 2007—Sondaj de opinie privind Holocaustul din România și percepția relațiilor interetnice" [Survey 2007, Survey Regarding the Holocaust in Romania and the Perception of Inter-ethnic Relations], *INSHREW,* http://www.inshr-ew.ro/ro/proiecte/sondaje .html.

55. "Sondaj 2010—Sondaj de opinie privind Fenomenul discriminării în România" [Survey 2010—Survey Regarding the Phenomenon of Discrimination in Romania], *INSHREW,* http://www.inshr-ew.ro/ro/files/proiecte/Sondaje/sondaj2010.pdf.

56. See, for example, US State Department, *Romania: Country Reports on Human Rights Practices 1999,* http://www.state.gov/j/drl/rls/hrrpt/1999/354.htm.

57. Shapiro, *What Is in the Air?,* 158.

58. Florian, *Teme antisemitie și de negare a Holocaustului,* 119–138.

59. "Holocaust denier appointed as minister," *The Coordination Forum for Countering Anti-Semitism*, http://antisemitism.org.il/article/73898/holocaust-denier-appointed-minister.

60. Andrew Hollinger, "The United States Holocaust Memorial Museum Objects to Cristea Coin," press release, 20 August 2010, http://www.ushmm.org/information/press/press-releases/the-united-states-holocaust-memorial-museum-objects-to-cristea-coin.

61. Vlad Stoicescu, "Academia Română cosmetizează aplauzele prin care a girat un discurs antisemit" [The Romanian Academy Cosmeticize the Applause Which Backed an Anti-Semitic Speech], *Adevărul*, http://Adevărul.ro/news/societate/academia-Română-cosmetizeaza-aplauzele-girat-discurs-antisemit-1_512fbd4400f5182b85b562f1/index.html#.

9

THE ROMANIAN ORTHODOX CHURCH AND HOLOCAUST MEMORY AFTER 1989

AFTER THE FALL OF THE Ceaușescu's regime there were three clear instances in which the Romanian Orthodox Church discussed its involvement in the Holocaust. The first one was represented by the publication in 1990 of an article that reinforced the cover-up of 1945 and added new nationalist elements developed during the Communist era. The second instance was the ceremony organized at the Palace of the Patriarchate in 2004 in which the Israeli ambassador to Romania awarded Father Gheorghe Petre the Righteous Among the Nations medal. This occasion allowed Patriarch Teoctist to boast of the alleged positive behavior of the Church toward Jews during the war. The Holocaust was also mentioned in 2002 and 2003 in the discussions of the Holy Synod regarding financial help for Roma Holocaust survivors. The attitude of the Orthodox Church toward Holocaust memory also appeared in an exchange of letters between the USHMM and the patriarchate regarding a 2001 incident in which a monument dedicated to Ion Antonescu was unveiled in an Orthodox church.

HIDING THE PROBLEMATIC ASPECTS OF THE CHURCH'S INVOLVEMENT
IN THE HOLOCAUST: THE REINFORCEMENT OF THE WHITEWASHING
NARRATIVE AFTER 1989

1990 is a significant year for understanding the Romanian Orthodox Church's attitude toward the Holocaust. Two important events that happened that year were a clear signal that the Church would continue the propaganda developed under Communism in which any serious and comprehensive analysis of its involvement in the events of the war was avoided. The first was the publication of an article dealing directly with the Holocaust. The second was the decision of the Holy Synod to rehabilitate Visarion Puiu, the former metropolitan of Transnistria and Bukovina, and Valerian Trifa, the former bishop of the Romanian Orthodox Church in America. Both these events continued the cover-up campaign, hiding any compromising information about the active involvement of the Church in the destruction of the Romanian Jews, and both presented the Church as interested in, even as the savior of, the Jews, and as a victim of Communism.

An article discussing the Romanian Orthodox Church's attitude during the Holocaust was published in the July–October 1990 issue of *BOR*. It was written by Alexandru Ioniță,[1] who was not a member of the Church's high hierarchy, and was entitled "The Attitude of the Romanian Orthodox Church toward Jews from 1918 to 1945 in Muntenia [Wallachia, southern part of the Old Kingdom of Romania] as It Appears in Publications of That Time and in Archival Documents."[2] Although the title suggests that the article addresses the fate of the Jews in the southern part of Romania, most of them saved as a result of Romania's change of policy toward deportation to Belzec in 1942, general assumptions about the whole of Greater Romania are made throughout it.

The article, which is eight pages long, copies many arguments from articles published in December 1945 by Bishop Antim Nica and by Teodor Manolache, but it also brings forward language and arguments developed during the last decades of the Communist era. For example, in the first sentences the author claims that the Romanian people were Christian from the country's birth; he also writes about the alleged tolerance of the Romanians from time immemorial and about Romanians' hospitality toward others. All of these statements, reminiscent of Communist historiography, contribute to the construction of the main argument: "All these foreigners ... the Romanians received with benevolence and humanness, helping them and securing them freedom of action [carte blanche] both in the material and spiritual domains. Armenians, Bulgarians, Germans, Magyars, Serbians, Turks, Tatars, and Jews found on the Romanian territory quietness, a place to work, the possibility to acquire a house, and also the full freedom to practice their religious beliefs."[3] Like Bishop Antim Nica in his 1945 article, the author entirely avoids mention of negative aspects, leaving the reader with the impression that Romanians were always tolerant and hospitable.

He says nothing about Church laws that expressed anti-Semitism or about episodes of religious intolerance against minorities. The author then quotes Nica and his argument regarding the baptism of Jews by the Romanian Orthodox Church as a way of proving the tolerance of the Church. But in contrast to Nica, who gave a detailed account of the evolution of conversion during the interwar period, Ioniță skips through this period very quickly. He avoids mentioning Patriarch Miron Cristea, his anti-Semitism, his role in the implementation of the law for the revocation of citizenship, and his role in Romanianization policies.

While in 1945 Nica acknowledged the measures of Romanian governments against Jews from 1938 onward, Ioniță promotes another narrative, developed during the last decades of Communism, according to which the Romanian authorities and the entire Romanian population fought against Germany and defended the Jews: "While the zeal of many governments in Europe in implementing the 'Final Solution' was without limits . . . the cities and villages of Romania offered safe shelter to Jews who successfully evaded the ghettos."[4] Ioniță does not explain whether he is referring to the ghettos of Transnistria, to which Romanian authorities deported and killed hundreds of thousands of Romanian and Ukrainian Jews, or to other ghettos across Europe.

In addition, the author trots out the classic arguments about Romanian noninvolvement in the Holocaust, arguments that present, at the same time, Ion Antonescu in a favorable light. He uses respectable work, such as that of historian Israel Gutman, speaking about the October 1942 moment, when the Romanian authorities changed their minds and refused German requests to deport all remaining Romanian Jews to Belzec. Ioniță does not say anything about the policies of the Antonescu regime prior to October 1942 and does not explain the political reasons behind the decision to halt the deportation of Jews to Belzec, namely the desire to use them as future bargaining chips with the Allies, should the direction of the war change. Instead, he presents a narrative in which there was no involvement of Romanians in the Holocaust and in which Romania became a shelter for all Jews from surrounding countries who wanted to escape destruction. Some of the arguments he uses in his article are from articles written during Communism in the context of the anti-Horthyst/Hungarian narrative. They show things in black and white: Romanians helped Jews and offered them shelter, while the Hungarians sent them to Auschwitz.[5] In this way the author aligns with the chauvinistic nationalist narrative described by Randolph Braham. This version of events uses some examples of Romanian humanitarianism to whitewash the past and to portray Hungarians in a negative light.[6]

When dealing directly with the attitude of the Romanian Orthodox Church toward Jews during the interwar and war period, Ioniță uses many examples from Bishop Nica's article and produces some new, Communist-inspired ones. For example he uses, as Nica did, the examples of Gala Galaction and Gheorghe Ispir, two respected interwar Orthodox theologians, to suggest that the entire Church had a favorable attitude toward Jews, and gives a new example: that of Father Petre Chiricuță, who wrote a book condemning anti-Semitism in 1926. Chiricuță was a rare exception in a Church in which the majority of clergy, students, professors at the Orthodox faculties of theology, and members of the hierarchy, led by Patriarch Miron Cristea, openly espoused anti-Semitism. Ioniță also mentions another priest from Bucharest, Toma Chiricuță, who during the German bombardments after August 23, 1944, defended some Jews who were asked by the Romanians to leave a bomb shelter.[7]

Ioniță uses only the favorable examples, which were rare. He does not mention that the Holy Synod rejected requests for help from converted and nonconverted Jews, or the anti-Semitic articles published in the central and regional journals of the Church. He says nothing about Patriarch Nicodim's open support for the war against the USSR and the strong anti-Judeo-Bolshevik campaign promoted by the Church, which legitimized state policies against Jews. Ioniță writes about the Holy Synod's protest against the March 1941 law banning the conversion of Jews, and the role of Metropolitan Bălan in that instance, but forgets to say that the last sentence of the Holy Synod's resolution (which he deliberately skips) favors compliance with the racial policies of the state. Ioniță also mentions two more interventions in the Holy Synod, both in 1942, discussing the Jewish problem, but he does not specify whether those interventions resulted in favorable decisions.[8] He also analyzes in detail, as did Nica and Manolache (see chapter 4), the alleged positive attitude of Patriarch Nicodim and the episode related in the Jewish newspaper *Neamul Evreesc*, in March 1945. Ioniță ends his article by saying "we can affirm that our Orthodox Church always had and practiced a Christian-humane attitude toward Jews who settled in Romania. This truth has been recognized by the Jews themselves. Jacques Pineles wrote the following: 'Romanian clergy always had a noble and benevolent attitude toward Jews.'"⁹ Bishop Antim Nica used this argument too, but while Nica mentioned that Pineles wrote in 1928, before the right-wing anti-Semitism of the 1930s and the Holocaust, Ioniță lets the reader believe that Pineles's assertion was not bound by time and space. (For a more detailed analysis of Pineles's claim, see chapter 4.)

Similar to the articles published in 1945, the article written by Alexandru Ioniță and published in 1990 in *BOR* promotes a fiction in which any compromising information is hidden, selects only favorable historical data, and, using only a few rare positive examples, portrays the Romanian Orthodox Church as always having had a favorable attitude toward Jews and as a savior of Jews. At the same time, the article neglects to say anything about anti-Semitic articles, refusal to help converted and unconverted Jews, encouragement of Antonescu's policies, or direct involvement of priests in physical violence against Jews. Moreover, compared with Nica and Manolache, Ioniță goes further, promoting the Communist myth of Romanian noninvolvement in the Holocaust and presenting Ion Antonescu as a savior of the Jewish community. This view of the Church's attitude toward Jews is completed by myths such as Romanians' permanent tolerance toward other minorities, or Romanians' hospitability and humane attitude toward foreigners.

The publication of the article soon after the fall of the Ceaușescu regime was most likely a deliberate decision. Many people in the Church hierarchy were old enough to know the truth about the involvement of the Church in the destruction of Romanian Jewry. Some of them, such as Patriarch Teoctist and Bishops Antim Nica and Bartolomeu Anania, had been personally involved in one way or another. Others, such as Bishop Nicolae Corneanu of Oradea, knew how the facts of the Holocaust were used in internal battles for ecclesiastical supremacy from 1945 to 1948. They understood that in the new, free society, sooner or later the Holocaust would become a topic of general public debate. As the Communist support vanished in 1989, people inside the Church reinforced the old myths to keep the Church from being dragged into this debate, exactly in a period of political liberalization when such discussions could be expected. The publication of the article in 1990 forestalled any claims that the narrative of 1945 was created by the Communists, and represented it as the true history of the Church's attitude toward Jews during the war.

The second event that took place in 1990 and shaped the attitude of the Romanian Orthodox Church toward Holocaust memory was the public rehabilitation of Visarion Puiu, former metropolitan of Bukovina and Transnistria, and of Valerian Trifa, the former Romanian Orthodox bishop in America. The Holy Synod voted in favor of rehabilitation in both cases, in the same session on September 25, 1990.[10] In doing so, the Church avoided any serious analysis of their involvement in the Holocaust. Instead, Puiu and Trifa were presented as victims of Communism. That the Church aimed, through this decision, to avoid the Holocaust debate is further suggested by the lack of a consistent agenda regarding the two former Orthodox hierarchs.

The rehabilitation decisions of 1990 were not followed by other specific actions. In Serbia for example, the rehabilitation of the controversial Bishop Nicolai Velimirović led to his canonization.[11] In Romania, although yearly conferences commemorating Visarion Puiu have been held in his native town, and although there is a large support group calling for him to be recognized as a saint, no clear steps have been made in this direction. Articles praising Visarion Puiu are regularly published in the lay and religious press,[12] and a Romanian MP has asked for his body to be returned from France,[13] but no direct actions have been taken so far. In the case of Valerian Trifa, the situation is even more interesting. After rehabilitation by the Holy Synod in 1990 his name has been almost entirely forgotten in both the religious and lay press. There is no public remembrance of him and no action group asking for his memorialization. The Romanian Orthodox Church's official silence in relation to Puiu's and Trifa's involvement in the Holocaust shows its duplicity. After 1990 the Church walked a tightrope: Puiu and Trifa were mentioned in favorable contexts when the Church wanted to present itself as a victim of Communism, and not mentioned in unfavorable contexts when their attitude during the Holocaust resurfaced.

The position of the Church regarding controversial individuals has also appeared in an exchange of letters between the USHMM and the Romanian Orthodox patriarchate. In June 2001 Miles Lerman, chairman emeritus of the United States Holocaust Memorial Council, wrote to Patriarch

Teoctist in relation to a monument dedicated to the wartime leader Ion Antonescu that was unveiled in the Sfinții Împărați Constantin și Elena church, in Bucharest, on June 1, 2001: "The recent monument to the glory of Ion Antonescu was inaugurated at the initiative of the Party Greater Romania, an openly fascist political organization which received a strong showing in the recent elections. The Party of Greater Romania advocates the rehabilitation of Romanian war criminals and is at the forefront of Holocaust denial. The fact that the Romanian Orthodox Church tolerated on its land a monument to the glory of a major war criminal is extremely worrisome." Mr. Lerman, after highlighting the positive role of Metropolitan Bălan in stopping the deportations of 1942, concludes his letter by saying that "this is why we are respectfully asking you to investigate the circumstances of the raising of this monument on the Orthodox Church grounds which in our view contradicts the very essence of your mission of peace and understanding between nationalities and religions."[14]

Patriarch Teoctist replied on July 13, 2001. After confirming that the problem raised was true, "even though not exactly in the form in which you have presented it," Teoctist, in a second paragraph, points out the Romanian Orthodox Church's participation in commemorations of the Holocaust, including ceremonies in Romania and in Poland. In the third paragraph he explains that the church was built at the initiative of and with funds provided by Ion Antonescu and his family and hence, "the Parish Assembly and parish Council are in charge of the administration of a place of worship and have responsibility for its maintenance." Here the patriarchate seemed to pass the responsibility to an inferior authority, in this case the parish assembly and council. In the last paragraph Teoctist expresses his hope that "this case will not, in any way, change the good relations established between the Romanian Orthodox Church and the Jewish people." In the last sentence of the letter the Patriarch wrote, "Additionally, it ought to be mentioned that the Romanian society of today is extremely divided as far as the person of Ion Antonescu is concerned."[15] Although Miles Lerman explained in his letter the negative role of Ion Antonescu in the Holocaust in Romania, the patriarch appears reluctant to accept the version of the USHMM regarding the former leader of the country. This last sentence and the fact that Teoctist does not address at all Lerman's allegations that the monument was raised with the participation of the anti-Semitic Greater Romania Party shows that in 2001 the Orthodox Church, through its patriarch, was reluctant to distance itself from those promoting extreme rightwing anti-Semitism.

The problematic attitude of the Romanian Orthodox Church toward individuals known for their anti-Semitism is revealed in other cases too. For example, Ilie Cleopa, a Romanian monk with a large audience after the fall of Communism, who shared and expressed publicly Legionary and anti-Semitic views in his writings published after 1989, was held in high regard. He suffered during some periods of the Communist regime, but he also enjoyed periods in which his articles were published in Church journals.[16] One of his books was published by the Orthodox publishing house in 1985, at the height of Ceaușescu's rule.[17] After 1989 not only did he have a great influence on the Orthodox faithful, but his books were introduced by important members of the hierarchy. In one of the books published in 2004 with the blessing of Metropolitan Daniel of Moldova (which was printed as a foreword on the first page), now the patriarch of the Romanian Orthodox Church, Cleopa describes Judaism as "the Jewish faith given to them by Moses, the prophet. They do not believe in Jesus Christ, the Redeemer of the world, refusing the new Covenant brought by Him. This is why they persecute the Christians."[18] The book uses aggressive language against other religious minorities. In the Iron Guard's tradition, the neo-Protestant denominations are described as "Satan's houses" and the neo-Protestant believers as "Satan's servants," "the forerunners of the Anti-Christ," or "the forerunners of Satan." In Cleopa's view, anyone who is not Orthodox is not a Romanian: "Stephen the Great was not a Baptist, Mircea the Old was not an Evangelical, or an Adventist. Alexander the Good was not a Jehovah's Witness like these fools who appear nowadays." In one passage he mirrors the Orthodox nationalism of the interwar years, writing "You cannot be a Christian and Romanian citizen if you do not have the right faith in Christ. You are a foreigner. You are not a son of the fatherland, since the true son of Romania is the one who is an Orthodox faithful, because the Orthodox Church has been predominant in this country in the last two thousand years."[19] It is very likely that Metropolitan Daniel did not share all the views expressed by Cleopa, but his blessing of controversial books containing clear rightwing anti-Semitic and nationalist propaganda encouraged the spread of this discourse.

The same can be said about Iustin Pârvu, the archimandrite from the Neamț Monastery, who although known for his Iron Guard past and his pro-Legionary attitudes after 1989, was still very much revered in Orthodox circles.[20] The Orthodox Church's duplicitous position in his case is detailed in the introduction to this book.

The duplicity of the Church's hierarchy toward anti-Semitism and Holocaust memory is also suggested by its attitude toward the student unions of the Orthodox faculties of theology. Continuing the tradition of the interwar period (remember that Valerian Trifa participated in the January 1941 pogrom of Bucharest in his position as the president of the National Union of Christian Students), these unions were active after 1990 in supporting the far-right agenda in general and anti-Semitism in particular.[21] According to some sociologists, "organizations like the Association of Christian Orthodox Students in Romania [Asociația Studenților Creştin Ortodocşi din Romania, ASCOR] were used to fight important battles that the Synod could not directly wage."[22]

In 2008, a conflict erupted between several organizations affiliated with the Orthodox Church and INSHREW. INSHREW successfully demanded the closure of an exhibition organized in Iaşi titled "The Fate of Martyrs." The exhibition was set up by several Christian Orthodox associations and celebrated some controversial, anti-Semitic, former Iron Guard priests who were arrested and prosecuted after the war, considered in some circles to be Orthodox martyrs. As a result of the closure, sixteen organizations, the majority of them Orthodox, such as ASCOR and the Friends of Mount Athos Association, wrote an open letter to the Romanian president, government, and parliament, attacking INSHREW. The letter openly defended Iron Guard members and sympathizers and exonerated them, without proper arguments, of their role in the destruction of Romanian Jewry. It went further and questioned the 2002 law against public expressions of anti-Semitism, considering it a violation of free speech. The letter also extensively used what Michael Shafir calls "comparative trivialization,"[23] comparing the Holocaust to the Communist "genocide." It attributed closure of the exhibition to the alleged religious hatred of INSHREW and its director, Alexandru Florian, against the Orthodox Church, but the arguments for this assumption increased the controversy. For example, the fact that the *Final Report* mentioned the presence of the cross on the frontispiece of the Romanian Parliament assembly room as a negative aspect was considered an expression of hatred because it denied, in the letter's view, the fact that Romania was a Christian nation. Another example of alleged hatred against the Orthodox Christians was that "it [there is no mention of who the letter is referencing here, but, considering the immediate context, "it" could refer to the *Final Report* and INSHREW] describes the Romanians' belief that Jews were responsible for the killing of Jesus as anti-Semitism." The letter made some recommendations, the most important being the elimination of the word "anti-Semitism" from the 2002 law and the redefinition of the word "Holocaust" to include the "systematic persecution against Christians during the totalitarian Communist regime."[24]

When asked to respond to this unprecedented attack against IN-SHREW, the Jewish community, and Holocaust memory, the Orthodox patriarchate refused to make any comment. After the fall of Communism, the Church kept away from promoting anti-Semitic discourse in its official statements and journals and continued the good relations with both the Romanian Jewish Community and the state of Israel. Nevertheless, it did not condemn the way in which Orthodox priests, students at the faculties of theology, and their organizations behaved toward the Jewish community and Holocaust memory.

Throughout the 1990s and 2000s, official declarations of Patriarch Teoctist and other members of the Church hierarchy lauded interwar personalities who promoted anti-Semitism.[25] Many well-known anti-Semites were either praised in the journals of the Church or had their articles published. Even Patriarch Miron Cristea was celebrated in several articles.[26] The memory of his anti-Semitism and of his measures against the Jews was wiped out, and only the positive aspects, such as his influential role as the first patriarch of the Church, were remembered. Annual commemorations of legionary "heroes" like Ion Moța and Vasile Marin were organized with the participation of Orthodox priests.[27] This rehabilitation of the rightwing anti-Semites, as in the case of Visarion Puiu and Valerian Trifa, was often done through the presentation of Legionaries as martyrs/victims of Communism, an aspect visible in the conflict generated by "The Fate of Martyrs" exhibition.[28] As in other cases mentioned above, the past involvement of such individuals in the destruction of Romanian Jewry was generally obscured. Alexandru Florian rightly points out that "the association of the Legionaries with the Orthodox Church is meant to sanitize the ideology and the political movement of the Legion and to rehabilitate it in the eyes of the public."[29] At the same time it should be mentioned that no official steps were made by the Church or by the Romanian state to rehabilitate the Iron Guard itself.

AWARENESS OF THE HOLOCAUST: THE DISCUSSIONS OF THE HOLY
SYNOD OF THE ROMANIAN ORTHODOX CHURCH REGARDING THE
ROMA SURVIVORS OF THE HOLOCAUST AND THE PARTICIPATION OF THE
CHURCH IN THE JEWISH-CHRISTIAN DIALOGUE

The attitude of the Romanian Orthodox Church toward Holocaust memory was, after 1989, duplicitous. Whenever it involved a discussion of its negative participation in the destruction of the Romanian Jewry, the Orthodox Church successfully avoided the topic. When the context was favorable, the Holocaust was even mentioned in meetings of the Holy Synod. Take, for example, the debate about providing financial help to Roma Holocaust survivors asked for by the International Organization for Migration (IOM). The topic was first mentioned in a 2002 Holy Synod meeting. According to this document, a protocol for collaboration between the IOM and the Romanian Orthodox patriarchate in matters such as human trafficking had been signed in 2001. On the basis of this accord, the IOM proposed involving the Orthodox patriarchate in a program of support for 4,000 Roma Holocaust survivors. The Holy Synod agreed to participate in the 2002–2003 initiative, considering that "the involvement of the Orthodox Church in such a program can prove once more that it cares for all its sons, no matter their ethnicity, social status, or political opinion."[30] The subject was discussed again in 2003 and the Holy Synod decided to continue the financial support for another year. The 2003 decision offered more details about the Roma Holocaust survivors, all of them living in different counties of Romania, and about the level of help, which for the first eight months of the program amounted to $409,384.[31] The subject ceased to appear in the minutes of the Holy Synod in the following years.

In all the Church's central and regional journals researched, covering a large period of time (1938 to 2012) and hundreds of issues, this was the only mention of Romas in the context of the Holocaust. Although anti-Semitism was often promoted before and during the war, there was no anti-Roma discourse in such journals. The cover-up campaign of 1945 and its subsequent Communist and post-Communist embodiments were entirely focused on Jews, without any mention of Romas. Even in articles promoting the tolerance propaganda about the permanent positive behavior of the Romanian Orthodox Church toward other minorities, Romas are nonexistent. Some arrogance of the Church in relation to this ethnic group can be sensed in the

Holy Synod's declaration mentioned above. The scarce space dedicated to Roma in this book reflects the Orthodox Church's lack of interest on this topic, except for the 2002–2003 discussions regarding Roma Holocaust survivors.

The participation of the Romanian Orthodox Churches in the Jewish-Orthodox dialogue is also suggestive of the way in which the Church dealt with Holocaust memory after the Second World War. The Romanian Orthodox Church became a part of the World Council of Churches (WCC) in 1961. In this capacity it participated at conferences on Jewish-Christian relations, but during the Communist era the reports about these events, published in the main journal of the Church, avoided any mention of Judaism, anti-Semitism, or the Holocaust.[32] The only major exception to this rule was the series of articles published in the second part of the 1960s discussing the Second Vatican Council's Nostra Aetate declaration. As discussed in chapter 7, those articles appeared in *Ortodoxia*, the journal of the patriarchate and not in *BOR*, the journal of the Holy Synod, the main journal of the Church. It should also be noted that those articles, which started as a mere interest of the Orthodox Church in the Catholic declaration, increasingly promoted the Communist myths of Church tolerance and hospitability. They advocated a dichotomist view in which the Orthodox Christians were portrayed as always having had a positive attitude toward Jews and other minorities, and the Catholics as intolerant and promoters of anti-Semitism.

It appears there was a Jewish-Orthodox meeting in Bucharest in 1979,[33] organized under the patronage of Patriarch Iustin and Chief Rabbi Moses Rosen. Papers such as "Tradition and Society in Judaism" and "The Role of the Bible in Orthodox Tradition" were presented.[34] The meeting was kept secret before and after the fall of Communism and nothing about it appears in any of the Church journals. The reasons for this before 1989 might have had to do with the Communist regime's problematic approach to topics such as Judaism, anti-Semitism, and the Holocaust. But the lack of any mention about it after 1989 suggests that the Orthodox Church was reluctant to mention the Jewish-Orthodox dialogue.

After 1990 the Romanian Orthodox Church participated in some Jewish-Orthodox conferences and missed others. For example, in 2007 the participation of the Church at the Sixth Academic Meeting between Judaism and Orthodox Christianity in Jerusalem was acknowledged in *BOR*.[35]

According to documents on the website of the Constantinople patriarchate, the Romanian Orthodox Church did not participate in the third, fifth, and seventh academic meetings (1993, 2003, and 2009). In 2003 the Romanian Orthodox Church participated in the Jewish-Christian meeting organized by the representatives of the WCC and the Progressive Judaism Society in New York. A report given to the Holy Synod by Dr. Ion Chivu reveals that the Romanian Orthodox delegation highlighted the Church's participation in the Jewish-Christian dialogue and the alleged ecumenical spirit between the Romanian Orthodox Church and the Jewish community, a "spirit tested in the harsh periods of our history."[36] This is a clear attempt to promote the whitewashing narrative in an international Jewish-Christian context but, given the fact that this example is probably unique, it seems that the Romanian Orthodox Church has not had a sustained agenda of promoting this narrative outside the country.

Most notably, the Romanian Orthodox Church was not present at the Christian Roundtable of Eastern Orthodox priests and cultural representatives from Greece, Georgia, Italy, Russia, and Ukraine visiting Jerusalem, April 20–24, 2007. The meeting issued one of the strongest declarations of Eastern Orthodoxy denouncing anti-Semitism and mentioned directly the death of the six million Jews in the Holocaust:

> For centuries Jews and Christians have been both united and separated by the relation to Christ. . . . For centuries the links of Jesus to His people have been in the shadows. Yet it is the words "you delivered" that came in the foreground and became the basis for an ideology, for contempt, for rejection, for the ghetto, the pale, the hate, the pogroms, and ended in the Holocaust. . . . As we go over the tragedy of the Holocaust, we are being called on to discover something on a truly evangelic scale: to know Christ who is being crucified with His people. The Holocaust is an obvious sign that points at the anti-Christ nature of the replacement theology. It must lead us to atonement and search for new paths, including theological ones. It is time that we called anti-Semitism a grave sin against God and man. . . . The conflict between the two Israels does not follow from the Revelation and is not etched forever in the Christian consciousness.[37]

This statement established an atmosphere in line with similar declarations of Catholic and Protestant institutions. The absence of any Romanian Orthodox representative at this meeting is again suggestive of the Church's reluctance to look into the past and to address its involvement in the Holocaust.

It should also be noted that while other Orthodox countries were more vocal in condemning anti-Semitism, such as the declaration of the Holy Synod of the Serbian Orthodox Church regarding anti-Semitic posters,[38] or the declarations of Bartholomew, the Constantinople patriarch,[39] the Romanian Orthodox Church has been reluctant to follow suit. On the few occasions when the Church has condemned anti-Semitism, the declarations were issued late and as a result of public pressure. In such instances the Church seems to lack the initiative and enthusiasm to condemn such expressions of prejudice.

Moreover, the Church did not distance itself from the people involved in the scandals. The case of Iustin Pârvu is an excellent example. Although the Church issued a declaration in 2011 condemning the Legionary songs sang at Pârvu's birthday celebrations, when he died in 2013 he was buried in a large Orthodox ceremony, as an emblematic figure of the Church. The Romanian Orthodox Church has also been reluctant to comment on and to condemn the aggressive tone of organizations affiliated with the Church that fought against Holocaust memory. The 2008 conflict between the Elie Wiesel Institute and several Orthodox organizations, detailed earlier in this chapter, is symptomatic of the Church's attitude after 1990: general avoidance of discussing the Holocaust, silence about organizations and individuals affiliated with the Church who promote anti-Semitism, and general avoidance of international meetings touching on the Shoah.

THE RELATIONS OF THE ROMANIAN ORTHODOX CHURCH WITH THE JEWISH COMMUNITY AND THE STATE OF ISRAEL AFTER 1989 AND THE MEMORY OF THE HOLOCAUST

"Continuity" would be the best word to describe the relations of the Romanian Orthodox Church with the Jewish community of Romania and with the state of Israel before and after 1989. While the Jewish community forced, after the fall of Ceaușescu, a historical reevaluation of the role played by many public figures and institutions in the Holocaust, it did not do the same in the case of the Romanian Orthodox Church. The harmonious relations developed under Communism went on almost entirely unchanged after 1989. An example in this sense is the memoir of Chief Rabbi Moses Rosen in which he speaks very briefly about the relations with the Romanian Orthodox patriarchs. He describes his relationship with Justinian and Teoctist as excellent. It is obvious from Church journals that Moses Rosen's connection with Patriarch Iustin Moisescu (1977–1986) was not as good, and he suggests in his memoir that Iustin had anti-Semitic and anti-Israel prejudices.[40] About Patriarch Teoctist (1986–2007), Moses Rosen says that "he is a very fine priest, a servant of love and brotherhood. Our relationship is excellent. Following the tradition established by his predecessors, Justinian and Iustin, who came to the Coral Synagogue to congratulate me on the twentieth and thirtieth anniversaries of my Chief Rabbinate, he was our honored guest in 1988, when I celebrated forty years as Chief Rabbi."

At one point the former chief rabbi acknowledges that the Romanian Orthodox Church before the war was "a nest of hatred and agitation against the Jews," but, he says, "I must stress the great difference between the situation nowadays and that prior to the Second World War."[41] This conciliatory approach, in which history is split between now and then, is symptomatic of most of the Jewish community's approach to the involvement of the Church in the Holocaust. The knowledge itself about "then" is partial and it mostly reflects the Communist narrative. For example, Rosen mentions only the attitude of the Church before the war, without any concern regarding the attitude of the Romanian Orthodox Church during the Holocaust. He does not challenge at all the narrative developed under Communism in which the Church was portrayed as a savior of Jews, in spite of historical evidence proving the opposite.

This attitude could be explained, although not entirely, by the lack of research on the topic and by the Church's constant promotion of the positive narrative, which worked in many cases as a smokescreen. Nevertheless, at the same time it is obvious that the former chief rabbi and the Jewish community made a deliberate decision to continue the politics of good relations it enjoyed with the Orthodox Church during the Communist regime. The reasons for this can be found both inside and outside Romania. Inside, this could be explained by a Jewish community's tradition of taking a conciliatory approach toward the majority Romanian Orthodox Church, an approach sometimes hard to understand. This attitude is visible in the actions of few Jewish leaders who, immediately after the war, advocated the idea the Church had been supportive of Jews, despite massive evidence to the contrary. This happened in other parts of Europe as well. According to Michael Phayer, immediately after the war several Jewish leaders, among them the secretary general of the World Jewish Congress and the chief rabbi of Palestine, hurried to thank Pope Pius XII and the Holy See for their efforts to save the Jews. This despite the fact that the attitude of the Catholic Church toward Jews during the war was still unclear.[42] It should be also noted that it was mostly historians who lived outside Romania, such as Jean Ancel, Radu Ioanid, Leon Volovici, and Paul Shapiro, who started research into the anti-Semitism of the Orthodox Church during the interwar period.

The outside factor that could explain these amiable relations is related to the attitude of the state of Israel toward Holocaust memory in Romania, and more precisely to its relations with the Romanian Orthodox Church. During the Ceaușescu era the state of Israel did not openly challenge the narrative of Romanian noninvolvement in the Holocaust. This amiable attitude continued to some extent after the fall of Communism. It was mainly the Romanian Jewish community who raised the topic of Romanian involvement in the destruction of Jews at the beginning of the 1990s. Israel joined these efforts and in 2003, after the scandal of officials' declarations denying the Holocaust in Romania, Israel recalled its ambassador as a sign of protest. However, the strong reaction of Israel in 2003 faded away in the following years. In 2010, Shimon Peres made the first visit to Romania of an Israeli president since the creation of the state in 1948. In his official speech, he thanked Romania for saving 400,000 Jews during the war, but said nothing about the other 280,000–380,000 Jews who were killed in territories under Romanian control. This political downplaying of the Romanian involvement in the Holocaust was reminiscent of the Communist-era relations between the two states. The first institution to react to this mistake was the Simon Wiesenthal Center.[43] Efraim Zuroff, the Israeli director of the center, said, "Although President Peres obviously wanted to highlight a positive aspect in the history of Romanian Jewry, an aspect that had a positive effect on development of the state of Israel, the fact that he did not condemn the horrendous crimes of the Antonescu regime against Jews will have poisonous consequences in Romania and across Eastern Europe where there is a tendency, in post-Communist societies, to deny or minimize the role of Nazi collaborators."[44] As foreseen by Zuroff, the speech was used by Holocaust deniers, such as Ion Coja, and by far-right circles, to demonstrate that Antonescu was a savior of Jews and that the Romanians were not involved in the Holocaust.[45]

Political, social, and economic interests shaped the way in which the state of Israel related to the problematic history of Romania's involvement in the Holocaust, and more research is needed to understand more clearly the various facets of this attitude. In December 1989, the Israeli government issued a general statement "welcoming the 'Emergency Democracy' in Romania, condemning the terrible massacre, and expressing hope that the remaining 20,000 Romanian Jews would not be harmed."[46] The economic relationship between Romania and Israel grew constantly after 1989. In 1989, the volume of trade was $40 million; by 1992 this had doubled to $80 million. Israel also played an important role in the modernization of the Romanian army in the first half of the 1990s.[47] For a few years after the fall of Communism, the Romanian authorities continued to play the role of negotiator in the Israeli-Palestinian conflict. In 1994, the Crans-Montana Forum brought Shimon Peres and Yasser Arafat to Bucharest. Their meeting at the People's Palace was used by Romania to showcase its diplomatic strength.[48] The Romanian regime sought to maintain good relations with Israel and the Arab states at the same time, but later on in the 1990s Romania's role in the peace process faded away.[49]

When it comes to the Orthodox Church itself, the state of Israel encouraged the travel of Romanian Orthodox pilgrims to the Holy Land. This was promoted in Church journals.[50] News about the excellent relations between the Romanian Orthodox Church and the state of Israel were regularly published as a way of advertising the Holy Land.[51] As many as 40,000 Romanian Orthodox pilgrims visit Israel every year.[52]

In 2004, the year in which the Elie Wiesel Commission issued the *Final Report*, Orthodox priest Gheorghe Petre was awarded Righteous Among the Nations status for his contribution in helping Jews during the Holocaust. He was involved in smuggling food and other supplies to those who had been deported to the Crivoi Ozero and Trei Dube ghettos in Transnistria (see more details in chapter 2).[53] Some Romanian Orthodox websites boast about the fact that Petre is the only Orthodox priest to be given the award,[54] but this is not actually accurate.[55] The official ceremony took place at the Palace of the Patriarchate in the presence of Patriarch Teoctist and of the Israeli ambassador to Romania, Rodica Radian-Gordon.[56] According to the Israeli ambassador, "Father Gheorghe Petre was a righteous among people in one of the darkest hours of humankind, in a place known as 'The Kingdom of Death.' The sentencing to death of hundreds of thousands of Jews—men, women, and children—who were deported to Transnistria, was done on one basis only: they were Jews. We have a responsibility that the horrors of the twentieth century never repeat again."[57]

While the award for a Romanian Orthodox priest was a positive factor, demonstrating that there were a few members of the clergy involved in saving Jews, the fact that the ceremony took place at the Palace of the Patriarchate was highly controversial. The Orthodox Church used the event to present itself as interested in the fate of Jews during the Holocaust. Patriarch Teoctist seized the moment to promote in his speech all the major elements of the whitewashed narrative built from 1945 onward: "I feel indebted to say that, as some of you already know, during those hard times, many Orthodox clergy, from regular priests to metropolitans and Patriarchs, intervened to the authorities to attenuate the sufferings of Jews with whom Romanians always lived in harmony."

In his brief speech, Teoctist mentioned the alleged help given to Jews by Metropolitan Nicolae Bălan and by Patriarch Nicodim, examples that had been used since the cover-up campaign of 1945. At one point he claimed that "they [the members of the Church's hierarchy who helped Jews] made efforts to redeem and attenuate the harsh and drastic measures taken against our fellow neighbors, the Jews of Romania, who were, as a matter of fact, our friends and our parents' friends."[58] The patriarch described the Romanian Orthodox Church as always having been favorable to the Jews. The Communist myths of tolerance and hospitality were presented as unquestionable truths. Any compromising information was avoided and, based on Gheorghe Petre's example and on the examples brought forward since 1945, the narrative of the Church as a savior of Jews was greatly emphasized.

The 2004 ceremony at the Palace of the Patriarchate came at a controversial time. In 2001 rumors were circulating that Patriarch Teoctist had been an Iron Guard sympathizer in his youth and that he had been involved in the Bucharest pogrom of 1941. Several historians claimed to have seen, in the former Securitate's archives, documents (later unavailable) showing that "the twenty-six-year-old Teoctist ransacked a Bucharest synagogue, together with other priests and Iron Guard members." It [the document] said that Teoctist was "once an active legionary, participant in the rebellion, and in the devastation of the synagogue on Antim Street."[59]

A few months after the ceremony celebrating Father Gheorghe Petre's rescue actions, an article by Ion Coja, one of the main Holocaust deniers in Romania, was published in BOR. This article was not about the Holocaust, but Coja's very presence in the pages of BOR was controversial.[60] The article presents the Church as the national church, attacks the EU which, according to the author, had at its core the same internationalist view (maybe an indirect attack of Jews) as the Communist International. In 2006, in another central journal of the Church, *Studii Teologice*, a celebratory review of a book about Teodor Popescu was published. He was presented as a martyr of the cross, a victim of Communism.[61] All these highlight the uninspired decision to organize the ceremony honoring Father Gheorghe Petre at the Palace of the Patriarchate, as the Romanian Orthodox Church continued to promote in its journals controversial anti-Semites and a strong nationalism reminiscent of that of the interwar period.

NOTES

1. At the time of publication Ioniță was a doctoral student at the Faculty of Orthodox Theology, University of Bucharest. After the fall of Communism he enjoyed a successful academic career at the University of Constanta, publishing several books, most of them continuing the nationalist narrative he had developed under Communism.

2. Alexandru Ioniță, "Atitudinea Bisericii Ortodoxe Române față de evrei între 1918–1945 în Muntenia, reflectată în publicațiile vremii și în documente de arhivă" [The Attitude of the Romanian Orthodox Church toward Jews from 1918 to 1945 in Muntenia (Wallachia, southern part of the Old Kingdom of Romania) as It Appears in Publications of That Time and in Archival Documents], *BOR* 108, nos. 7–10 (July–October 1990): 203–211.

3. Ibid., 203.

4. Ibid., 205.

5. Ibid., 205.

6. Randolph L. Braham, "A TV Documentary on Rescue during the Holocaust. A Case of History Cleansing in Romania," *Eastern European Quarterly* 28, no. 2 (June 1994): 196.

7. Ioniță, *Atitudinea Bisericii Ortodoxe Române față de evrei*, 207.

8. Ibid., 209.

9. Ibid., 211.

10. Dumitru Velenciu, "Visarion Puiu, Mitropolit al Bucovinei (1935–1944), Un Martir al Demnității Ortodoxe," *Analele Bucovinei* 11, no. 1 (2004): 64.

11. See Jovan Byford, *Denial and Repression of Antisemitism: Post-Communist Remembrance of the Serbian Bishop Nikolaj Velimirović* (New York: Central European University Press, 2008), 12.

12. See, for example, Florian Bichir, "Mitropolitul Visarion Puiu și organizarea bisericească" [Metropolitan Visarion Puiu and Church Organization], *Evenimentul Zilei* [The Event of the Day], 18 March 2012, http://www.evz.ro/detalii/stiri/mitropolitul-visarion-puiu-si-organizarea-bisericeasca-971967.html.

13. Pavel Târpescu, "Evocarea Vieții și Activității Mitropolitului Visarion Puiu" [Remembrance of Metropolitan Visarion Puiu's Life and Activity], *Dezbateri Parlamentare, Sedința Camerei Deputaților din 11 Martie 2003*, http://www.cdep.ro/pls/steno/steno.stenograma?ids=5392&idm=1,18&idl=1.

14. Miles Lerman to H. H. Patriarch Teoctist, 13 June 2001, courtesy of Dr. Radu Ioanid, director of the International Archival Program, Center for Advanced Holocaust Studies, USHMM.

15. Teoctist, Patriarch of the Romanian Orthodox Church, to Mr. Miles Lerman, 13 July 2001, USHMM, courtesy of Dr. Radu Ioanid.

16. Ilie Cleopa, "Viața religioasă din unele mănăstiri ale Bisericii Ortodoxe Române" [Religious Life of Some Romanian Orthodox Church Monasteries], *Studii Teologice*, series 2, vol. 5, nos. 5–6 (May–June 1953): 429–443.

17. Ilie Cleopa, *Despre credința ortodoxă* [About the Orthodox Faith] (Bucharest: Institutul Biblic și de Misiune al Bisericii Ortodoxe Române, 1985).

18. Ilie Cleopa, *Ne vorbește părintele Cleopa* [Father Cleopa Is Speaking to Us], 3rd ed. (Neamț, Romania: Mănăstirea Sihăstria, 2004), 10.

19. Ibid., 39, 41.

20. When Pârvu died in June 2013, he was buried as an emblematic figure of the Church, the funeral service being officiated by the Metropolitan of Moldova. See Florin Jbanca, "Părintele Iustin, jelit de o mare de credincioși" [A Sea of Church-goers Mourn for Father Iustin], *Adevărul*, 20 June 2013, http://adevarul.ro/locale/piatra-neamt/foto-parintele-iustin -jelit-mare-credinciosi-1_51c3322dc7b855ff56af1006/index.html.

21. Lavinia Stan and Lucian Turcescu, *Religion and Politics in Post-Communist Romania* (New York: Oxford University Press, 2007), 50.

22. Ibid. Here Stan and Turcescu quote the opinion of Gabriel Andreescu, human rights activist and political scientist.

23. Michael Shafir, "Romania's Torturous Road to Facing Collaboration," in *Collaboration with the Nazis: Public Discourse after the Holocaust*, ed. Roni Stauber (London: Routledge, 2011), 260.

24. "Scrisoarea celor 16 organizații prin care se semnalează acte grave de instigare la ură religioasă și națională, precum și încălcarea libertății religioase și de gândire a creștinilor Ortodocși pe teritoriul României" [The Letter of 16 Organizations Drawing Attention to Grave Acts of Incitement to Religious and National Hatred as well as the Infringement of Orthodox Believers' Religious Freedom and Freedom of Thought in Romania], *Asociatia Rost*, http://www.rostonline.org/blog/claudiu/2008/11/scrisoare-către-Președintele-basescu .html. The letter is no longer on the site, but I have a copy of it thanks to the generosity of Dr. Alexandru Florian, the director of the INSHREW.

25. Gheorghe Vasilescu, "In ziua învierii a plecat dintre noi Arhiepiscopul Antim Nica al Dunării de Jos" [On the Day of the Resurrection the Archbishop of Lower Danube, Antim Nica, Passed Away], *BOR* 112, nos. 1–6 (January–June 1994): 200, 202. Patriarch Teoctist's speech appears in Vasilescu's article.

26. See for example Virgil Teodorescu, "Patriarhul Miron Cristea, contemporanul nostru" [Patriarch Miron Cristea, Our Contemporary], *BOR* 116, nos. 7–12 (July–December 1998): 231–242.

27. Alexandru Florian, "Teme antisemitie și de negare a Holocaustului în media din România anului 2007" [Anti-Semitic and Holocaust Denial Themes Used in Romanian Media during 2007]. *Holocaust. Studii si Cercetări* 1, no. 2 (2009): 132–133.

28. Ibid., 135.

29. Ibid., 132–133.

30. Comitetul de Redacție [Editorial Board], "Partea Oficială" [Official Section], *BOR* 120, nos. 1–6 (January–June 2002), 621.

31. Ibid., 121, no. 1–6 (January–June 2003): 745–748.

32. See for example, "Partea Oficială, Tem. nr. 14.455/1961, Participarea delegației Bisericii Ortodoxe Române la Lucrările celei de-a treia Adunări Generale a Consiliului Ecumenic al Bisericilor" [Official Section, Theme No 14.455/1961, the Participation of the Romanian

Orthodox Church's Delegation at the Third General Assembly Meeting of the Ecumenical Council of Churches], *BOR* 80, nos. 1–2 (January–February 1962): 176–177.

33. See Normon Solomon, "Jewish-Christian Relations," *Jewish Virtual Library*, accessed 22 February 2013, http://www.jewishvirtuallibrary.org/jsource/judaica/ejud_0002_0011_0_10125.html; see also "Documents and Statements: Jewish and Orthodox Christian Dialogue (October 29, 1979)," Sacred Heart University, Documents and Statements, accessed 22 February 2013, http://www.sacredheart.edu/faithservice/centerforchristianandjewishunderstanding/documentsandstatements/jewishandorthodoxchristiandialogueoctober291979/. The meeting is also confirmed on the Ecumenical Patriarchate website, "Inter-Religious Dialogues Organized by the Ecumenical Patriarchate," accessed 22 February 2013, https://www.patriarchate.org/dialogue.

34. John S. Romanides, "Jewish and Christian Orthodox Dialogue. Bucharest, Romania, October 29–31, 1979, a follow-up of the dialogue held in March of 1977 in Lucerne, Switzerland," *The Romans*, accessed 22 February 2013, http://www.romanity.org/htm/rom.24.en.jewish_and_christian_orthodox_dialogue.htm.

35. Comitetul de Redacție [Editorial Board], "Partea Oficială—Viața Bisericească" [Official Section—Church Life], *BOR* 125, nos. 1–6 (January–June 2007): 240–241.

36. Ibid., 121, nos. 1–4 (January–March 2004): 399–400.

37. Christian Roundtable of Eastern Orthodox Priests and Cultural Representatives, "To Recognize Christ in His People," April 20–24, 2007, Council of Centers of Jewish-Christian Relations, accessed 22 February 2013, http://www.ccjr.us/dialogika-resources/documents-and-statements/e-orthodox/1011-eoroundtable2007june1.

38. Holy Synod of Bishops of the Serbian Orthodox Church, "The Serbian Orthodox Church Regarding Anti-Semitic Posters (March 24, 2005)," Sacred Heart University, Documents and Statements, accessed 22 February 2013, http://www.sacredheart.edu/faithservice/centerforchristianandjewishunderstanding/documentsandstatements/theserbianorthodoxchurchregardingantisemiticpostersmarch242005/.

39. Patriarch Bartholomew, "Address of His All Holiness Ecumenical Patriarch Bartholomew: Meeting with the Members Religious and Lay Leaders of the Jewish Community, Park East Synagogue, Direct Archdiocesan District, New York, October 28, 2009," Ecumenical Patriarchate of Constantinople, video version of His speech, accessed 22 February 2013, https://www.patriarchate.org/-/ecumenical-patriarch-bartholomew-meets-with-jewish-religious-and-lay-leaders?inheritRedirect=true; see also "Greetings of Ecumenical Patriarch Bartholomew to the Third Academic Meeting between Orthodoxy and Judaism: Continuity and Renewal," Ecumenical Patriarchate of Constantinople, accessed 22 February 2013, https://www.patriarchate.org/addresses/-/asset_publisher/npz6Rwvho3aC/content/greetings-of-ecumenical-patriarch-bartholomew-to-the-third-academic-meeting-between-orthodoxy-and-judaism.

40. Moses Rosen and Joseph Finklestone, *Dangers, Tests and Miracles: The Remarkable Life Story of Chief Rabbi Rosen of Romania* (London: Weidenfeld & Nicolson, 1990), 290.

41. Ibid., 293.

42. Michel Phayer, *The Catholic Church and the Holocaust, 1930–1965* (Bloomington: Indiana University Press, 2000), 160.

43. Associated Press, "Wiesenthal Center Criticizes Peres for Thanking Romania," The Jerusalem Post, 13 August 2010, http://www.jpost.com/Breaking-News/Wiesenthal-Center-criticizes-Peres-for-thanking-Romania.

44. Redacția, "Evreii români, nemulțumiți de discursul președintelui israelian Shimon Peres" [Romanian Jews Unhappy with the Speech of Israeli President Shimon Peres], Historia.ro, accessed 22 March 2012, http://www.historia.ro/exclusiv_web/actualitate/articol/evreii-romani-nemultumiti-discursul-Președintelui-israelian-shimon.

45. See Ion Coja, "Decalogul junelui naționalist: România, colonie a Israelului?" Ioncoja. ro (blog), 28 August 2010, http://www.ioncoja.ro/carte-pentru-dumirire-%c8%99i-indreptare /decalogul-junelui-na%c8%9bionalist-5/.

46. Jacob Abadi, "Israel and the Balkan States," *Middle Eastern Studies* 32, no. 4 (October 1996): 309.

47. Ibid., 310.

48. See Chris Hedges, "Peres and Arafat in Talks to Complete Accord," *New York Times*, 22 April 1994, http://www.nytimes.com/1994/04/22/world/peres-and-arafat-in-talks-to -complete-accord.html.

49. Abadi, "Israel and the Balkan States," 309.

50. See, for example, Biroul de Presă al Patriarhiei, "Ministrul turismului din Israel în vizită la Patriarhia Română" [The Israeli Tourism Minister in Visit at the Romanian Patriarchate], press release, *Ziarul Lumina*, 7 April 2011, http://ziarullumina.ro/ministrul-turismului -din-israel-in-vizita-la-patriarhia-romana-12750.html.

51. See Biroul de Presă al Patriarhiei, "Ambasadorul Israelului, în vizită la Patriarhia Română" [The Ambassador of Israel in Visit at the Romanian Patriarchate], press release, *Ziarul Lumina*, 8 September 2011, http://ziarullumina.ro/ambasadorul-israelului-in-vizita-la -patriarhia-romana-5540.html.

52. Dumitru Manolache, "Seminar pe tema pelerinajelor la Locurile Sfinte," *Ziarul Lumina*, 9 October 2010, http://ziarullumina.ro/seminar-pe-tema-pelerinajelor-la-locurile -sfinte-21496.html.

53. The Righteous Among the Nations, Petre Gheorghe, accessed 19 June 2013, http://db .yadvashem.org/righteous/family.html?language=en&itemId=4420764.

54. Arhiepiscopia Râmnicului, "Parintele Gheorghe Petre Govora a trecut la Domnul" [Father Gheorghe Petre Govora Has Passed to the Lord], CrestinOrtodox.ro, accessed 5 March 2013, http://www.crestinortodox.ro/stiri/crestinortodox/parintele-gheorghe-petre -govora-trecut-domnul-135107.html.

55. See, for example, the case of Vladimir Imshennik, an Orthodox priest from Poland (now Belarus), who was awarded Righteous Among the Nations status in 1993: "Vladimir and Galina Imshennik," Yad Vashem, accessed 19 June 2013, http://www.yadvashem.org/righteous /stories/imshennik. See also the case of Aleksey Glagolev, an Orthodox priest from Ukraine who was recognized as Righteous in 1991: "Glagolev Family," Yad Vashem, accessed 19 June 2013, http://db.yadvashem.org/righteous/family.html?language=en&itemId=4044305.

56. Gheorghe Vasilescu, "Un preot Ortodox Român 'Drept între Popoare'" [A Romanian Orthodox Priest "Righteous Among the Nations"] *BOR* 122, nos. 5–8 (May–August 2004): 206.

57. Ibid.

58. Ibid., 208.

59. See Stan and Turcescu, *Religion and Politics*, 73.

60. Ion Coja, "Securitatea a colaborat cu Biserica și nu invers" [Securitate Collaborated with the Church and not the Opposite], *BOR* 123, nos. 4–6 (April–June 2005): 531–534.

61. Alexandru Ionuț Tudorie, "Un Martir al Crucii; Viața și Opera lui Teodor Popescu" [A Martyr of the Cross; the Life and Work of Teodor Popescu], *Studii Teologice*, series 3, vol. 2, no. 3 (July–September 2006): 189–193.

CONCLUSION

THE MEMORY OF THE HOLOCAUST in Romania was built in the context of several political changes that occurred after the Second World War. Immediately after 1945, as in other countries that came under Soviet dominance, a deliberate decision was made to avoid the mention of Jewish suffering and to replace Jewish identity with language that suited the Communist narrative, such as "anti-fascist fighters," "other nationalities," and "coinhabitant minorities."[1] During the Communist era, the involvement of the Romanians in the Holocaust was entirely forgotten in a process labeled by Michael Shafir as "the state organized forgetting of the Holocaust." The Holocaust itself was not entirely hidden; books about the death camps and Nazi and Hungarian atrocities were published after 1965. What was hidden was the role of Romanian authorities in the Holocaust.

We should see the Romanians' avoidance of responsibility for collaboration with the Nazi regime in a larger context. For many years France avoided taking responsibility for its role in the destruction of French Jewry, casting the blame entirely on the Germans, in what has become known in historiography as "the Vichy syndrome." This narrative, which places great emphasis on the Resistance, secured the continuity of France's glorious national myth.[2] The Germans themselves for many years were inclined to blame their country's violent attitude against Jews on a small group of Nazi leaders.[3] This process of replacing responsibility with victimhood in order to maintain a myth of national glory has appeared not only on a large scale among European nations, but on a smaller scale among institutions within the nations. In Germany, for example, until recently almost nobody carefully analyzed the myth of the "Clean Wehrmacht,"[4] according to which the German army was not involved in killing Jews and other atrocities, and even if sporadic cases were brought forward, they were considered as small exceptions. Different churches in Europe, because of the lack of research, portrayed themselves as having acted heroically in the Holocaust, which recent research contradicts.[5] The Catholic Church immediately after the war presented itself as a victim of Nazism, hoping to deflect responsibility for the results of its silence about the plight of the Jews.[6] Only after the death of Pope Pius XII and the election of Pope John XXIII who, as a papal nuncio in Turkey and Greece during the war, saw the full impact of Catholic prejudice against Jews, did the Catholic Church start a process of self-analysis.

Katherine Verdery, in her excellent analysis on nationalism in Romania, speaks about the East European predilection for the victimhood narrative:

> All across the region, local historiographies represented nations as innocent victims, victimized nearly always by other nations, rather than by their own members. . . . Poland appears time and again in Polish historical works as the "Christ of nations," whom the nations around it unjustly crucified, carving it up for over a century; generations of Czechs have been raised with the image of their nation as martyr; Hungary's and Romania's historians have presented their nations as suffering for the salvation of western civilization, sacrificed on an Ottoman altar so that the glory of western Christendom might endure. . . . Famous Romanian émigré Mircea Eliade wrote in 1953 that "few peoples can claim that they had so much ill fortune in history as the Romanian people."[7]

In Communist Romania, the process of hiding the past and promoting a victimhood narrative in relation to the Holocaust was not challenged by inside or outside forces. The Romanian Jewish community strove to fulfil its other, more immediate needs, like securing safe travel for Jews who wanted to emigrate, or promoting harmonious relations with other religious communities, a process imposed by the Communist regime. Nor did any intellectual or religious movement challenge the narrative of Romanian non-involvement in the Holocaust. In Romania there were no cases like those of some Catholic intellectuals in Poland, who before 1989 challenged the narrative promoted by the Polish Communist authorities about the destruction of Jewry.[8] As to outside factors that might have influenced the Romanian approach to Holocaust memory, the most important one, the state of Israel, was more concerned with maintaining good relations with Romania than with pressing for a correct assessment of the Romanians' involvement in the Holocaust. As with the Jewish community, the state of Israel needed to solve more stringent problems, such as keeping the gates open for the emigrating Romanian Jews. In addition, the fact that Romania remained the only Communist country to maintain diplomatic relations with Israel after 1967 made it an important player in Arab-Israeli negotiations.

Part of the fault for this false collective memory of the Holocaust in Romania lies with the growing promotion of nationalism after 1955. In the context of Stalin's death and of the withdrawal of Soviet troops, Romanian authorities took clear steps toward creating a more nationalist Communism. This process, which grew steadily during the Ceaușescu era, involved the promotion of a specific historiography in which historical facts were not important anymore. What was important was the creation of a past that corresponded with the political agenda of national Communism, a history in which Romanians were portrayed as always tolerant and hospitable. In this myth, the Romanians were never presented as perpetrators, only as victims. The political dimensions of this myth were even clearer in the Hungarian-Romanian dichotomy. In Communist historiography Hungarians were portrayed as perpetrators of the Holocaust, and the Romanians as those who offered safe haven for Jews persecuted in Hungary.[9]

After the fall of Ceaușescu, the nationalism promoted during Communism continued to influence the building of Holocaust memory in Romania. The rehabilitation of interwar nationalists during the last decades of the Ceaușescu era became the basis for the reemergence of a strong anti-Semitism in the 1990s. Although the Communist authorities generally avoided mention of these individuals' anti-Semitism, it was in the air awaiting the proper moment to be rediscovered. Octavian Goga, Nicolae Iorga, Mircea Eliade, and most importantly Ion Antonescu, the Romanian leader during the war, became heroic figures after 1990. Their aura had been constructed long before 1989. The Holocaust debate that took place in Romanian academia in the 1990s was centered on these individuals. Even after the issuance of the *Final Report* (2004), Ion Antonescu remained an important political figure and there were TV programs such as "The 100 Greatest Romanians"[10] and educational programs by the Elie Wiesel Institute that increased public knowledge about Antonescu's actions against Jews during the war.

All these elements were essential factors in the building of Holocaust memory in Romania, but this analysis would be incomplete without a deeper understanding of the glorification/victimization narrative in the Romanian context. The core of this narrative should be sought in traditions dating back to medieval times. A famous Romanian ballad, *Miorița* (The Little Ewe Lamb),[11] which has its origins in Moldova, the eastern part of Romania, tells the story of three shepherds: one Moldavian, one Wallachian, and one Hungarian. The Wallachian and the Hungarian shepherds plan to kill the Moldavian shepherd. When the Moldavian hears about the plan he does nothing and speaks to one of his sheep. From this allegorical dialogue springs the idea of an implacable destiny, which cannot be fought against. The Moldavian shepherd is a victim who makes peace with his tragic fate. The ballad suggests that there is something glorious in this peaceful acceptance of a tragic destiny, what literary critics call "Mioritic fatalism."[12]

Mioritic fatalism appears in another popular ballad, *Mănăstirea Argeș*, which originated in Wallachia, the southern part of Romania. The ballad tells the story of the construction of one of the oldest and most famous monastic buildings in Romania, the Argeș Monastery. In a tale similar to other European myths, what the workers build during the day collapses overnight. The workers make a pact according to which the first human being to come to them would be walled up alive in the building, thus securing its resistance. The first person to arrive is Ana, the wife of the main builder. Like the Moldavian shepherd, Ana embraces her fate with content.

A careful historical analysis reveals a swing in the way in which these ballads, and the messages they convey, were used over time. The interwar nationalists, for example, challenged the medieval narrative of victimhood and the peaceful acceptance of a tragic fate, the Mioritic fatalism. In 1930 Mihail Sadoveanu, starting from the theme of *Miorița*, published a famous novel called *Baltagul* (The Hatchet). While in *Miorița* the shepherd dies without questioning his fate or seeking revenge, in *Baltagul*, after the shepherd's death, his wife, Victoria Lipan, kills her husband's murderers. Victoria Lipan thus became a model hero as Romania approached the period of the Holocaust. The creation of Greater Romania after 1918 led many Romanians to believe that peaceful acceptance of victimhood had to make room for self-determination. It is not by chance that immediately prior to and during the Second World War many voices started to question the viability of the fatalist narrative promoted in *Miorița*. In 1938 sociologist H. H. Stahl tried to demythologize the poem, reconsidering its philosophical meanings and interpreting it in a purely historical and economic context.[13] In 1942,

Victor Eftimiu, a well-known Romanian drama writer, declared that "Miorița, the famous ballad which is considered by some to be the most beautiful Romanian poem, should be taken out from the school books because it contains a monumental lesson of cowardice and capitulation."[14] The aggressive violence of the Romanians toward Jews and other religious and ethnic minorities before and during the Second World War was based in part on this belief that Romanians had to break free of this mythical fatalism that had kept them victims for centuries, and assume control of their nationhood. Romanians believed that they should overcome the Moldavian shepherd's pattern and "defend" themselves, take fate into their own hands.

For Romanians the war against the USSR was not just a war against Communism, or a war for the recuperation of the territories lost in 1940, it was a war of self-determination, of breaking old patterns. The violence against Jews was not just a political or social decision. It was a mythological fight against the "other." It was as though the Moldavian shepherd suddenly realized that he had to fight back and revolt against his destiny. In Victor Eftimiu's words, "if they [the Moldavians/Romanians] were not so languid [as the shepherd from *Miorița*], they would have never been mounted [*încălecați*] by the Jews."[15] The portrayal of Jews as the archenemies of the Romanian people, as Satan's soldiers, espoused by members of the Orthodox hierarchy who were held in high esteem by the people, including by Patriarch Nicodim, fed into this myth. It was precisely this friend-enemy discourse and the reverberations it had in popular folklore that allowed scenes of extreme violence to pass the radar of conscience.

The swing back to an emphasis on *Miorița* can be sensed soon after the war. The poem suited the victimhood narrative, which was increasingly promoted by the Communist regime. Like the Moldavian shepherd, Romanians were portrayed as having behaved humanely toward the "others," while the others (especially the Hungarians in the Communist narrative) took advantage and plotted behind their backs to destroy them. It was a return to the medieval roots of the ballad. After the fall of Communism, the two approaches to *Miorița* were promoted simultaneously. On the one hand, Romanians refused to accept that in the recent past they had been the aggressors, despite growing evidence proving this. They continued to believe the Communist narrative, which was embedded in their national identity after several decades of Communist indoctrination, and which did not leave room for repentance or confessions of guilt. On the other hand, as during the interwar period, a growing sense of revolt against the victimhood pattern was visible after the fall of Ceauşescu. Rediscovering the interwar nationalists in the 1990s, many Romanians started to believe again that they had to fight back, they had to overcome fate and revolt against their enemies. After 1990 "the others" took different forms, but most often they were the Hungarians, Jews, and Christian "sects" (Evangelical denominations such as Baptists, Adventists, and Jehovah's Witnesses).[16] This view of the other as the enemy who wants to destroy the very existence of the Romanian people was encouraged, after 1989, by important theologians of the Romanian Orthodox Church such as Dumitru Stăniloae (see chapter 8).

As Alexandru Florian points out in an article discussing the Romanian public's lack of interest in the Holocaust, the reasons for this should be sought in the Communist education, which entirely denied any Romanian involvement in the Holocaust.[17] Even today the Holocaust is not perceived as having anything to do with the Romanians—it is not yet part of the Romanians' collective memory. And not just the Holocaust, but any negative aspect of Romanian history is of no interest. The victimhood narrative continued almost unchallenged after the fall of Communism. Even when historians tried to challenge the way Romanian historiography was written in the last century,[18] pointing to problematic aspects of nationalist historiographies, the old narrative remained dominant.[19]

The Romanian Orthodox Church and Holocaust memory: Understanding the lack of an Orthodox Holocaust theology

The process of making the Holocaust relevant for a Romanian audience has also been hindered by the way in which the Orthodox Church and other Christian denominations in Romania relate to Holocaust memory. Romania is a deeply religious country. About 90 percent of Romanians profess themselves religious and believing in God. The Romanian Orthodox Church was for more than twenty years the most trusted Romanian institution, with outstanding figures in major polls. As one of the country's most important institutions, with a major influence in the social, political, and educational realm, the Church could have a major impact on the lay Romanian's understanding of the Holocaust. As religious institutions, the Christian churches could challenge the glorification-victimization myth and bring negative aspects of the past into the open by discussing concepts such as guilt, responsibility, and repentance. While the collective psyche of a nation is easily tempted to avoid such painful analysis, the Churches could set the tone for another approach. It was not by chance that the growing interest in the Holocaust and the acceptance of responsibility for collaboration with the Nazis in countries such as France and West Germany grew when Catholic and Protestant churches began openly discussing anti-Semitic prejudices and past misdeeds.

The Romanian Orthodox Church in particular has several times acknowledged the need for repentance and the benefits of accepting responsibility for past mistakes. In an article published in *Studii Teologice* in 1955 Niculae Balca discusses the benefits of repentance from a psychological and soteriological point of view. Although focusing on individual sin and guilt, and avoiding discussion of the collective guilt of the Church, Balca accepts the need to confess guilt: "Repentance is a deep necessity of the human soul which is subjected to mistakes, errors, and sin."[20]

In the next issue of the *Studii Teologice* an article by Irineu Crăciunaş analyzes the problem of moral responsibility. After highlighting our juridical, political, social, and medical responsibilities, the author defines moral responsibility as "essentially different from the other ones by the fact that it is linked to the moral conscience. This moral conscience declares us morally responsible before the decision of any other authority. It obliges us to an inner acknowledgement of our guilt, of our bad deeds, to an acceptance of any consequences and to an effort to repair them."[21] In comparison to the Balca article, Irineu Crăciunaş openly touches on collective responsibility but specifically points out that "the Church in its essence and in ecumenical unity cannot be made responsible because it is infallible."[22] Although the collective responsibility of the Church is denied in these articles, they at least offer a basis for a serious discussion about moral responsibility in society as a whole. The victimhood narrative, which avoided any discussion about guilt, could be challenged from the perspective of repentance and moral responsibility.

These important declarations, published in 1955, were not followed through by the Romanian Orthodox Church. Instead of encouraging an open discussion about a problematic past, the Church continued to promote a whitewashed narrative both in its relation to the Holocaust and to Communism. The refusal of the Orthodox Church to responsibly address these issues springs from its inability to deal with and fear of the past. As discussed in chapters 1 and 2, the church-state relationship before and during the war, and its cultivated anti-Semitism, had a poisonous effect on the attitude of the Romanian Orthodox Church toward Jews. The close links with political power meant that the Church supported, in its official press and through the actions of its organizations and clergy, all the major steps in the destruction of Romanian Jewry.

Knowing these dark aspects of the past, the Romanian Orthodox Church concealed its negative involvement in the Holocaust in 1945. Bishop Antim Nica's article was essential in this process. During the Communist era, new concepts such as the permanent tolerance of the Church toward Jewish and other minorities were added to this narrative which was based on history cleansing and selective memory. After 1989 the Romanian Orthodox Church successfully avoided dealing with its involvement in the Holocaust. The Church continued to present itself as favorable to the Jews, as their savior, as always tolerant and hospitable toward foreigners. This fiction, using extensively the 1945 cover-up, was reinforced by Alexandru Ioniță's 1990 *Biserica Ortodoxă Română* article and by Patriarch Teoctist's speech at the 2004 celebration of Father Gheorghe Petre. The lack of academic research on the involvement of the Romanian Orthodox Church in the destruction of Romanian Jewry and the conciliatory approach of both the Jewish community and the state of Israel helped the Church avoid scrutiny.

The fact that the Church promoted the cover-up fiction and portrayed itself as always tolerant and hospitable does not mean that after 1989 it kept away from extreme nationalism, anti-Semitism, and intolerance of minorities. On the contrary, in the 1990s the Romanian Orthodox Church was at the forefront of Romanian nationalism, encouraging extreme discourse in which everyone who was not Orthodox was seen as not being a true Romanian, a discourse directly linked to the interwar notion of Românianism. Important Romanian theologians such as Dumitru Stăniloae and the patriarch of the Church, Teoctist, promoted such themes in their articles and public speeches.

Two important aspects mentioned by Michael Shafir in reference to postcommunist Romania, the resistance myths and the Vichy syndrome[23] were also present in the Romanian Orthodox Church's post-1989 narrative. The Church presented itself as a victim of Communism, and portrayed itself in a glorious light in relation to its involvement in the Holocaust. Both myths were enforced through the obstruction of access to documents that would have allowed a proper investigation.

Although the Romanian Orthodox Church avoided official expressions of anti-Semitism after 1989, actions such as the rehabilitation of Puiu and Trifa, and the defense of controversial priests who were linked with the Iron Guard, led to an increase of grassroots anti-Semitism. The fact that controversial books had forewords written by members of the Church hierarchy led to the impression that although no official declarations were made against Jews, the general rightwing anti-Semitism of the interwar period, which was rediscovered in them, was blessed by the hierarchy. All these factors had a paradoxical effect on the way in which the Romanian Orthodox Church related to Holocaust memory. On the one hand, it presented itself as a savior of Jews, promoting without remorse the narrative developed since 1945. On the other hand, it encouraged the promotion of anti-Semitism and defended those clergy who were involved in violent actions against Jews. Instead of analyzing their behavior toward the Jews and whether or not their prosecution by the Communist authorities after the war was legitimate, these priests were presented as martyrs and victims of Communism.

It is true that knowledge about the anti-Semitism of the Romanian Orthodox Church during the interwar period increased after the fall of Communism. Several postcommunist works mention the anti-Semitism of Patriarch Cristea, or the links between the Iron Guard and the Church. As a result, in some instances, such as the issuance of the five special coins celebrating the five patriarchs of the Church, organizations from inside and outside Romania have protested. But knowledge about the attitude of the Romanian Orthodox Church during the Holocaust has been almost entirely nonexistent.

As Saul Friedländer reminds us, in his excellent book entitled *Memory, History, and the Extermination of the Jews of Europe*, the passage of time is an implacable force that will in the end awaken our awareness of past misdeeds.[24] The Romanian Orthodox Church has to look into its past and, based on a theology of repentance than can be sensed in the 1955 articles published in *Studii Teologice*, to construct its own Holocaust theology. As in the case of the Catholic and Protestant churches, the Romanian Orthodox Church has to more clearly define its theology about Judaism, supersession (replacement theology), deicide, anti-Semitism, anti-Semitic writings of the Church fathers, and its own history of anti-Semitism. It also has to be more open in allowing historians to look into its past. If a decision to fully open its Second World War archives is not possible, the Orthodox Church should at least follow the example of the Catholic Church, which published twelve volumes of documents regarding the "Jewish problem" during the war. Taking a truthful approach to the past, bringing negative aspects to light and dealing with them would allow the Church to honestly celebrate the real examples of rescue. There were priests who, on their own initiative, defended the Jews during the Holocaust, some losing their lives in the process. These examples are almost entirely forgotten today because the Church is afraid of looking into the past.

It is time to open new avenues into analyzing the role of other Eastern European Orthodox Churches during the Holocaust. Due to the lack of academic research, many Orthodox Churches present themselves in a glorious light. In all Eastern European Orthodox countries an analysis of Orthodox anti-Semitism and the way in which it influenced Eastern-Europeans' attitudes toward Jews during the war is essential. As Geoffrey Wigoder points out, Orthodoxy is still embedded in medieval traditions, unwilling to revise its anti-Semitic doctrines and generally reluctant to accept steps forward taken by other Christian denominations in the Jewish-Christian dialogue.[25] Although Wigoder's book was published in 1988, not much has changed in this matter since then. An analysis of the way in which various national Orthodox churches behaved during the Holocaust and their role in supporting local or Nazi policies would be crucial, as would a careful research into these Churches' role in the building of Holocaust memory and the resurgence of anti-Semitism after 1990. In Eastern Europe, old nationalist and anti-Semitic discourses in which the Church is reinvested as the core of peoples' identity are increasingly being brought to light.[26] Anti-Semites of the interwar period are silently legitimized yet again. In this context, without clearly and properly addressing the dark episodes of the Holocaust, Orthodox Churches could become again agents of anti-Semitic hatred and the dark demons of the past could be resurrected.

NOTES

1. For a comparative case, see Jeffrey Herf, *Divided Memory: The Nazi Past in the Two Germanys* (Cambridge, MA: Harvard University Press, 1997), 178–179.

2. Henry Rousso, *The Vichy Syndrome: History and Memory in France since 1944* (Cambridge, MA: Harvard University Press, 1991), 301–306.

3. See Saul Friedländer, *Memory, History, and the Extermination of the Jews of Europe* (Bloomington: Indiana University Press, 1993), 14–15. See also Abraham Peck, ed., *Jews and Christians after the Holocaust* (Philadelphia: Fortress, 1982), 40.

4. See Wolfram Wette, *The Wehrmacht: History, Myth, Reality*, trans. Deborah Lucas Schneider (Cambridge, MA: Harvard University Press, 2006), especially "The Wehrmacht and the Murder of Jews," 90–138, and "The Legend of the Wehrmacht's 'Clean Hands,'" 195–250. See also Geoffrey Megargee, "Burying the Myth of the 'Clean' Wehrmacht," review of *The Wehrmacht: History, Myth, Reality*, by Wolfram Wette, *H-Net Reviews*, August 2008, http://www.h-net.org/reviews/showpdf.php?id=14799.

5. The Serbian Orthodox Church, for example, like the Romanian Orthodox Church, presents itself as having always been tolerant and favorable to Jews. See Bishop Jovan Ćulibrk, "A View of Theologians of the Serbian Orthodox Church on the Suffering of Jews during the War" (presentation at Theological Contemplations and Debates vis-à-vis the Holocaust in Real Time, Yad Vashem, Jerusalem, 9–12 July 2012). For a more scholarly approach, see Jovan Byford, *Denial and Repression of Antisemitism: Post-Communist Remembrance of the Serbian Bishop Nikolaj Velimirovic* (New York: Central European University Press, 2008).

6. Phayer, *The Catholic Church and the Holocaust, 1930–1965* (Bloomington: Indiana University Press, 2000), 144.

7. Verdery, "Nationalism and National Sentiment in Post-socialist Romania," *Slavic Review* 52, no. 2 (Summer 1993): 195–196.

8. See Anna Sommer, "Auschwitz Today: Personal Observations and Reflections about Visitors to the Auschwitz-Birkenau State Museum and Memorial," in *Les Cahiers Irice, Le Future d'Auschwitz*, proceedings of the workshop, 11 May 2010, Paris, 91–92, http://irice.univ-paris1.fr/IMG/pdf/pdf_Volume_integral_Cahier_7_-_copie.pdf.

9. Randolph L. Braham, "A TV Documentary on Rescue during the Holocaust. A Case of History Cleansing in Romania," *Eastern European Quarterly* 28, no. 2 (June 1994): 196.

10. See Televiziunea Naționala a României [Romanian National Television], "Cine este in top 100 Mari Români" [Who is in top 100 Greatest Romanians], accessed 26 February 2013, http://www.tvr.ro/cine-este-in-top-100-mari-romani_2103.html#view.

11. English translation by W. D. Snodgrass, accessed 2 July 2013, http://spiritromanesc.go.ro/Miorita%20-eng.html.

12. Adrian Fochi, *Miorița: Tipologie, Circulație, Geneză* (Bucharest: Editura Academiei Române, 1964), 152–153. Fochi refers to the fatalist interpretation of Liviu Rusu, *Le sens de l'existence dans la poésie populaire roumaine* (Paris: Alcan, 1935).

13. M. Eliade, *De la Zamolxis la Gengis Han* [From Zalmoxis to Genghis Khan] (Bucharest: Editura Științifică și Enciclopedică, 1980), 233. Here Eliade refers to the work of H. H. Stahl, "Filozofarea despre filozofia poporului Român," *Sociologia Românească* 3, nos. 3–4 (1938): 104–119.

14. Victor Eftimiu, *Opere* [Works], vol. 18, *Amintiri și polemici* [Memories and Polemics] (1942; Bucharest: Minerva, 1996), 159.

15. Ibid.

16. Verdery, "Nationalism and National Sentiment," 196.

17. Alexandru Florian, "Evreii din România în Timpul celui de-al doilea război mondial: o problema de cultură și conștiință civica," *Holocaust. Studii și Cercetări* 1, no. 1 (2009): 139.

18. See, for example, Florin Constantiniu, *O istorie sinceră a poporului român* [An Honest History of the Romanian People], 3rd ed., rev. (Bucharest: Univers Enciclopedic, 2002), or Lucian Boia, *Istorie și mit in conștiința românească* [History and Myth in Romanian Consciousness] (Bucharest: Humanitas, 1997).

19. For an analysis of the evolution of Romanian historiography since the fall of Communism, see Cristina Petrescu and Dragos Petrescu, "Mastering or Coming to Terms with the Past: A Critical Analysis of Post-Communist Romanian Historiography," in *Narratives Unbound: Historical Studies in Post-Communist Eastern Europe,* ed. Antohi Sorin, Trencsényi Balázs, and Apor Péter (New York: Central European University Press, 2007), 311–408.

20. Niculae Balca, "Etapele psihologice ale mărturisirii," *Studii Teologice,* series 2, vol. 7, nos. 1–2 (January–February 1955): 30.

21. Irineu Crăciunaş, "Responsabilitatea morală," *Studii Teologice,* series 2, vol. 7, nos. 3–4 (March–April 1955): 183.

22. Ibid., 192.

23. Shafir, "Romania's Torturous Road to Facing Collaboration," *in Collaboration with the Nazis: Public Discourse after the Holocaust,* ed. Roni Stauber (London: Routledge, 2011), 245.

24. Friedländer, *Memory, History, and the Extermination of the Jews,* 37.

25. Geoffrey Wigoder, *Jewish-Christian Relations since the Second World War* (Manchester, UK: Manchester University Press, 1988), 6.

26. Verdery, "Nationalism and National Sentiment," 196.

APPENDIX

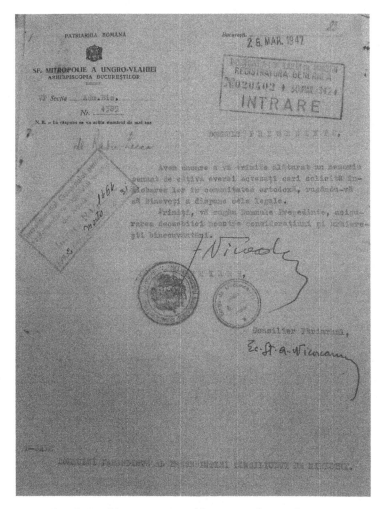

Letter dated March 28, 1942, signed by Patriarch Nicodim, inquiring about the status of baptized Jews.

The text reads: "We have the honor to send you attached a written pleading signed by few baptized Jews who ask to be integrated into the Orthodox community, and we request your legal decision. Please receive, Mister President, the assurance of our distinguished consideration and our priestly blessings."

Source: CSIER III, 1068, f. 83

Iles Lerman, Chairman Emeritus
and James Holocaust Memorial Council

June 13, 2001

Preafericitul Parinte Patriarh Teoctist:
Cancelaria Sfintului Sinod
Strada Antim 29
Bucuresti, Romania

Dear Patriarch Teoctist:

On June 1, 2001, in the Bucharest church *Sfinții Împarați Constantin si Elena* founded by Romania's wartime dictator and Hitler ally, Marshall Ion Antonescu, a monument dedicated to him was unveiled.

As you also know, Ion Antonescu, Romania's ruler during World War II was one of the main allies of Nazi Germany, who made his country a member of the Axis and who declared war on the United States. Romania was the main ally of Germany on the Eastern front. Antonescu's troops participated in the mobile killing operations. Antonescu initiated pogroms against the Jews, massive massacres, and the full-scale deportations of the Romanian Jews from Bessarabia and Bukovina. He also handed over the Romanian Jews to the Germans in the Ukraine and Western Europe. Antonescu and his regime are responsible for the death of at least 250,000 Romanian and Ukrainian Jews. Ion Antonescu's direct involvement in the physical destruction of the Romanian and Ukrainian Jews in Moldova, Bessarabia, Bucovina and Transnistria is clearly demonstrated by many historical World War II documents which originate from the Romanian archives.

The recent monument to the glory of Ion Antonescu was inaugurated at the initiative of the Party of Greater Romania, an openly fascist political organization which received a strong showing in the recent elections. The Party of Greater Romania advocates the rehabilitation of Romanian war criminals and is in the forefront of Holocaust denial.

The fact that the Romanian Orthodox Church tolerates on its land a monument to the glory of a major war criminal is extremely worrisome. The Romanian Orthodox Church had an important role through the Archbishop Balan of Transylvania in the cancellation of the planned deportation of the Romanian Jews from Regat and Southern Transylvania to Belzec in 1942 contributing in an essential way to the saving of many Jewish lives. This important rescue action should not be tarnished by the very same iniquition which accomplished it.

That is why we are respectfully asking you to investigate the circumstances of the raising of this monument on the Orthodox Church grounds which in our view contradicts the very essence of your mission of peace and understanding between various nationalities and religions.

We strongly believe that the cult of Ion Antonescu, severely damages Romania's image abroad as well as the development of Romania toward a stable and democratic society.

Looking forward to your answer, I am,

Sincerely yours,

Miles Lerman

100 Raoul Wallenberg Place, S.W., Washington, D.C. 20024-2126, Telephone (202) 488-0400, Fax (202) 314-7881, www.ushmm.org
1450 East Chestnut Avenue, Building 1, Suite A, Vineland, N.J. 08361, Telephone (856) 691-7605, Fax (856) 692-3826

Letter from Miles Lerman, Chairman Emeritus USHMM, to the Romanian Orthodox Patriarch, June 13, 2001, complaining about the unveiling in an Orthodox church of a monument dedicated to Ion Antonescu.

Aleea Patriarhiei, 2
70526 — BUCUREŞTI 4
ROMÂNIA

Aleea Patriarhiei, 2
70526 — BUCHAREST 4
ROMÂNIA

No. 2973/2001
13.07.2001
For Your Information.

Mr. MILES LERMAN
Chairman Emeritus
United States Holocaust Memorial Council

Dear Mr. Lerman,

We have very carefully studied your letter and after making the necessary inquiries we have come to the sad conclusion that what you have informed us of were true, even though not exactly in the form in which you have presented it.

As it is well known, the Romanian Orthodox Church proved in very many circumstances in which its hierarchs and leaders participated, its spirit of rapprochement towards Jewish people in Romania, through the participation of our forerunners and of ours personally in various occasions hosted in the Coral Temple in Bucharest and in the commemoration of the victims of the progrom in Iaşi. Even outside Romania we recently participated, in November 2000, in a commemoration of the victims of the extermination camp of Majdanek, Poland, when we prayed together with Rabbi Elio Toaff for the remembrance of those innocent people who lost their lives in that terrible place. It is also worth mentioning the long standing and close relationship with rabbi Arthur Schneier, president of the "Appeal to Conscience" Foundation.

As far as the place of worship you refer to in your letter, that was built at the initiative and the funds provided by Ion Antonescu and his family. Our church regulations stipulate among other things that the Parish Assembly and parish Council are in charge with the administration of a place of worship and the responsibility of its maintenance. These two bodies take also decisions including the works for restoration and development of the place of worship. According to the tradition of our church the founders of a place of worship enjoys a special appreciation throughout the existence of the respective place of worship.

While expressing our regret for the possible problems that may have emerged, we hope that this case will not in any way change the good relations established between the Romanian Orthodox Church and the Jewish people from Romanian and from other parts of the world. Additionally, it ought to be mentioned that the Romanian society of today is extremely divided as far as the person of Ion Antonescu is concerned.

With best wishes,

TEOCTIST

PATRIARCH OF THE ROMANIAN ORTHODOX CHURCH

Patriarch Teoctist's reply to Miles Lerman's letter, July 13, 2001.

Letter from Metropolitan Nicolae Bălan of Transylvania to the Ministry of Religions about Law 711 banning the conversion of Jews, April 2, 1941.

Source: USHMM, RG25.021M, reel 100, f. 35-37

Patriarch Miron Cristea, Armand Călinescu, and other members of the Romanian government at the Palace of the Patriarchate. Romanian army parade, 1938.

Credit: Romanian National Archives

Reference number: BU-F-01073-2-03181-02

Miron Cristea and Octavian Goga in front of the Palace of the Patriarchate, 1939.

Credit: Romanian National Archives

Reference Number: BU-F-01073-2-03006

Patriarch Nicodim Munteanu surrounded by priests and military personnel during a ceremony, 1940.

Credit: Romanian National Archives

Reference Number: BU-F-01073-2-00388

Patriarch Nicodim Munteanu, Gheorghe Tătărescu, Alexandru Vaida-Voevod (in uniforms of the Front of National Rebirth), and others during a parade, 1940.

Credit: Romanian National Archives

Reference number: BU-FD-01073-1-10978-065

Mihai Antonescu giving a speech in the presence of Patriarch Nicodim Munteanu, 1940–1944.

Credit: Romanian National Archives

Reference number: BU-F-01073-2-00439-1

King Michael, Ion Antonescu, the queen mother, and Horia Sima on the stairs of the Palace of the Patriarchate, 1940.

Credit: Romanian National Archives

Reference number: BU-F-01073-1-10932—24

The General Consistory Meeting of the Romanian Orthodox Church for the election of a new patriarch (June 30, 1939, Nicodim Munteanu), 1939–1940.

Credit: Romanian National Archives

Reference number: BU-F-01073-2-00387

THE PATRIARCHS OF THE ROMANIAN ORTHODOX CHURCH

- Miron Cristea (1925–1939)
- Nicodim Munteanu (1939–1948)
- Justinian Marina (1948–1977)
- Iustin Moisescu (1977–1986)
- Teoctist Arăpașu (1986–2007)
- Daniel Ciobotea (since 2007)

BIBLIOGRAPHY

I. Archival Material

Unpublished

**United States Holocaust Memorial Museum Archive
(USHMM): https://www.ushmm.org/.**

RG 25.084 Selected Records from the National Council for the Study of Securitate Archives

RG 25.021 Selected Records Relating to the Holocaust in Romania, 1941–2002, especially reels 1, 2, 4, 8, 13, 16, 22, 97, 100, 101, 103

RG 25.047 Selected Records of the Foreign Information Service of Romania (SIE)

RG 25.002 Selected Records from the Romanian National Archives, reels 1, 6, 7, 35

RG 10.297 Charles Kremer Collection

RG 25.051 Records of the World Jewish Congress in Romania

Jewish Press Periodicals from the Collection of the Romanian Academy Library

**Consiliul National pentru Studierea Arhivelor Securității
(CNSAS): http://www.cnsas.ro/.**

Fond Documentar [Documentary Fund]

D10419 Procesul Masacrului de la Iași [The Trial of the Jassy Massacre], 3 volumes

D11374 Comunitatea Evreilor din România, 1942–1943 [The Jewish Community of Romania, 1942–1943]

D11381 Comunitatea Evreilor din România, 1943–1949 [The Jewish Community of Romania, 1943–1949]

D11387 Problema Evreiască, 1943–1947 [The Jewish Problem, 1943–1947]

D11433 Instrucțiuni și ordine referitoare la reglementarea cetățeniei evreiești 1930–1939 [Instructions and Orders Related to the Regulation of Jewish Citizenship 1930–1939]

D11915 Situația Social-Politică, Economică, Starea de Spirit a Populației, 1941–1950 [The Socio-Political and Economic Situation, the Morale of the Population, 1941–1950]

D12088 Chestiunea Preoțească în Vechiul Regat, 1947–1948 [The Priesthood Issue in the Old Kingdom, 1947–1948]

D12207 Organizarea și Activitatea Populației Evreiești din Romania, 1918–1953 [The Organization and Activity of the Jewish Population of Romania, 1918–1953]

D12208 Activitatea Sionistă a Unor Organizatii Evreiești din România. Starea de Spirit a Populației Evreiești, Emigrarea în Palestina, Tezaurul unor Organizații Sioniste, 1936–1964 [The Zionist Activity of Some Jewish Organizations from Romania. The Morale of the Jewish Population, Emigration to Palestine, the Treasury of Some Zionist Organisations, 1936–1964]

D12210 Măsurile Represive împotriva Evreilor din Moldova, 1941–1942 [The Repressive Measures against the Jews from Moldova, 1941–1942], 2 volumes

D12216 Revenirea în Moldova a Evreilor Deportați in Transnistria in 1944 [The Return to Moldova of Jews Deported to Transnistria in 1944]

D13029 Procesul Complotist Antistatal în Frunte cu Rudolf Slansky [The Trial of the Anti-State Plot Headed by Rudolf Slansky], volumes 1 and 5

D13158 Criminalii de Război, 1950–1952 [War Criminals, 1950–1952]

D13273 Preoți Operați 1945 [Priests Filed in 1945]

D14480 Procesul de la Nuremberg. Criminalii de Război Hitleriști [The Nuremberg Trial. The Hitlerist War Criminals]

D14578 Urmărirea Foștilor Legionari de către Organele de Securitate din fostul Județ Ilfov [The Surveillance of the Former Legionaries by the Securitate in the Former County of Ilfov]

D14673 Culte și Secte după 23 August 1944 [Religions and Sects after 23 August 1944]

D164 Problema Evreiască, Anii 1948–1957 [The Jewish Problem, 1948–1957]

D169 Problema Evreiască pe Anul 1952 [The Jewish Problem, Year 1952]

D184 Emigrația Politică Română [Romanian Political Immigration]

D3388 Declarații cu Privire la Deportarea Evreilor în Transnistria. Tratamentul Aplicat Evreilor în Lagăre, 1948–1950 [Declarations Regarding the Deportation of Jews to Transnistria. The Treatment of Jews in Lagers, 1948–1950]

D3415 Cultul Ortodox—Materiale Informative și Diverse Verificări [The Orthodox Church—Informative Materials and Various Checks]

D3455 Crime de Război și Acțiuni Antisemite Săvârșite de Militari și Polițiști [War Crimes and Anti-Semitic Actions Done by Military Personnel and by Policemen]

D56 Problema Preoțească în Vechiul Regat, 1945–1947 [The Priesthood Problem in the Old Kingdom, 1945–1947]

D68 Nunciatura Papală, 1948–1949

D7349 Buletin Informativ Anul 1946 [Informative Bulletin, 1946]

D74 Starea de Spirit, Evidența și Activitatea Dușmănoasă a Preoților Cultului Ortodox in anii 1948–1951 [The Morale, Evidence, and Hostile Activity of Orthodox Priests in 1948–1951]

D8171 Urmărirea și Judecarea Criminalilor de Război Militari si Funcționari din Aparatul de Stat în anii 1944–1945 [The Prosecution and Trial of Military War Criminals and State Functionaries, 1944–1945]

D8172 Urmărirea și Judecarea Criminalilor de Război, 1944–1945 [The Prosecution and Trial of War Criminals, 1944–1945]

D8174 Arestarea și Judecarea Persoanelor Civile și Militare Vinovate de Dezastrul Țării— Crime de Război [The Arrest and Trial of Civilians and Military Individuals Guilty of the Country's Disaster—War Crimes]

D8175 Referitor la foștii guvernanți și funcționari din Transnistria învinuiți pentru crime de război, cf. art. 14 din Convenția de Armistițiu—documente din perioada 1944–1945 [Regarding the Former Government Officials and Functionaries of Transnistria Prosecuted for War Crimes According to Article 14 of the Armistice Convention— Documents from 1944–1945]

D8177 Identificarea, Arestarea și Judecarea Criminalilor de Război. Masacrul Impotriva Evreilor, 1944–1950 [Identification, Arrest, and Trial of War Criminals; The Massacre against Jews, 1944–1950]

D8743 Sinteza Privind Cercetările Efectuate în Problema Sionistă, 1952 [Overview of the Inquiries into the Zionist Problem, 1952]

D8750 Tabelele Nominale cu Rudele și Membrii de Familie, Criminali de Război, Intocmite de DGSS și Organe din Subordine in 1952 [Nominal Tables with Relatives and Family Members, War Criminals, Compiled by DGSS and Auxiliary Agencies in 1952]

D8889 Fond Documentar Privind Sioniștii, 1948 [Documentary File Regarding the Zionists, 1948]

D8891 Federația Sioniștilor din România (1945–1946) [The Zionist Federation of Romania (1945–1946)]

D8925 Problema Preoțească în Vechiul Regat, 1948–1949 [The Priesthood Problem in the Old Kingdom, 1948–1949]

D8927 Chestiunea Preoțească în Vechiul Regat, 1940–1943 [The Priesthood Issue in the Old Kingdom, 1940–1943]

D12378 Problema Culte si Secte [The Cults and Sects Problem], 4 volumes

DIE 142 Privitor la Visarion Puiu [Regarding Visarion Puiu]

DIE 82 Privitor la Valerian Trifa[Regarding Valerian Trifa]

Fond de Urmărire [Surveillance Fund]

R 319280 Dosar Personal al Agentului, Numele Conspirativ "VALER" [Personal File of the Agent, Code Name "VALER"]

Fond Operativ [Operative Fund]

I234510 Arbore P Ion

I86960 Sofian Ignatie

I86248 Teodorescu Costache

Institutul Naţional pentru Studierea Holocaustului din România, Elie Wiesel (INSHREW): http://www.inshr-ew.ro/.

The USHMM copied microfilmed archive

RG-25.004M, Selected records from the Romanian Information Service, reels 19–22, 23–26, 27, 28

RG 25.002, Selected records from the Romanian National Archives, reels 14, 33

The institute's library, including its journals archival collection: *Holocaustul. Studii şi Cercetări* and *Studia et Acta Historiae Iudaeorum Romaniae*

Arhivele Naţionale ale României (ANR) [The National Archives of Romania]: (English Language Version): http://www.arhivelenationale.ro/?lan=1.

ANR 2720, Ministerul Cultelor si Artelor [Ministry of Religions and Arts], 1933–1944: 2/1943, 47/1943 94/1943, 134/1943, 180/1943

ANR 3323, Ministerul Cultelor si Artelor [Ministry of Religions and Arts], 1948–1968: 6/1951, 8/1957

Centrul pentru Studiul Istoriei Evreilor din România (CSIER) [The Center for the Study of the History of Romanian Jews]: http://www.csier.ro/.

Fond III: 9, 12, 60, 473, 623, 858, 1049, 1068, 1092

Fond V: 76, 160, 186, 242, 243, 246, 249, 262, 266

Biblioteca Centrală Universitară, especially the Church journals archival collection: *Biserica Ortodoxă Română, Ortodoxia, Studii Teologice, Analele Bucovinei*

Biblioteca Academiei Române, especially the Church journals archival collection: *Cuvântul Preoţesc, Luminătorul, Transnistria Creştină, Apostolul*

Institutul de Istoria Artei „George Oprescu," Church journals archival collection: *Biserica Orthodoxă Română* (1938–1989), *Studii Teologice*

Published

Ancel, Jean. *Documents Concerning the Fate of Romanian Jewry during the Holocaust.* New York: Beate Klarsfeld Foundation, 1986.

Benjamin, Lya, ed. *Problema evreiască în stenogramele Consiliului de Ministri* [The Jewish Question in the Minutes of the Council of Ministers], vol. 2 of *Evreii din România între anii 1940–1944* [The Jews of Romania, 1940–1944]. Bucharest: Hasefer, 1996.

Carp, Matatias. *Cartea Neagra* [The Black Book]. Bucharest: Atelierele grafice Socec, 1946–1948. English edition: Carp, Matatias. *Holocaust in Romania: Facts and Documents on the Annihilation of Romania's Jews, 1940–1944.* Harbor, FL: Simon, 2000.

Mircu, Marius. *Pogromurile din Bucovina si Dorohoi* [The Pogroms in Bukovina and Dorohoi]. Bucharest: Glob, 1945.

Taneva, Albena, ed. *The Power of Civil Society in a Time of Genocide: Proceedings of the Holy Synod of the Bulgarian Orthodox Church on the Rescue of the Jews in Bulgaria, 1940–1944*. Sofia: Sofia University Press, 2005.

Trașcă, Ottmar. *Al III-lea Reich și Holocaustul din România: 1940–1944. Documente din arhivele germane* [The Third Reich and the Holocaust in Romania: 1940–1944. Documents from German Archives]. Bucharest: INSHREW, 2007.

II. Journals

Analele Bucovinei. Bucharest, Rădăuți: Editura Academiei Române, 1994–

Apostolul, Jurnalul Arhiepiscopiei Bucureștilor. Bucharest: Tipografia Cărților Bisericești, 1924–1940

Biserica Ortodoxă Română, Revista Sfântului Sinod. Bucharest: Tipografia Institutului Biblic și de Misiune al Bisericii Ortodoxe Române, 1874–

Cuvântul Preoțesc. Rădăuți: Văd. Blondovschi, 1934–1942

Holocaustul. Studii și Cercetări, Jurnalul INSHREW, 2009–

Luminătorul, Revista Eparhiei Chișinăului Si Hotinului. Chișinau: Tip. Eparhiala, 1923–1944

Ortodoxia, Revista Patriarhiei Române. Bucharest: Editura Institutului Biblic si de Misiune Ortodoxă, 1956–1995

Studia et Acta Historiae Iudaeorum Romaniae. Bucharest: Hasefer, 2002–

Studii Teologice, Publicație a Facultății de Teologie din București. Bucharest: Editura Bucovina, 1929–1940

Studii Teologice, Revista Institutelor Teologice din Patriarhia Româna. Bucharest: Editura Institutului Biblic și de Misiune Ortodoxă, 1949–

Transnistria Creștină, Revista Misiunii Bisericești Pentru Transnistria. Odessa: 1942–1943

III. Speeches and official declarations/telegrams

Comitetul de Redacție [Editorial Board]. "Razboiul Sfânt de Dezrobire" [The Holy War of Restoration]. *Biserica Ortodoxă Română (BOR)* 59, nos. 5–6 (May–June 1941): 337.

Cristea, Miron Patriarhul României. "Apelul Guvernului către țară." *Apostolul* 14, no. 4 (15 February 1938): 43–45.

"Cronica interna, telegrama trimeasă Domului Mareşal Ion Antonescu" [Internal Chronicle, the Telegram Sent to Marshal Ion Antonescu]. *BOR* 59, nos. 9–10 (September–October 1941): 600–601.

"Crucea biruitoare" [The Victorious Cross]. *BOR* 61, nos. 1–3 (January–March 1943): 1–10.

"Declarația IPS Sale Mitropolitul Nicolae Bălan" [The Declaration of His Holiness Metropolitan Nicolae Bălan]. *Apostolul* 15, no. 12 (1–30 July 1939): 141–142.

"Schimb de telegrame între Prea Fericitul Părinte Iustinian Patriarhul Bisericii Ortodoxe Române și Eminența Sa, Dr. Moses Rosen, șef rabinul cultului mozaic din România" [Exchange of Telegrams between His Holiness Iustinian, the Patriarch of the Romanian Orthodox Church, and His Eminency, Dr. Moses Rosen, the Chief Rabbi of the Jewish Community (Mosaic Religion) of Romania]. *BOR* 92, nos. 5–6 (May–June 1974): 560–561.

Nicodim, Patriarhul României. "Cuvânt pentru post, pentru oștire și pentru ogor" [Message for the Fast, Army and Land]. *BOR* 60, nos. 1–4 (January–April 1942): 3–12.

———. "Cuvântul Bisericii pentru Războiul Sfânt" [The Church's Message on the Holy War]. *BOR* 59, nos. 7–8 (July–August 1941): 377–381.

———. "Cuvântul de Binecuvântare al Bisericii pentru Anul Nou 1944" [The Church's Message of Blessing for the New Year 1944]. *BOR* 62, nos. 1–3 (January–March 1944): 1–5.

———. "Indemnul IPS Patriarh Nicodim catre Popor" [The Appeal of H. H. Patriarch Nicodim to the People]. *BOR* 63, nos. 1–3 (January–March 1945): 88–89.

———. "Pastorala cu Ocazia Incheierii Armistițiului dintre România și Statele Aliate din 23 August 1944" [The Pastoral Letter Concerning the Signing of the Armistice between Romania and the Allies, 23 August 1944]. *BOR* 62, nos. 7–12 (July–December 1944): 219–223.

Rosen, Moses. "Mesajul Eminenței Sale Dr. Moses Rosen Șef Rabinul Cultului Mozaic din România." *BOR* 86, no. 6 (June 1968): 540–541.

Sfântul Sinod al Bisericii Ortodoxe Române. "Pastorala din Partea Sinodului Bisericii Ortodoxe Române" [The Pastoral Letter of the Holy Synod of the Romanian Orthodox Church]. *BOR* 63, nos. 7–8 (July–August 1945): 289–292.

Simedrea, Tit. "Cuvântarea IPSS Tit Simedrea Mitropolitul Bucovinei cu prilejul dechiderii adunarii eparhiale" [The Speech of His Holiness Tit Simedrea, the Metropolitan of Bukovina, at the Opening of the Church Assembly]. *Cuvântul Preoțesc* 9, no. 5 (May 1942): 1–3.

IV. Testimonies and Memoirs

Imbrescu, Ilie. *Biserica și Mișcarea Legionară* [The Church and the Legionary Movement]. Bucharest: Cartea Româneacă, 1940.

Mircu, Marius. *Oameni de omenie în vremuri de neomenie* [Humane People in In-Humane Times]. Bucharest: Hasefer, 1996.

Rosen, Moses, and Joseph Finklestone. *Dangers, Tests and Miracles: The Remarkable Life Story of Chief Rabbi Rosen of Romania*. London: Weidenfeld & Nicolson, 1990.

Safran, Alexandre. *Resisting the Storm, Romania 1940–1947: Memoirs.* Jerusalem: Yad Vashem, 1987.

V. Selected Books and Articles

Selected books

Ancel, Jean. *Contribuții la istoria României: problema evreiască* [Contributions to the History of Romania: The Jewish Problem]. Bucharest: Hasefer, 2001.

————. *Transnistria, 1941–1942: The Romanian Mass Murder Campaigns.* Tel Aviv: Tel Aviv University, 2003.

Anghelescu, Gheorghe F., and Cristian Untea. *Father Dumitru Stăniloae: A Worthy Disciple of the Classical Patristics: Bio-bibliography.* Bucharest: Editura Enciclopedică, 2009.

Bănică, Mirel. *Biserica Ortodoxă Română: stat și societate în anii '30* [The Romanian Orthodox Church—State and Society in the 1930s]. Iași, Romania: Polirom, 2007.

Bauer, Yehuda. *American Jewry and the Holocaust: The American Jewish Joint Distribution Committee, 1939–1945.* Detroit: Wayne State University Press, 1982.

Bobango, Gerald J. *The Romanian Orthodox Episcopate of America: The First Half Century, 1929–1979.* Jackson, MI: Romanian-American Heritage Center, 1979.

Boia, Lucian. *Istorie și mit in conștiința românească* [History and Myth in Romanian Consciousness]. Bucharest: Humanitas, 1997.

Braham, Randolph L. *The Treatment of the Holocaust in Hungary and Romania during the Post-Communist Era.* New York: Columbia University Press, 2004.

————. *The Vatican and the Holocaust: The Catholic Church and the Jews during the Nazi Era.* New York: Rosenthal Institute for Holocaust Studies, 2000.

Buzilă, Boris. *Din istoria vieții bisericești din Basarabia 1812–1944* [A History of the Bessarabian Church 1812–1944]. Bucharest: Fundațiile Culturale Române, 1996.

Byford, Jovan. *Denial and Repression of Antisemitism: Post-Communist Remembrance of the Serbian Bishop Nikolaj Velimirović.* New York: Central European University Press, 2008.

Cajal, Nicolae, and Hary Kuller, eds. *Contribuția evreilor din România la cultură și civilizație* [The Contribution of Romanian Jews to the Culture and Civilization]. Bucharest: Hasefer, 2004.

Caravia, Paul. *The Imprisoned Church: Romania 1944–1989.* Bucharest: National Institute for the Study of Totalitarianism, 1999.

Cleopa, Ilie. *Despre credința ortodoxă* [About the Orthodox Faith]. Bucharest: Editura Institutului Biblic și de Misiune al Bisericii Ortodoxe Române, 1985.

————. *Ne vorbește părintele Cleopa* [Father Cleopa Is Speaking to Us]. 3rd ed. Neamț, Romania: Mănăstirea Sihastria, 2004.

Coja, Ion. *Protocoalele kogaionului: teze și ipoteze, consemnate și autentificate de Ion Coja pentru a se înțelege și evalua corect contenciosul româno-evreiesc, inclusiv—așa numindu-I unii—holocaustul din România* [The Protocols of Zion: Thesis and Hypothesis, Recorded and Authenticated by Ion Coja for a Good Understanding of the Jewish-Romanian Discord, Including the So-Called Holocaust in Romania]. Bucharest: Țara Noastră, 2004.

Constantiniu, Florin. *O istorie sinceră a poporului român* [An Honest History of the Romanian People], 3rd ed., rev. Bucharest: Univers Enciclopedic, 2002.

Costache, Silviu. *Evreii din Romania: studiu de geografie umană* [The Jews of Romania - Study of Human Geography]. Bucharest: Bucharest University Press, 2004.

Crainic, Nichifor. *Ortodoxie și etnocrație* [Orthodoxy and Ethniocracy]. Bucharest: Cugetarea, 1938.

Cristian, S. C. *Patru ani de urgie: notele unui evreu din România* [Four Years of Wrath: Notes of a Jew from Romania]. Bucharest: Timpul, 1944

Cross, Lawrence. *Eastern Christianity: The Byzantine Tradition*. Philadelphia: E.J. Dwyer, 1988.

Deletant, Dennis. *Communist Terror in Romania: Gheorghiu-Dej and the Police State, 1948–1965*. London: Hurst, 1999.

———. *Hitler's Forgotten Ally: Ion Antonescu and His Regime, Romania 1940–1944*. London: Palgrave Macmillan, 2006.

Dumitriu-Snagov, Ion. *România în diplomația Vaticanului 1939–1944*. Bucharest: Garamond, 1991.

Ericksen, Robert P., and Susannah Heschel. *Betrayal: German Churches and the Holocaust*. Minneapolis: Augsburg Fortress Press, 1999.

Fochi, Adrian. *Miorița: Tipologie, Circulație, Geneză*. Bucharest: Editura Academiei Române, 1964.

Friedländer, Saul. *Memory, History, and the Extermination of the Jews of Europe*. Bloomington: Indiana University Press, 1993.

Gillet, Olivier. *Religie și naționalism. Ideologia Bisericii Ortodoxe Române sub regimul comunist* [Religion and Nationalism: The Ideology of the Romanian Orthodox Church under the Communist Regime]. Bucharest: Compania, 2001.

Govrin, Yosef. *Israeli-Romanian Relations at the End of the Ceaușescu Era: As Seen by Israel's Ambassador to Romania, 1985–1989*. London: Frank Cass, 2002.

Haumann, Haiko. *A History of East European Jews*. New York: Central European University Press, 2002.

Herf, Jeffrey. *Divided Memory: The Nazi Past in the Two Germanys*. Cambridge, MA: Harvard University Press, 1997.

Hilberg, Raul. *The Destruction of the European Jews*. Chicago: Quadrangle Books, 1961.

Hitchins, Keith. *Rumania 1866–1947*. Oxford: Clarendon, 1994.

Iancu, Carol. *Les juifs en Roumanie (1919–1938): de l'émancipation a la marginalisation*. Paris, Leuven: Peeters, 1996.

———. "The Struggle for the Emancipation of Romanian Jewry and Its International Ramifications." In *The History of the Jews in Romania*, vol. 2, *The Nineteenth Century*. Edited by Liviu Rotman and Carol Iancu, 111–149. Tel Aviv: The Goldstein-Goren Diaspora Research Center, 2005.

Ioanid, Radu. *The Holocaust in Romania: The Destruction of Jews and Gypsies under the Antonescu Regime: 1940–1944*. Chicago: Ivan R. Dee, 2000.

———. *Holocaustul în România: distrugerea evreilor și romilor sub regimul Antonescu, 1940–1944*. Bucharest: Hasefer, 2006.

———. *The Ransom of the Jews: The Story of the Extraordinary Secret Bargain between Romania and Israel*. Chicago: Ivan R. Dee, 2005.

Ionescu, Ștefan Cristian. *Jewish Resistance to "Romanianization," 1940–44*. London: Palgrave Macmillan, 2015.

Iorga, Nicolae. *Istoria bisericii românești și a vieții religioase a Românilor* [The History of the Romanian Church and of Romanians' Religious Life]. Vălenii de Munte, Romania: Neamul Românesc, 1908.

Karețki, Aurel, and Maria Covaci. *Zile însîngerate la Iași: 28–30 iunie 1941* [Bloody Days in Iași: 28-30 June 1941]. Bucharest: Editura Politică, 1978.

Kuller, Hary. *Evreii în România anilor 1944–1949: evenimente, documente, comentarii* [The Jews in Romania 1944–1989: Events, Documents, Comments]. Bucharest: Hasefer, 2002.

Leuștean, Lucian N. *Orthodoxy and the Cold War: Religion and Political Power in Romania, 1947–65*. London: Palgrave Macmillan, 2009.

Livezeanu, Irina. *Cultural Politics in Greater Romania: Regionalism, Nation Building, and Ethnic Struggle, 1918–1930*. Ithaca, NY: Cornell University Press, 1995.

Manuilă, Sabin, ed. *Recensământul general al populației româniei din 29 decemvrie 1930* [The Census of Romania's Population, 29 December 1930], vol. 2. Bucharest: Institutul Central de Statistică, 1938.

Mendelsohn, Ezra. *Jews of East Central Europe between the World Wars*. Bloomington: Indiana University Press, 1983.

Nastasă, Lucian, ed. *Antisemitismul universitar în România (1919–1939): mărturii documentare* [Academic Antisemitism in Romania (1919–1939) Documentary Evidence]. Cluj-Napoca, Romania: Kriterion, 2011.

Neumann, Victor. *Istoria evreilor din România: studii documentare și teoretice* [The History of the Jews of Romania: Documentary and Theoretical Studies]. Timișoara, Romania: Amarcord, 1996.

Nicolescu, Gheorghe, Gheorghe Dobrescu, and Andrei Nicolescu. *Preoți in tranșee 1941–1945* [Priests in Trenches, 1941–1945]. Bucharest: Fed. Print, 1999.

Ornea, Zigu. *The Romanian Extreme Right: The Nineteen Thirties*. Boulder, CO: East European Monographs, 1999.

Păiușan-Nuică, Cristina, and Radu Ciuceanu. *Biserica Ortodoxă Română sub regimul comunist, 1945–1958* [The Romanian Orthodox Church under the Communist Regime, 1945–1958]. Bucharest: Institutul National pentru Studiul Totalitarianismului, 2001.

Pană, Georgeta. *Antisemitismul religios din perspectivea holocaustului* [Religious Anti-Semitism from a Holocaust Perspective]. Bucharest: Bucharest University Press, 2008.

Peck, Abraham J., ed. *Jews and Christians after the Holocaust*. Philadelphia: Fortress, 1982.

Petcu, Adrian Nicolae, ed. *Partidul, Securitatea și cultele, 1945–1989* [Party, Securitate, and Religions, 1945–1989]. Bucharest: Nemira, 2005.

Petrescu, Cristina, and Dragoș Petrescu. "Mastering or Coming to Terms with the Past: A Critical Analysis of Post-Communist Romanian Historiography." In *Narratives Unbound: Historical Studies in Post-Communist Eastern Europe*. Edited by Antohi Sorin, Trencsényi Balázs, and Apor Péter. New York: Central European University Press, 2007.

Phayer, Michel. *The Catholic Church and the Holocaust, 1930–1965*. Bloomington: Indiana University Press, 2000.

Pineles, Jacques. *Istoria Evreilor: din cele mai vechi timpuri până la declaratia Balfour* [The History of Jews: From Ancient Times to the Balfour Declaration]. Iași, Romania: Lumea, 1935.

Quinlan, Paul Daniel. *Regele Playboy: Carol al II-lea de România* [The Playboy King, Carol II of Romania]. Bucharest: Humanitas, 2001.

Rezachevici, Constantin. "The Jews in the Romanian Principalities, Fifteenth to Eighteenth Centuries." In *The History of the Jews in Romania, vol. 1, From the Beginnings to the Nineteenth Century*. Edited by Paul Cernavodeanu. Tel Aviv: Goldstein-Goren Diaspora Research Center, 2005.

Rittner, Carol, Stephen D. Smith, and Irena Steinfeldt, eds. *The Holocaust and the Christian World: Reflections on the Past, Challenges for the Future*. London: Kuperand, 2000.

Rosen, Moses. *Chief Rabbi of Romania Dr. Moses Rosen on His Eightieth Birthday Anniversary*. Bucharest: Hasefer, 1992.

Rotman, Liviu. *The Communist Era until 1965*. Vol. 4 of *The History of the Jews in Romania*. Tel Aviv: The Goldstein-Goren Diaspora Research Center, 2005.

———. *Evreii din România în perioada comunistă, 1944–1965* [The Jews of Romania during Communism, 1944–1965]. Iași, Romania: Polirom, 2004.

Rousso, Henry. *The Vichy Syndrome: History and Memory in France since 1944*. Cambridge, MA: Harvard University Press, 1991.

Shachan, Avigdor. *Burning Ice: The Ghettos of Transnistria*. New York: Columbia University Press, 1996.

Shafir, Michael. *Between Denial and "Comparative Trivialization": Holocaust Negationism in Post-Communist East Central Europe*. Jerusalem: Hebrew University of Jerusalem, 2002.

———. "Romania's Torturous Road to Facing Collaboration." In *Collaboration with the Nazis: Public Discourse after the Holocaust*. Edited by Roni Stauber, 245–278. London: Routledge, 2011.

Shapiro, Paul. "Faith, Murder, Resurrection, the Iron Guard and the Romanian Orthodox Church." In *Antisemitisim, Christian Ambivalence, and the Holocaust*. Edited by Kevin P. Spicer, 136–170. Bloomington: Indiana University Press, 2007.

Solonari, Vladimir. *Purifying the Nation, Population Exchange and Ethnic Cleansing in Nazi-Allied Romania*. Washington, DC: Woodrow Wilson Center, 2010.

Stan, Lavinia, and Lucian Turcescu. *Religion and Politics in Post-Communist Romania*. New York: Oxford University Press, 2007.

Stavrache, Dumitru. *Mitropolitul Visarion Puiu: documente din pribegie (1944–1963)* [Metropolitan Visarion Puiu: Documents from Wandering (1944–1963)]. Pașcani, Romania: Moldopress, 2002.

Steinacher, Gerald. *Nazis on the Run: How Hitler's Henchmen Fled Justice*. New York: Oxford University Press, 2011.

Teoctist, Patriarhul României. "Cuvânt Inainte" [Foreword]. In *Autocefalie, Patriarhie, Slujire Sfântă. Momente Aniversare în Biserica Ortodoxă Română* [Autoceaphaly, Patriarchate, Sacred Service. Aniversary Moments in the Life of the Romanian Orthodox Church]. Bucharest: Editura Institutului Biblic si de Misiune, 1995, 5–14.

Vago, Bela. *In the Shadow of Swastika: The Rise of Fascism and Anti-Semitism in the Danube Basin, 1936–1939.* Farnborough, Hampshire, UK: Saxon House, 1975.

Vasile, Cristian. *Biserica Ortodoxă Română în primul deceniu comunist* [The Romanian Orthodox Church during the First Decade of Communism]. Bucharest: Curtea Veche, 2005.

Voicu, George, ed. *Pogromul de la Iași (28–30 Iunie 1941): prologul Holocaustului din Romania.* Iași, Romania: Polirom, 2006.

Volovici, Leon. *Antisemitism in Post-Communist Eastern Europe: A Marginal or Central Issue?* Jerusalem: Hebrew University of Jerusalem, 1994.

———. *Ideologia naționalistă și „problema evreiască": eseu despre formele antisemitismului intellectual in Romania anilor '30.* Bucharest: Humanitas, 1995.

Wette, Wolfram. *The Wehrmacht: History, Myth, Reality.* Translated by Deborah Lucas Schneider. Cambridge, MA: Harvard University Press, 2006.

Wiesenthal, Simon. *Asasinii printre noi* [The Murderers Among Us]. Bucharest: Editura Politică, 1969.

Wigoder, Geoffrey. *Jewish-Christian Relations since the Second World War.* Manchester, UK: Manchester University Press, 1988.

Zernov, Nicolas. *Eastern Christendom.* London: Weidenfeld & Nicolson, 1961.

Selected articles:

Abadi, Jacob. "Israel and the Balkan States." *Middle Eastern Studies* 32, no. 4 (October 1996): 296–320.

Antonescu, George. "Impotriva Simoniei" [Against Simony]. *Cuvântul Preoțesc* 8, nos. 8–10 (1941): 4–5.

Balca, Niculae. "Etapele psihologice ale mărturisirii." *Studii Teologice,* series 2, vol. 7, nos. 1–2 (1955): 25–38.

Baleasnai, Andrei. "Ororile Bolsevismului" [Bolshevik Hideousness]. *Transnistria Creștină* 2, nos. 1–2 (January–February 1943): 79–82.

Benjamin, Lya. "Dreptul la convertire și statutul evreilor convertiți în perioada regimului antonescian." In *Studia et Acta Historiae Iudaeorum Romaniae,* edited by Silviu Sanie and Dumitru Vitcu, 3:245–262. Bucharest: Hasefer, 1998.

Bogdănescu, Titus. "Viața lui Iisus, Judeii" [The Life of Jesus, the Jews]. *Luminătorul* 75, nos. 3–4 (1942): 172–178.

Braham, Randolph L. "A TV Documentary on Rescue during the Holocaust. A Case of History Cleansing in Romania." *Eastern European Quarterly* 28, no. 2 (June 1994): 193–203.

Brătescu-Voinești, Ioan Al. "Comunismul." *Apostolul* 14, no. 21 (1–15 December 1938): 303–306.

Byford, Jovan. "From 'Traitor' to 'Saint': Bishop Nikolaj Velimirović in Serbian Public Memory." *Analysis of Current Trends in Antisemitism* no. 22 (2004): 1–41.

Cănănău, Nic. "Ce spun canoanele despre primirea în Creștinism a Iudeilor?" [What Do the Canons Say about the Conversion of Jews to Christianity?]. *Luminătorul* 75, nos. 3–4 (1942): 196–205.

Chirot, Daniel. "Social Change in Communist Romania." Special issue, *Social Forces* 57, no. 2 (December 1978): 457–499.

Comitetul de Redacție [Editorial Board]. "Excelenta sa Dr. Moses Rosen, Șef Rabinul Cultului Mozaic din România, Președintele Federației Comunităților Evreiești din România a Adus Omagiul Său Personalității Patriarhului Justinian" [His Excellency Dr. Moses Rosen, the Chief Rabbi of the Jewish Community (Mosaic Religion) of Romania, the President of the Federation of Jewish Communities of Romania Has Paid Homage to the Personality of Patriarch Justinian]. *BOR* 96, no. 4 (April 1977): 250–251.

Comitetul de Redacție [Editorial Board]. "Participarea Prea Fericitului Patriarh Teoctist la aniversarea Eminentei Sale Dl. Șef Rabin Moses Rosen" [The Participation of His Holiness Patriarch Teoctist at the Anniversary of His Eminency Mister Chief Rabbi Moses Rosen]. *BOR* 106, nos. 7–8 (July–August 1988): 25.

Crăciunaș, Irineu. "Responsabilitatea morală." *Studii Teologice*, series 2, vol. 7, nos. 3–4 (March–April 1955): 182–196.

Cristea, Miron Patriarhul României. "Renașterea spirituală a Românismului prin tainele și luminile Bisericii Creștine" [The Spiritual Rebirth of Romanianism (Romanian nationalism) through the Sacraments and the Light of the Christian Church]. *Apostolul* 14, nos. 1–2 (1–31 January 1938): 1–2.

Dură, Ioan. "Ierarhi ai Bisericii Ortodoxe Române îndepărtați din scaun și trimiși în recluziune monastică de către autoritățile comuniste în anii 1944–1981" [Clergy of the Romanian Orthodox Church Sacked and Sent into Monasteries by Communist Authorities from 1944 to 1981]. *BOR* 120, nos. 110–112 (October–December 2002): 302–322.

Enache, George-Eugen, Adrian-Nicolae Petcu, Ionuț-Alexandru Tudorie, and Paul Brusanovski. "Biserica Ortodoxă Română în anii regimului comunist. Observații pe marginea capitolului dedicat cultelor din Raportul final al comisiei prezidențiale pentru analiza dictaturii comuniste" [The Romanian Orthodox Church during the Communist Regime. Observations Regarding the Religions Chapter from the *Final Report of the Presidential Commission for the Analysis of the Communist Dictatorship*]. *Studii Teologice*, series 3, vol. 5, no. 2 (April–June 2009): 7–105.

Fecioru, Dumitru. "La șase ani de patriarhat ai Înalt PS Nicodim" [Six Years of the Patriarchate of His Holiness Nicodim]. *BOR* 63, no. 6 (June 1945): 210–212.

Florian, Alexandru. "Evreii din România în Timpul celui de-al doilea război mondial, o problema de cultură și conștiință civica" [The Jews of Romania during the Second World War: An Issue of Civic Culture and Consciousness]. *Holocaust. Studii și Cercetări* 1, no. 1 (2009): 139–149.

———. "Teme antisemite și de negare a Holocaustului în media din România anului 2007" [Anti-Semitic and Holocaust Denial Themes Used in Romanian Media during 2007]. *Holocaust. Studii si Cercetări* 1, no. 2 (2009): 119–138.

Gheorghiu, Mihai Dinu, William Totok, Elena-Irina Macovei, and Simona-Gabriela Sînzianu. "Naționalism, rasism, antisemitism și xenofobie pe platformele electronice ale unor publicații românești difuzate pe internet" [Nationalism, Racism,

Anti-Semitism, and Xenophobia on the Internet Electronic Platforms of Romanian Publications]. *Holocaust. Studii și Cercetări* 1, no. 2 (2009): 139–154.

Grumăzescu, IC. C. "Iisus și războiul" [Jesus and the War]. *Luminătorul* 74, nos. 5–6 (May–June 1941): 296–300.

Gușu, Cosmina. "Reflectarea Holocaustului în revista Magazin Istoric" [The Holocaust as it Appears in 'The Historical Magazine' Review]. *Holocaustul. Studii și Cercetări* 1, no. 1 (2009): 151–160.

Henry, Patrick. "The French Catholic Church's Apology." *French Review* 72, no. 6 (May 1999): 1099–1105.

Iacob, Lazăr. "Biserica și transformările sociale" [The Church and the Social Changes]. *BOR* 63, nos. 7–8 (July–August 1945): 302–311.

Ioanid, Radu. "The Pogrom of Bucharest, 21–23 January 1941." *Holocaust and Genocide Studies* 6, no. 4 (1991): 373–382.

Ionescu, Barbu, Gr. "A Treia Sesiune a Conciliului al II-lea de la Vatican" [The Third Session of the Second Vatican Council]. *Ortodoxia* 16, no. 4 (October–December 1964): 471–503.

Ioniță, Alexandru. "Atitudinea Bisericii Ortodoxe Române față de evrei între 1918–1945 în Muntenia, reflectată în publicațiile vremii și în documente de arhivă" [The Attitude of the Romanian Orthodox Church toward Jews from 1918 to 1945 in Muntenia (Wallachia, southern part of the Old Kingdom of Romania) as It Appears in Publications of That Time and in Archival Documents]. *BOR* 108, nos. 7–10 (July–October 1990): 203–211.

Lavi, Theodor. "The Vatican's Endeavors on Behalf of Rumanian Jewry during the Second World War." *Yad Vashem Studies* no. 5 (1963): 405–418.

Manolache, Teodor N. "Din dragoste și din simțul datoriei: fapte mai puțin cunoscute din activitatea IPS Nicodim in timpul razboiului" [From Love and Duty: Lesser-Known Deeds Performed by H. H. Nicodim during the War]. *BOR* 63, nos. 11–12 (November–December 1945): 670–677.

"Masacrul bolsevic de la Winnitza văzut de delegatiile bisericești străine" [The Winnitza Bolshevik Massacre as Seen by the Foreign Churches' Delegates]. *BOR* 61, nos. 7–9 (July–September 1943): 437–448.

Nica, Antim. "Episcopul M. S. Alexander." *BOR* 63, no. 10 (October, 1945): 412–415.

———. "Pe urmele apostolatului românesc" [Retracing the Romanian Apostolate]. *BOR* 63, nos. 11–12 (November–December 1945): 571–589.

Nicodim, Patriarhul României. "Ispita. 21–23 Ianuarie 1941" [Temptation. 21–23 January 1941]. *BOR* 59, nos. 3–4 (March–April 1941): 129–131.

Oldson, William. "Alibi for Prejudice: Eastern Orthodoxy, the Holocaust, and Romanian Nationalism." *East European Quarterly* 36, no. 3 (Fall 2002): 301–311.

Păcurariu, Mircea. "Mitropolitul Nicolae Bălan al Ardealului. La 100 de ani de la Naștere" [Metropolitan Bălan of Transylvania : One Hundred Years since His Birth]. *BOR* 100, nos. 5–6 (May–June 1982): 494–518.

———. "Biserica Ortodoxă Română, slujitoare a păcii în istoria poporului roman" [The Romanian Orthodox Church, a Servant of Peace in the History of the Romanian People]. *BOR* 98, nos. 9–10 (September–October 1980): 120–147.

Pană, Gina. "Inchisoarea legionară Aiud" [Aiud, the Legionary Prison]. *Holocaust, Studii și Cercetări* 1, no. 1 (2009): 21–27.

Paperno, Irina. "Exhuming the Bodies of Soviet Terror." *Representations* 75, no. 1 (Summer 2001): 89–118.

Popa, Ion. "Miron Cristea, the Romanian Orthodox Patriarch: His Political and Religious Influence in Deciding the Fate of the Romanian Jews (February 1938–March 1939)." *Yad Vashem Studies* 40, no. 2 (2012): 11–34.

Popa, Ion. "Visarion Puiu, the Former Romanian Orthodox Metropolitan (Archbishop) of Transnistria—A Historical Study on His Life and Activity before, during and after the Holocaust (1935–1964)." *Holocaust Study and Research* 6, no. 1 (2013): 182–203.

Popescu, Teodor. "Anticreștinismul comunist" [The Communist Anti-Christianity]. *BOR* 60, nos. 1–4 (January–April 1942): 13–50.

———. "Privire istorică asupra schismelor, ereziilor și sectelor" [Historical Overview on Schisms, Heresies, and Sects]. *Studii Teologice*, series 2, vol. 2, nos. 7–8 (1950): 347–355.

Portase-Prut, David. "Bat clopotele până la Bug, Gânduri pascale" [The Bells Toll Up to the Bug [River], Easter Thoughts]. *Transnistria Creștină* 1, no. 1 (January–March 1942): 15–16.

Shapiro, Paul. "What Is in the Air?" *Holocaustul Studii si Cercetări* 1, no. 2 (2009): 157–171.

Sîrbu, Corneliu. "Poziții principale ale Ortodoxiei față de celelate religii" [The Main Considerations of Orthodoxy toward Other Religions]. *Ortodoxia* 21, no. 4 (October–December 1969): 507–523.

Stăniloae, Dumitru. "Unitatea spirituală a neamului nostru și libertatea" [Our Nation's Spiritual Unity and Freedom]. *BOR* 108, nos. 1–2 (January–February 1990): 47–49.

Târgovișteanu, Vasile. "Spiritul de Colaborare și Frățietate Dintre Poporul Român și Naționalitățile Conlocuitoare" [The Spirit of Collaboration and Brotherhood between the Romanian People and the Co-Inhabitant Nationalities]. *BOR* 105, nos. 5–6 (May–June 1987): 5–12.

Teodorescu, Virgil. "Patriarhul Miron Cristea, contemporanul nostru" [Patriarch Miron Cristea, Our Contemporary]. *BOR* 116, nos. 7–12 (July–December 1998): 231–242.

Tomescu, Constantin. "Trans Nistrum." *Transnistria Creștină* 2, nos. 1–2 (January–February 1943): 1–8.

Tudorie, Alexandru Ionuț. "Un martir al crucii; viața și opera lui Teodor Popescu" [A Martyr of the cross; the life and work of Teodor Popescu]. *Studii Teologice*, series 3, vol. 2, no. 3 (July–September 2006): 189–193.

Vasilescu, Emilian. "Declarații asupra Religiilor Necreștine" [Declarations on Non-Christian Religions]. *Ortodoxia* 19, no. 1 (January–March 1967): 134–143.

———. "Preocupări în teologia ortodoxă română în legătură cu religiile necreștine" [Considerations in Romanian Orthodox Theology Regarding Non-Christian Religions]. *Ortodoxia* 23, no. 1 (January–March 1971): 27–41.

Vasilescu, Gheorghe. "Un preot Ortodox Român 'Drept între Popoare'" [A Romanian Orthodox priest "Righteous Among the Nations"]. *BOR* 122, nos. 5–8 (May–August 2004): 206–208.

———. "In ziua învierii a plecat dintre noi Arhiepiscopul Antim Nica al Dunării de Jos" [On the Day of the Resurrection the Archbishop of Lower Danube, Antim Nica, Passed Away]. *BOR* 112, nos. 1–6 (January–June 1994): 200, 202.

Velechiu, Dumitru. "Mitropolitul Visarion Puiu, un martir al demnitatii ortodoxe" [Metropolitan Visarion Puiu a Martyr of Orthodox Worthiness]. *Analele Bucovinei* 11, no. 1 (2004): 41–82.

Verdery, Katherine. "Nationalism and National Sentiment in Post-socialist Romania." *Slavic Review* 52, no. 2 (Summer 1993): 179–203.

Vîlcu, N. "Romano-Catolicismul şi religiile necreştine după documentele conciliului al II-lea de la Vatican" [Roman-Catholicism and the Non-Christian Religions According to the Documents of the Second Vatican Council]. *Ortodoxia* 20, no. 3 (July–September 1968): 395–406.

"Vizita conducătorilor de partid şi de stat la Mănăstirea Dealu" [The Visit of the Party and State Leaders to the Dealu Monastery]. *BOR* 85, nos. 5–6 (May–June 1967): 517–521.

VI. Official Reports

Comisia Prezidenţială pentru Analiza Dictaturii Comuniste din România [Presidential Commission for the Analysis of the Communist Dictatorship in Romania]. *Raport Final.* Bucharest: Humanitas, 2006.

Friling, Tuvia, Radu Ioanid, and Mihai Ionescu, eds. *The Final Report of the Elie Wiesel Commission for the Study of the Holocaust in Romania.* Bucharest: Polirom, 2005.

VII. Web Pages

Aderet, Ofer. "Behind the Scenes of Anwar Sadat's Historic Visit to Jerusalem." *Ha'aretz*, 27 November 2012. http://www.haaretz.com/news/national/behind-the-scenes-of-anwar-sadat-s-historic-visit-to-jerusalem.premium-1.480957.

Christian Roundtable of Eastern Orthodox Priests & Cultural Representatives. "To Recognize Christ in His People." Council of Centers of Jewish-Christian Relations, 20–24 April 2007. http://www.ccjr.us/dialogika-resources/documents-and-statements/e-orthodox/1011-eoroundtable2007june1.

Commission for Religious Relations with the Jews. *We Remember: A Reflection on the Shoah.* Accessed 16 July 2013. http://www.vatican.va/roman_curia/pontifical_councils/chrstuni/documents/rc_pc_chrstuni_doc_16031998_shoah_en.html.

Constantinople Patriarchate. http://www.Patriarchate.org/.

Corlăţan, Mirela. "Un mitropolit român a adus Yad Vashem în faţa instanţei" [A Romanian Metropolitan Has Taken Yad Vashem to the Court]. *Evenimentul Zilei*, 1 February 2011. http://www.evz.ro/un-mitropolit-roman-a-adus-yad-vashem-in-fata-instantei-919902.html.

"Documents and Statements." Sacred Heart University Center for Christian and Jewish Understanding. Accessed 22 February 2013. http://www.sacredheart.edu/faithservice/centerforchristianandjewishunderstanding/documentsandstatements/.

Dugan, George. "Jews Occupy Building and Urge Ouster of Prelate." *New York Times*, 15 October 1976. http://select.nytimes.com/gst/abstract.html?res=9E06EFDE173CE336A05756C1A9669D946790D6CF&scp=28&sq=trifa&st=p.

European Commission. "Regular report from the Commission on Romania's progress towards accession 1998." Bulletin of the European Union Supplement 9 (1998), 17 December 1998. http://aei.pitt.edu/44598/.

Fantaziu, Ionuț. "Arhive: 'Sub o conductă de apă au fost îngropați 2.500 de evrei'" [Archives: Under a Water Pipe Were Buried 2,500 Jews (An Interview with Radu Ioanid)]. *Evenimentul Zilei*, 1 July 2011. http://www.evz.ro/radu-ioanid-steaua-romaniei-ramane-la-vadim-sau-la-wiesel-936170.html.

Federatia Comunităților Evreiești din România. https://www.jewishfed.ro/.

Fototeca Ortodoxiei Românești. http://fototecaortodoxiei.ro/.

Goldman, Ari. "Valerian Trifa, an Archbishop with a Fascist Past, Dies at 72." *New York Times*, 29 January 1987. http://www.nytimes.com/1987/01/29/obituaries/valerian-trifa-an-archbishop-with-a-fascist-past-dies-at-72.html?scp=1&sq=trifa&st=nyt.

"Greetings of Ecumenical Patriarch Bartholomew to the Third Academic Meeting between Orthodoxy and Judaism: Continuity and Renewal." Ecumenical Patriarchate of Constantinople. Accessed 22 February 2013. https://www.patriarchate.org/addresses/-/asset_publisher/npz6Rwvho3aC/content/greetings-of-ecumenical-patriarch-bartholomew-to-the-third-academic-meeting-between-orthodoxy-and-judaism.

Ha'aretz staff and Associated Press. "Romanian President Backtracks on Holocaust Remarks." *Ha'aretz*, 27 July 2003. http://www.haaretz.com/print-edition/news/romanian-president-backtracks-on-holocaust-remarks-1.95414.

Holy Synod of Bishops of the Serbian Orthodox Church. "The Serbian Orthodox Church Regarding Anti-Semitic Posters (March 24, 2005)." Sacred Heart University, Documents and Statements. Accessed 22 February 2013. http://www.sacredheart.edu/faithservice/centerforchristianandjewishunderstanding/documentsandstatements/theserbianorthodoxchurchregardingantisemiticpostersmarch242005/.

Human Rights World Report 1990. "Romania: Human Rights Developments." http://www.hrw.org/reports/1990/WR90/HELSINKI.BOU-02.htm.

INSHREW. "Drepți între Popoare" [Righteous Among the Nations]. http://www.inshr-ew.ro/drepti-intre-popoare.

The International Raoul Wallenberg Foundation and Casa Argentina en Israel Tierra Santa, eds. *John XXIII—"The Good Pope."* 2009. http://www.raoulwallenberg.net/wp-content/files_mf/1310655046ebookroncalli-ENGLISHcorrected.pdf.

Patriarch Bartholomew. "Address of His All Holiness Ecumenical Patriarch Bartholomew: Meeting with the Members Religious and Lay Leaders of the Jewish Community, Park East Synagogue, Direct Archdiocesan District, New York, October 28, 2009." Ecumenical Patriarchate of Constantinople, video version of His

speech. Accessed 22 February 2013. https://www.patriarchate.org/-/ecumenical
-patriarch-bartholomew-meets-with-jewish-religious-and-lay-leaders
?inheritRedirect=true.

Romanides, John S. "Jewish and Christian Orthodox Dialogue. Bucharest, Romania,
October 29–31, 1979, a follow-up of the dialogue held in March of 1977 in Lucerne,
Switzerland." *The Romans*. Accessed 22 February 2013. http://www.romanity.org/htm
/rom.24.en.jewish_and_christian_orthodox_dialogue.htm.

Romanian Orthodox Church. http://www.patriarhia.ro/.

Samoilă, Gheorghe. "Grigore Resmeriță (1896–1941)—preot martir." http://frgheorghe
.wordpress.com/grigore-razmerita-1896-1941-preot-martir/.

Sfântul Sinod. "Hotărârea nr 5944 din 5 iulie 2012 a Sfântului Sinod al Bisericii Ortodoxe
Române privind modul de aprobare a accesului la documentele aflate în Arhiva
Sfântului Sinod și în arhivele centrelor eparhiale, pentru cercetarea științifică,
publicistică sau de altă natură." Hotărâri ale Sfântului Sinod [Decisions of the Holy
Synod]. Accessed 2 July 2013. http://patriarhia.ro/images/pdf/HotarariSinodale/2012
/5944_Comunicare_documente_Arhiva.pdf.

Ștef, Mugur. "Press Statement of the NBR Spokesman." Press release, 19 August 2010.
http://www.bnr.ro/page.aspx?prid=4413.

Stoicescu, Vlad. "Reacția Patriarhiei în cazul 'Refrene legionare la «Petru Vodă»': Nu e
responsabilitatea noastră" [The Reaction of the Patriarchate in the Case 'Legionary
Songs at Petru Vodă': It is not Our Responsibility]. *Evenimentul Zilei*, 21 February 2011.
http://www.evz.ro/reactia-patriarhiei-in-fata-controversei-de-la-petru-voda-nu-e
-responsabilitatea-noastra-921.html.

"The United States Holocaust Memorial Museum Objects to Cristea Coin." Press release, 20
August 2010. https://www.ushmm.org/information/press/press-releases/the-united
-states-holocaust-memorial-museum-objects-to-cristea-coin.

US Department of State. Romania Human Rights Practices 1993. 31 January 1994. http://
www.hri.org/docs/USSD-Rights/93/Romania93.html.

———. "Romania—International Religious Freedom Report 2005." Accessed 4 March 2013.
http://www.state.gov/j/drl/rls/irf/2005/51575.htm.

INDEX

religious anti-Semitism and, 98; of
Romanian government, 98, 153, 197
Crainic, Nichifor, 43, 46, 161
Crans-Montana Forum, 184
Cristea, Miron (patriarch), 23, 147, 207, 208;
anti-Semitism of, 27, 31–33, 39n61, 41, 95,
133, 170, 177, 198; church-state relationship
and, 31–33; death of, 34; Deportation and
Romanianization policies of, 32–33, 41;
influence of, on fate of Jews, 31–33, 41; as
prime minister, 1, 8–9, 20, 28–29, 53, 65, 90
Cristian, S. C., 94–95
Crusaders, 141
Cushing, Richard James (cardinal), 140–141
Cuza, Alexandru C., 23, 26, 28, 31, 33
Cuza, Alexandru Ioan, 25, 26

Daniel (patriarch), 4, 154, 175
Defense of Peace program, 122, 124, 143
deicide, 138
Dej, Gheorghiu, 117, 120, 122–123
denial, of Holocaust, 7, 160, 162–164, 174,
182
Deportation and Romanianization policies,
of Cristea, 32–33, 41
deportations, 157; to Belzec, 30, 35, 57, 67, 74,
169–170; halting of, 58; of Romanian Jews,
30, 32–33; to Transnistria, 55, 73, 85, 92
destruction: of French Jewry, 190; of
Romanian Jewry, 1, 11, 20, 21, 29, 62, 172,
176, 197
Displaced Persons Act, 135
documents: about anti-Semitism, 137; about
conversion, 88–91; about Holocaust,
137–145
Dumitriu-Snagov, Ion, 10

Eastern Europe: church-state relations
in, 27; Holocaust memory in, 2, 183;
nationalism in, 2, 158; Orthodox churches
of, 3, 11, 46, 199
economic and racial anti-Semitism, 47, 66
economy, between Israel and Romania, 184
Elie Wiesel International Commission on
the Holocaust in Romania, Final Report
of, 7, 27, 73, 152–153, 157, 162, 184
Elie Wiesel National Institute for the
Study of the Holocaust in Romania
(INSHREW), 1, 13, 14, 15, 158–159, 162–163,
176–177
emigration (1948–1989), 120, 153

Faculty of Theology, in Bucharest, 35, 56, 176
fall: of Ceaușescu, 152, 153, 156, 168, 181, 192,
195; of Communism, 2, 3, 7, 9, 12, 153–158,
177, 182, 198
"Fate of Martyrs," 176, 177
Fecioru, Dumitru, 86, 87, 99
Federation of Jewish Communities of
Romania (FCER) (Federația
Comunităților Evreiești din România), 23,
58, 75–76, 122, 157, 158
*Final Report of the Presidential Commission
for the Analysis of Communist Dictatorship*,
123
Final Solution, 170
Filderman, Wilhelm, 57, 58, 75, 117
First Solution, 41
Florian, Alexandru, 16, 162, 163, 176, 177, 195
*Four Years of Wrath. Notes of a Jew from
Romania. See Patru Ani de Urgie. Notele
Unui Evreu din România*
France, Puiu in, 134
French Catholic Church, 9
French Jewry, destruction of, 190
Friedländer, Saul, 11, 198
*"From 'Traitor' to 'Saint': Bishop Nikolaj
Velimirović in Serbian Public Memory"*
(Byford), 11

gendarmerie, Romanian, 30, 38n43
Gillet, Olivier, 14, 27–28
glorification-victimization myth, 195
Goga, Octavian, anti-Semitism of, 33, 133,
143, 146, 192, 208
Goga-Cuza government, 20, 28, 31–32, 90
government cover up campaign, 98, 153
Govora Law, 24, 89
Govrin, Yosef, 15, 119
Great Union, 25, 26
Greater Romania, 25, 159, 169, 193
Greater Romania Party, 159, 174
Greek Orthodox Church, 73, 124
Groza, Petru, 72, 78, 98, 103

The History of Jews from Ancient Times to
the Balfour Declaration. See *Istoria
Evreilor din cele mai vechi timpuri până la
Declarația Balfour*
Holocaust: awareness of, 178–181; Catholic
Church involvement of, 10; debate on,
152–153; denial of, 7, 160, 162–164, 174, 182;
growing interest in, 196; hasty

74–75; decrease in, 73, 120; emigration of, 120, 153; as refugees, 74; restitution for, 74; survivors of, 73–74, 157

John XXIII (pope), 191

John Paul II (pope), 9

journals, of Romanian Orthodox Church, 13–16, 133; central, 42–46; regional, 47–49; whitewashing process in, 87–88

Judaism: mention of, 179; theological approach to, 142

Judeo-Bolshevik propaganda, 43–45, 49, 51, 66, 84

Justinian (patriarch), 122–123, 124, 127, 146

Karetski, Aurel, 15, 119

killing, of Jews, in Transnistria, 44–46, 48–49, 73, 89, 110, 153, 170

Kramer, Charles, 14, 135, 136

Lavi, Theodor, 10

Law for the Revision of Citizenship, 20, 33, 41

Legionnaires, 29, 177

Legionary Rebellion, 50, 107, 135

Legionary State, 35, 64, 107

Lerman, Miles, 173–174, 204, 205

Leuștean, Lucian, 25, 27–28, 83, 95n1

The Little Ewe Lamb. See Miorița

Maniu, Iuliu, 104

Manolache, Teodor, 88, 91–95, 169, 171–172

martyrology, competitive, 160

Mein Kampf, 160

memory. See Holocaust memory

Messiah, 47–48

metropolitans, in Romania, 23–24, 26

Michael the Brave, 146

Miorița (The Little Ewe Lamb), 193–194

missionary campaign, in Transnistria, 49, 52–56, 66

Moisescu, Iustin (patriarch), 123, 125, 126, 179, 182

monument, to Antonescu, 174, 204

moral conscience, 196

moral responsibility, 196

Morley, John, 10

Munteanu, Nicodim (patriarch), 24, 34, 41, 93, 209, 210, 211; Antonescu and, 26, 36; appointment of, 35, 39n75; with cover up campaign, 98–99, 194; death of, 72–73, 79; intervention efforts of, 60–61, 63–65, 185;

replacement of, 100; Safran and, 94, 111–112; whitewashing message of, 83–86; writings relating to, 43, 45, 87–88, 203

The Murderers Among Us (Wiesenthal), 118

Museum of Jewish Culture and Civilization in Bucharest, 119

Museum of the History of the Jewish Community of Romania, 144

National Bank of Romania (NBR), 1

National Christian Defense League, 124

National Christian Party, 28

national Communism, 123, 143, 145–148

National Council of Churches, 136

National Institute for the Study of Totalitarianism, 106

National Union of Christian Students, 135

nationalism, 9; of 1990s, 159; in Eastern Europe, 2; Orthodox, 1–2, 3, 128, 133, 145–148, 156; postcommunist, 158; Romanian Orthodox Church, anti-Semitism of, and, 152, 158–162, 197

Nazis: atrocities committed by, 133, 136, 190; collaboration with, 110–112, 183, 193, 196; genocide of, 9; myths about, 162–163, 193–194; regime of, 10, 45, 118, 199; Romanian Orthodox Church archives relating to, 137, 141, 144; Romanians as victims of, 128, 191; Trifa relating to, 135

New Generation Party, 155, 159

Nica, Antim (bishop), 15; conversion documents and, 88–91; with cover up campaign, 91–95, 99; in Transnistria, 61, 87, 99, 109; writings of, 169–170, 171, 197

non-Christian religions, 138, 141–142

Norwegian Lutheran mission, 61, 89

Nostra Aetate declaration, 116, 133, 137–145, 179

Old Kingdom, of Romania, 22, 23, 28, 31, 34, 61, 63, 74

Orthodox Church, 113n23; Christian-humane attitude of, 171; Coptic, 139; of Eastern Europe, 11, 46, 199; Greek, 73, 124; Holocaust relating to, 8, 15; non-Christian religions and, 138, 141–142; religious harmony agenda with, 101–105, 124–125, 126; ROCOR, 134; Russian, 3; Serbian, 8, 11, 181, 200n5. See also Catholic Church; Romanian Orthodox Church; Romanian Orthodox Church, anti-Semitism of

Ion Popa is a Claims Conference Saul Kagan Postdoctoral Fellow in Advanced Shoah Studies and an Honorary Research Fellow of the Centre for Jewish Studies, University of Manchester, UK. Over the years he has been the recipient of various international fellowships, among them the Tziporah Wiesel Fellowship at the Centre for Advanced Holocaust Studies, USHMM, Washington DC, the Claims Conference Saul Kagan Doctoral Fellowship, the Postdoctoral Fellowship at the Yad Vashem International Institute for Holocaust Research, and the DRS Postdoctoral Fellowship at Freie Universiät, Berlin.

Lightning Source UK Ltd.
Milton Keynes UK
UKOW01n0814071017

310514UK00009B/330/P